Qualitative Research Methods in Mathematics Education

edited by

Anne R. Teppo
Montana State University—Bozeman

National Council of Teachers of Mathematics

Copyright © 1998 by
THE NATIONAL COUNCIL OF TEACHERS OF MATHEMATICS, INC.
1906 Association Drive, Reston, Virginia 20191-1593

Library of Congress Cataloging-in-Publication Data:

Qualitative research methods in mathematics education / edited by Anne
R. Teppo.
        p. cm. — (Journal for research in mathematics education.
Monograph ; no. 9)
    Includes bibliographical references.
    ISBN 0-87353-459-X
    1. Mathematics—Sstudy and teaching—Research. I. Teppo, Anne R.
II. Series.
QA11.Q32 1998
510′.71—dc21   98-36575
                                                              CIP

Printed in the United States of America

Table of Contents

Authors

David J. Clarke
Associate Dean
Faculty of Education
University of Melbourne
Parkville, Victoria, 3052,
Australia

Beatriz S. D'Ambrosio
Associate Professor
School of Education
Indiana University Purdue
  University Indianapolis
Indianapolis, IN 46202

Paul Ernest
Reader in Mathematics Education
University of Exeter
Exeter EX1 2LU United Kingdon

Gerald A. Goldin
Professor of Education, Mathematics,
  and Physics
Center for Mathematics, Science and
  Computer Education and
Graduate School of Education
Rutgers University
New Brunswick, NJ 08903

Barbara Jaworski
University Lecturer in Educational
  Studies
Oxford Centre for Mathematics
  Education Research
Oxford 0X2 6PY United Kingdom

Judith Mousley
Senior Lecturer
Faculty of Education
Deakin University
Geelong, Victoria, 3217, Australia

Dagmar Neuman
Department of Education and
  Educational Research
Göteborg University
Göteborg, Sweden

Susan Pirie
Professor of Mathematics Education
Department of Curriculum Studies
University of British Columbia
Vancouver, BC V6T 1Z4

Peter Sullivan
Assistant Professor
Faculty of Education
Australian Catholic University—
  Christ Campus
Oakleigh, Victoria, 3166, Australia

Anne R. Teppo
Adjunct Instructor
Department of Mathematical Sciences
Montana State University—Bozeman
Bozeman, MT 59717

Andrew Waywood
Lecturer in Mathematics Education
Australian Catholic University—
  Christ Campus
Oakleigh, Victoria, 3166,
  Australia

Acknowledgments

The editor wishes to thank those who provided support and encouragement for the theme of this monograph in the early stages of the project. Their involvement in the field of mathematics education and their individual research interests helped clarify the nature of the product. Grateful thanks are extended to Deborah Ball, Catherine Brown, Jere Confrey, Robert Davis, Kathleen Heid, Carolyn Maher, Terezinha Nunes, Leslie Steffe, and Erna Yackel. Thanks are also due to the contributing authors whose ideas and continual input defined the focus and produced the end result.

Abstract

The chapters in this monograph describe qualitative research methods used to investigate students' and teachers' interactions with school mathematics. Each contributing author uses data from his or her own research to illustrate a particular technique or aspect of research design. The different chapters present a wide range of methods, representing a variety of goals and perspectives. Rather than a comprehensive reference manual, this monograph illustrates the diversity of methods available for qualitative research in mathematics education.

The monograph begins with a discussion of key elements that contribute to the dynamic and evolving domain of mathematics education research. Background information is then provided that relates to the philosophical and epistemological assumptions underlying all qualitative research. In the chapters that follow, actual studies present the contexts for discussions of research design and techniques. Issues of research design include the importance of making explicit the underlying theoretical assumptions; the selection of an appropriate methodology; the interpretative, intersubjective nature of analysis; and the establishment of reliability and validity. Specific data collection techniques include clinical interviews, stimulated recall interviews, open-ended survey questions, and field notes and video or audio taping to record classroom events. Methods of analysis include participant validation, the categorization of data through constant comparison and software indexing and retrieval, phenomemographic analysis, and the identification of empirical examples of theoretical constructs. The monograph ends with a discussion of general issues, including the role of theory and the establishment of criteria for judging the goodness of qualitative research.

Chapter 1

Diverse Ways of Knowing

Anne R. Teppo

The chapters in this monograph describe qualitative methods used in mathematics education research. Rather than write a comprehensive manual, contributing authors describe specific methods from their own studies to illustrate the range of techniques used to investigate students' and teachers' interactions with school mathematics. Each chapter focuses on only one aspect of the author's research to provide a more in-depth discussion of that particular facet of the overall design.

A goal of this book is to stimulate dialogue. Mathematics education research supports a variety of methodological perspectives and goals of inquiry, which makes communication across perspectives difficult and the need for dialogue imperative. Creating dialogue is not easy. Fenstermacher and Richardson (1994) suggest enjoying each speaker on his or her own ground. However, as Cobb (1995) points out, this task requires a decentering of participants to allow them to "appreciate the other's position ... even when it is difficult to argue for it from their own perspective" (p. 25). Such decentering involves developing a sensitivity to the contextual meaning of others and regarding each research result as the product of a particular line of inquiry that must be viewed in the context of that inquiry (Bredo, 1994).

This chapter begins with an examination of the general context within which qualitative research in mathematics education is placed and then discusses the particular contexts within which the contributing authors situate each chapter. To set the stage, key elements are described that contribute to the dynamic and evolving domain of qualitative research in mathematics education, including the acceptance of qualitative research as an important methodology in educational inquiry, a broadening of perceptions of the nature of mathematics and mathematics education, and a recognition of the complexity of classroom mathematics teaching and learning. Against this broad background, the chapter concludes with a summary of the contributions of the other authors and a brief discussion of the ways in which these contributions illustrate the diversity of qualitative research methods employed in mathematics education.

QUALITATIVE RESEARCH

Qualitative research has been described as a *field* of inquiry (Denzin and Lincoln, 1994) that cuts across disciplines and subject matter, finding application in such areas as anthropology, sociology, psychology, sociolinguistics, political science, and education. Qualitative research focuses on processes, meanings, and the socially constituted nature of reality and provides insights into the phenomena being studied that cannot be obtained by other means. Denzin and Lincoln, in their comprehensive *Handbook of Qualitative Research* (1994), offer the following generic definition that recognizes the cross-disciplinary nature of the field and the fact that qualitative research means many things to many people:

> Qualitative research is multimethod in focus, involving an interpretative, naturalistic approach to its subject matter. This means that qualitative researchers study things in their natural settings, attempting to make sense of, or interpret, phenomena in terms of meanings people bring to them. Qualitative research involves the studied use and collection of a variety of empirical materials—case study, personal experience, introspective, life story, interview, observational, historical, interactional, and visual texts—that describe routine and problematic moments and meanings in individuals' lives. (p. 2)

Qualitative Research in Education

Anthropologists and sociologists have employed qualitative research methods since the turn of the century, but only in the last 30 years has this type of research become regarded as a legitimate method for educational inquiry (LeCompte, Millroy, & Preissle, 1992). The road to acceptance has been at times confrontational. In a purposively provocative article, Gage (1989) described what he termed the "paradigm wars" of educational research in the 1980s (p. 10). Protagonists adhered to one of three alternative and competing research paradigms, which Gage characterized as the objective-quantitative of the natural sciences, the interpretative-qualitative of anthropology, and the critical-theoretic of sociology and political science. These debates were conducted along disciplinary lines as researchers within psychological, anthropological, and social science orientations argued over the hegemony of their particular methodological framework. Critics of the scientific paradigm decried educational psychology's long-held influence on research on teaching and learning (exemplified by process-product studies) and pushed for increased use of qualitative studies focused on personal meanings and socially constructed reality. (Ernest, Chapter 3 this volume, presents a comparison of the three alternative research paradigms and their underlying ontological and epistemological beliefs.)

Emerging from the methodological debates of the 1980s, educational researchers within the qualitative tradition have found "themselves in the peculiar position of having achieved orthodoxy" and have become part of the "dominant methodological establishment" (LeCompte, Millroy, & Preissle, 1992, p. xvi). The qualitative-quantitative debate has been replaced with a recognition that each paradigm offers a different way to focus research on the complexities of contemporary education (Cizek, 1995).

Paradigms are overarching worldviews that represent particular belief systems about the nature of knowledge and how that knowledge is acquired. Because of the differences in their fundamental beliefs, it is not easy to move between them. Hence, the characterization of "competing" paradigms. Within a paradigm, however, it is possible to hold differing perspectives or points of view. As the qualitative paradigm has moved into mainstream educational research, its multiple perspectives, which have long been a tradition within this paradigm, have opened up an overwhelming array of methodologies from which to choose. Educational research currently supports "a diverse array of voices speaking from quite different, often contradictory perspectives and value commitments" (Donmoyer, 1996, p. 19).

Diversity of Perspectives Within Mathematics Education Research

The diversity of qualitative research perspectives employed in mathematics education research, although not yet representative of the wide variation employed across the entire educational research field, presents sufficient range to elicit controversy. Recent commentaries (Cobb, 1994; Cobb, Jaworski, & Presmeg, 1996; Cobb & Yackel, 1996; Greer, 1996; Bredo, 1994) address the conflicting and complementary perspectives that cognitive science, sociocultural theory, and constructivism provide for studying learning within the broad paradigm of qualitative research. Greer (1996, p. 182) characterizes this situation as creating a "ferment of new ideas, liberalization of methodology, and [an] openness to concepts from many disciplines." The following brief discussion illustrates some of the range of points of view currently available from which to conduct mathematics-education inquiry.

Cobb (1994, 1995) describes the applicability of the separate, but complementary, perspectives of constructivism and sociocultural theory for mathematics-education research. Learning, from the constructivist perspective, is seen as an individual cognitive activity that involves the internal reorganization of mental schema. Although such learning takes place within a social setting, research is focused on the individual's mental constructions. In contrast, a sociocultural perspective views learning as the enculturation of an individual into a community of practice, and the focus of inquiry is placed on the individual's participation in social practice. These two perspectives provide complementary ways to frame inquiry, with each perspective providing the figure against the background for the other. Because each perspective tells "half the story," Cobb maintains that the selection of either the cognizing individual or the social interaction as the primary unit of analysis should be guided by the needs of any particular educational inquiry.

Cobb and Yackel (1996) have proposed a third perspective that uses the complementary nature of the constructivist and sociolocultural points of view. Their *social constructivist* or "emergent" framework is used to study mathematical learning as it occurs within the social contexts of the classroom. The development of individual meaning and the development of social meaning are taken as being reflexively related in that neither can exist independently of the other. Individual "constructions are seen to occur as students participate in and contribute to the practices of the local community" (p. 185).

Research methods of educational psychology and cognitive science have also been employed in mathematics education. The information-processing model of human cognition used by cognitive psychologists in the 1960s and 1970s is now recognized as inadequate for capturing the "complexity and richness of mathematical activity" (Greer, 1996, p. 181). Recent focus on detailed studies of the cognitive processes of individuals engaged in the performance of everyday mathematics (as opposed to academic mathematical tasks) reflects a change in educational psychology's perspective on the study of the mind to one of situated cognition. Mind is regarded as an aspect of a given person-environment interaction. Research from this perspective focuses on problems arising in the course of everyday activities in which an individual's social and physical interactions define the object of research (Bredo, 1994).

The preceding discussion touches only briefly on the range of perspectives and related research methodologies that is currently being employed in mathematics-education research. The disciplinary perspectives of sociology, anthropology, and cognitive science and the theoretical framework of constructivism present multiple vantage points from which to launch inquiry into the complexity and messiness of the classroom. In spite of this diversity, a common theme running across the different perspectives is the increasing importance being given to local context as the determinant of research design. When the contributions available from each perspective are considered, the issue should not be which point of view is better but which one is most useful and appropriate for the problem at hand. "Claims that [a particular] perspective captures the essence of people and communities should be rejected for pragmatic justifications that consider the contextual relevance and usefulness of a perspective" (Cobb, 1994, p. 13).

The wide range of frameworks of inquiry available for qualitative research reflects the diversity of the disciplines that have developed the various methodologies. Employing the techniques of a particular point of view involves more than simply adopting a set of research practices. Underlying each set are fundamental differences in how one views the world, how the objects of study fit into this view, and how knowledge about these objects can be acquired. Doing research also means understanding the underlying ways of thinking implicit in a given perspective (Steffe & Wiegel, 1996).

A Need for Dialogue

The burgeoning list of qualitative methods employed in educational research has helped create a field in which there is little consensus concerning the following questions: What is educational research? What should scholarly discourse look like? What role should research play in education? (Donmoyer, 1996; Fenstermacher & Richardson, 1994; Lester, Kehle, & Birgisson, 1996). The existence of a proliferation of approaches can be viewed as daunting. Alternatively, it can be taken as a sign that the field of educational research is alive and well. If we adopt the latter view, then dialogue and informed critique are needed to maintain the field's health in the face of diversity. (Goldin, Chapter 4 this volume, presents an example of how the explicitation of methodology facilitates dialogue.) Differences in points of view can be used as a mechanism for progress.

> It is by the very process of "misunderstanding" others—that is, interpreting their claims and beliefs in slightly different terms than they do themselves—that the process of communication actually moves forward to new understandings. ... We need to be similar enough to make dialogue possible, but we also need to be different enough to make it worthwhile. (Burbules & Rice, 1991, p. 409)

However, given the current diversity of perspectives and competing paradigms in educational research, consensus may not always be possible. The process of debate is worthwhile only to the extent that those engaged undergo some change in opinion—at the least, enabling those who disagree to gain greater insight into their own positions. What is important is to encourage "healthy confusion" (Fenstermacher & Richardson, 1994, p. 54)—to engage in open discussion; to allow new and interesting, along with old, voices to be heard; and to make explicit one's assumptions about one's research and related educational goals. "There are as many worlds as ways to describe them" (Eisner, 1993, p. 6), and we should celebrate the multiplicity of voices rather than seek synthesis into a single perspective.

AN OVERVIEW OF THE FIELD OF MATHEMATICS EDUCATION

Disciplinary Perspective

The context of inquiry is made up of a complex web in which our underlying beliefs are carried out within the local dynamics of a particular investigation. Not only is the individual situated within a given research setting, he or she is also situated within a particular epistemological, cultural, and gendered framework of beliefs and values that both facilitate and constrain how we perceive the world and what we select for study within it.

Eisner (1993), using an historical perspective, illustrates how particular perceptions can influence the framing and examination of educational practice.

> How we answer the question of whether history is the text historians write or the past historians write about is crucial to our own view of what history is and, therefore, to what is relevant for helping students understand it. If history is text, then text must continue to be central to the teaching of history: To understand history one has to understand text. But if history is the past about which historians write, then any form of representation that sheds light on the past is relevant, indeed a useful, way to understand history. (p. 9)

Mathematics educators face a similar problem in considering their field of inquiry. Underlying assumptions concerning the nature and role of mathematics in society and how it is to be taught and learned influence both educational practice and research (Dossey, 1992). A recognition of the changing face of 20th century mathematics, the emergence of computers and powerful handheld calculators, and the changing needs of contemporary society raise questions about the appropriateness of specific educational content. Emerging theories of learning suggest new approaches to traditional classrooms and question old assumptions about the kinds of mathematical knowledge that best promote understanding (R. B. Davis, 1994). One role of research in mathematics education is to illuminate these issues and provide an information base for their resolution (Research Advisory Committee, 1997). A great deal has been written about these issues (e.g., R. B. Davis, 1994; Dossey, 1992). The following discussion represents only the tip of an important disciplinary iceberg that bears careful scrutiny elsewhere.

The Nature of Mathematics

Mathematics has been described as the science of abstract patterns and characterized by its usefulness for organizing mental and empirical structures (Devlin, 1997; Steen, 1990; van Oers, 1996). This characterization only hints at the complex nature of a field that is valued by some for its intellectual beauty, by others for its utilitarian applications, and by still others for its emancipatory properties in an increasingly technological world. Mathematics can be regarded as the product of intellectual abstraction or as the processes that produce such a product. It can be regarded as a static entity or as a fallible, creative, evolving activity that permeates many aspects of our daily lives.

The subject of mathematics is multifaceted. Steen (1990) describes a set of diverse perspectives that "illustrate the complexity of structures that support mathematics" (p. 4). These perspectives, or "deep ideas that nourish the growing branches of mathematics" (p. 3), can be thought of as (a) specific mathematical structures, such as numbers or shapes; (b) mathematical attributes, such as linear or periodic; (c) actions, such as represent or prove; (d) abstractions, such as symbols or equivalence; (e) attitudes, such as wonder or beauty; (f) mathematical behaviors, such as motion or iteration; or (g) mathematical dichotomies, such as discrete versus continuous.

Another characteristic of the subject is that many mathematical entities exhibit a process/product duality reflecting an "interplay of form with content" (Freudenthal, 1991, p. 10). Symbolic representations of such entities can be perceived either as mathematical processes or as the products of these processes. Mathematical thought is characterized by the ability to generalize detail (process or form) into structure (product or content) and to create new conceptual entities from an abstraction of this structure (Sfard, 1991; Tall, 1991; Teppo & Esty, 1994, 1995). This movement from form to content makes it possible to deal with complexity by reducing detail through abstraction (Devlin, 1997; Dryfus, 1991).

In addition, the use of some form of external representation makes it possible think about and manipulate the concepts under consideration, which leads to new levels of thought. The search for, and development of, adequate symbols to express new levels of conceptualization are a characteristic of the generative powers of mathematics (van Oers, 1996).

The nature of mathematics is also reflected through the activity and disposition of its practitioners. *Doing* mathematics, which is different from the mathematics presented in professional journals, includes, among other actions, exploring situations, searching for patterns, inventing strategies, using intuition, generalizing, and abstracting—creating mathematics. Coupled with such activity is the development of a mathematical disposition—a particular way of perceiving and doing that enables a person to navigate his or her way around the domain. Breiter (1997) describes this as "a diffuse kind of knowledge or competence that makes performance possible" (p. 3). Cobb and Yackel (1996) identify a set of reflexively related beliefs, values, and "sociomathematical norms" that, developed through classroom interactions, enables students to engage in autonomous mathematical practice.

Mathematics exists as an aim in itself of concern to practicing mathematicians, as a tool applied in the pursuit of other disciplines or in everyday life, and as a social and cultural artifact. As an aim in itself, it is self-generating, serving as "a forceful motor for its own long-term development" (Freudenthal, 1991, p. 3). Within this area, mathematical objects serve as the raw material from which other mathematical objects are created. As a tool, it is used to mathematize aspects of human experience that exist outside the realm of mathematics (P. J. Davis, 1993; Restivo, 1992). When employed in the course of everyday activities, such as in building a house or selling goods, the term *ethnomathematics* has been developed to emphasize the cultural embeddedness of the tool (Nunes, 1992).

Our understanding of mathematics is grounded in practice that is implicitly social. In his sociology of mathematics, Restivo (1992) argues that mathematical objects do not exist "independent of the flux of history and culture" (p. 3). These objects are a human creation that are "embedded in and ... embody world views" (p. 103). It is necessary to think in terms of a "cultural conception of mathematics" (Radford, 1997, p. 28). Mathematics is also grounded in common sense and stems from the systematization, organization, and reorganization of contextually bound experiences (Freudenthal, 1991). "The effects of culture and society are fundamental to the way in which we come to know" (Radford, 1997, p. 29).

The Nature of Mathematics Education

It is important for researchers engaged in the processes of "giving meaning to educational events" to situate these meanings against one's "assumptions about the teaching and schooling that underlie those events" (Gitlin, 1990, p. 460). How one thinks about mathematics education, how one defines what it means for students to know and do mathematics in school, is, in turn, affected by one's views about the nature of mathematics, one's underlying epistemological perspective, and one's educational goals.

P. J. Davis (1993) argues that today's world is characterized by the large degree to which mathematizations permeate our daily lives, both in the humanistic areas and in the sciences. Everyone uses mathematics at some level. Consequently, it is the role of education to enable citizens to become aware of and assess these mathematizations—to develop "mathematical ëstreet smarts' that enable [them] to form judgments in the absence of technical expertise" (p. 192).

Breiter (1997) addresses the role of education from a more individual perspective, advocating the development of mathematical disposition—an "intuitive, perception-like understanding ... that makes lifelong learning in mathematics a possibility" (pp. 3, 5). Renz (1997) offers a similar vision for mathematics education, stating a minimal list of competencies required for an uncertain future. Students should know how to solve problems by asking others; should be able to communicate by speaking, writing, and drawing; should be aware of the existence of multiple solutions; and should understand that most problems do not have definite solutions. Cobb and Yackel (1996) introduce additional dispositional attributes from their social constructivist perspective. In particular, mathematics education should foster the development of sociomathematical norms including the development of student autonomy and the ability to judge mathematical solutions on the basis of their differences, sophistication, efficiency, and acceptability. A common theme running through the different educational criteria listed here is that what students believe and think about mathematics is important for succeeding both in and out of school and for facilitating future learning.

Mathematics education can be defined as formal schooling to distinguish it from the ethnomathematics of everyday learning. The operationalization of such education is then to take mathematical knowledge, which was originally developed to be used rather than taught, and transform it into a teachable form (Greer, 1996). This transformation process must consider not only what knowledge is to be learned, but also the nature of the knowledge and the kinds of experiences that students are to develop (R. B. Davis, 1994). The focus of the transformational process is on the development of appropriate educational tasks within effective learning environments.

The Netherlands has developed a program of realistic mathematics education that employs the processes of horizontal and vertical mathematicizing as the "teachable form" (Freudenthal, 1991; Treffers, 1991). Conceptual development proceeds from informal, context-bound experiences to mathematical formalisms. A given situation is horizontally mathematized by students into a model; through vertical mathematization, this model is transformed, again by students, into formal mathematical structure. The emphasis in realistic mathematics education is to use contextual situations that connect with children's existing methods of working and that promote natural, further generalizations and abstractions. Education is seen as the process of guided reinvention in which the learner reinvents "mathematising rather than mathematics; abstracting rather than abstractions; ... algorithmising rather than algorithms; verbalising rather than language" (Freudenthal, 1991, p. 49).

Learning mathematics is recognized as a social and cultural activity. Our schools serve as one of the places in which students are introduced to the "meaning of culturally approved mathematical signs, symbols, and techniques" (Crawford, 1996, p. 145). The question of whether this process is *enculturation* (the assimilation of an existing tradition) or *acculturation* (the process of intercultural borrowing to create a new and blended culture) is one of perspective. When a mathematics classroom is examined from the external vantage point of an educational system, that is, outside the culture of the classroom, the processes of education are seen as the enculturation of students as they interact with more knowledgeable others. From the point of view within the culture of the classroom, the differences in beliefs and values of the participants support a view of acculturation in which the intersubjective meanings of the students and teacher are negotiated in the process of constituting a classroom mathematics community (Cobb, Jaworski, & Presmeg, 1996; Cobb & Yackel, 1996). Learning environments can be thought of as being constructed by individuals in activity rather than as existing independently of the participants (Saxe & Bermudez, 1996).

Richards (1996) describes a type of mathematics classroom that fosters acculturation into a shared community through the use of what he calls, "inquiry math." In such a classroom, the students and teacher participate in mathematical discussion and act mathematically—asking questions, solving problems that are problematic to the solvers, posing conjectures, and listening to mathematical arguments. The classroom atmosphere allows taking risks and making mistakes, and the teacher is able to truly listen to the students because of his or her understanding of "the larger mathematical picture that provides a context for the students' questions" (p. 74). Mathematical communication and the negotiation of meaning take place at a level at which there are two sides, and each is able to listen to the other.

The preceding characterizations illustrate the diversity of perspectives from which school mathematics can be viewed. Each perspective highlights a different aspect of the complex reality of mathematics learning within a socially and culturally constituted environment. As R. B. Davis (1994) points out in his discussion of what mathematics students should learn, "people no more agree on what they most value in an act of mathematical problem solving than they do in paintings or poems or symphonies. I know people who can't see why anyone would want to listen to Bach" (p. 25).

Mathematics Education Research

The multiple perspectives from which the nature of mathematics is now being considered and the variations in processes and contexts that are increasingly being used to characterize school mathematics reflect a paradigm shift from a modernist to a postmodernist worldview. This shift represents a reconceptualization of the nature of knowledge from a single and external reality to a set of multiple and subjective realities. Current trends in research in mathematics education reflect a similar paradigm shift from an emphasis on scientific or quantitative studies to the use of qualitative, interpretative methodologies (see Ernest, Chapter 3, this volume). "Researchers today are looking at aspects of mathematical learning in ways that were, if not unthought of, at least not common 25 years ago" (Kieran, 1994, p. 583).

The goals of mathematics education research reflect the diversity and complexity of its subjects of inquiry. At a general level, the goal of research is to produce new knowledge. In a field that is still in the process of defining itself, this knowledge provides an important base for progress in mathematics education (Silver & Kilpatrick, 1994). How one characterizes such progress, however, depends on one's perspective. The field of mathematics education encompasses the study and implementation of classroom instruction (in all its complexity) as well as the formulation of theories of the development of mathematical understanding (in all its variations).

From a practical perspective, there is a need for research to address the concerns of practicing educators in the field and to present results that are accessible to them and are of immediate use (Kennedy, 1997). The questions and data from such studies also provide important examples of exemplary practice and resources to stimulate reflection on relevant issues (Research Advisory Committee, 1994; Renz, 1997). Research is also needed to facilitate the creation, implementation, and evaluation of innovative curricula that can move mathematics programs beyond simply making improvements to those that currently exist. In addition, researchers should consider what role they can, or should, play in the development of informed public discussion concerning educational progress (R. B. Davis, 1992; Research Advisory Committee, 1997).

Research on practice can also be used as an emancipatory vehicle. The processes of inquiry, when conducted by practicing teachers, give them voice and power and enable them to pursue lines of inquiry directly applicable to their needs. The teacher-researcher movement changes the nature of the traditional relationship between the researcher and those studied by recognizing the value of teachers' personal knowledge and providing them with a vehicle for effecting change and setting educational policy (Brown, 1997; Gitlin, 1990; Richardson, 1994).

The incorporation of qualitative methodologies into mathematics education research has made it possible to investigate the teaching and learning of mathematics at new and different levels of complexity and from multiple perspectives. A goal of much of this research is to investigate the processes of coming to know mathematics both from the perspective of the cognizing individual and from within the sociocultural interactions of the classroom. Such research aids in the development of explanatory models of what constitutes mathematical learning (Steffe, 1996).

Research has also been used to expand our own conceptions of mathematics and our perceptions of what is possible in mathematics education. Attending to students' expressions of their ways of thinking, doing, and describing, or "student voice," promotes reconceptualizations of one's own mathematical understanding and promotes diversity of mathematical perspective (Confrey, 1995b). Careful analysis of videotapes of groups of students working through problematic situations reveals students' abilities to develop powerful mathematical ways of thinking (Maher & Martino, 1996).

Multiple challenges face the field of mathematics education research. The availability of diverse perspectives for launching inquiry will require a greater acceptance of alternative research methodologies and a greater commitment for researchers to communicate with one another across divergent points of view. As we recognize and accept the complexity of the questions we wish to ask and the phenomenon we wish to study, new methods will need to be identified that can capture this complexity in meaningful ways—requiring a "new set of explanations and a new set of tools" (Schoenfeld, 1994, p. 703).

The dynamic nature of the field of mathematics education research is reflected in an interplay between emerging lines of inquiry and evolving research methods. At the same time, the growth in diversity of perspectives makes it more difficult to establish standards of scholarly inquiry on which all participants in the field can agree. As Silver and Kilpatrick (1994) point out,

> It may be neither possible nor desirable to forge a single perspective out of the many that are found in our field.... [What is needed is a] spirit of greater openness, tolerance, and respect for the work and ideas of those colleagues who share neither our culture nor our tradition. (p. 763)

DIVERSE WAYS OF KNOWING

A study of the field of mathematics education research or, in the case of this monograph, of a small part of one corner of the field, is a useful endeavor. Bishop (1992, p. 720), commenting on its international scope, notes "the immensely disparate and complex [nature of the] field" and recommends that those who are trying to understand mathematics education and the nature of its research compare and contrast their work with others. This book provides a forum for such an examination. It is not intended to serve as a reference manual. Rather, the intent is to illustrate the diversity of methods available for researchers.

The purpose of this monograph is primarily to examine the processes by which knowledge is generated (research methods). In so doing, that which is known (reported results) becomes more clear. Thus, we seek to extend our knowledge of mathematics education by examining the ways in which knowledge in the field is created. We can increase our understanding of what we know if we understand how we come to know it.

The chapters use information from actual studies to illustrate different components of qualitative research design, presenting a wide range of methods and representing a variety of goals and perspectives. Instead of focusing on the results of their research, the authors select one facet of their design and describe in detail how it contributes to the final product.

Chapters 2 and 3 orient the reader toward a critical examination of the monograph. In Chapter 2, Pirie raises the question "What makes this research?" in relation to the field of mathematics education and invites the reader to become a participant in the process of creating a definition. In Chapter 3, Ernest provides background information related to the philosophical and epistemological assumptions underlying all qualitative research. He describes the constructivist theory of learning that undergirds much of the research reported here and contrasts quantitative, qualitative, and critical research paradigms.

Chapters 4 and 6 raise key issues regarding research design. Goldin (Chapter 4) discusses the importance of making explicit the theoretical assumptions underlying the selection of the research task and the methods of data collection and analysis—describing how protocols for in-depth clinical interviews are used to study individual children's problem-solving skills. Pirie (Chapter 6) focuses on the decision-making steps, required for robust research design, that she used to meet her goal of developing theory to describe how pupil-pupil discussion facilitates mathematical understanding.

The other chapters present a wide range of approaches and focus on different aspects of the total research design. Neuman (Chapter 5), using a phenomenographic perspective, describes the model that she developed to characterize the variation in the ways that beginning school children experienced aspects of subtraction. She presents a detailed analysis of cognitive constraints that make some problems easy and others difficult in her discussion of the word problems she selected for her clinical interviews. Clarke (Chapter 7) describes a technique for creating integrated data sets consisting of transcripts of classroom videotapes, students' interpretations of episodes on these videotapes, and observer field notes. His analyses of these data sets illustrate the use of multiple perspectives for investigating what it means to "come to know" something in a mathematics classroom. Jaworski (Chapter 8) describes how she assigned significance to classroom events in her study characterizing an "investigative approach" to teaching. She offers examples of the detailed reports used to record not only each incident of interest, but its classroom context, the interpretations of this incident by herself and the teacher, and the relations of the incident to her underlying theoretical framework.

Mousley, Sullivan, and Waywood (Chapter 9) present information on the use of the computer program NUD•IST to analyze open-ended responses to a large-scale survey. The purpose of this analysis was to identify features that members of the mathematics education community believed were desirable components of a quality mathematics lesson. D'Ambrosio (Chapter 10) describes aspects of professional-development programs that focused on developing teacher-researchers. She presents the steps used to move a group of preservice students toward an understanding of the nature of qualitative research and provides examples of inservice teachers' reflections on their use of research within their own classrooms.

The sequencing of chapters represents a continuous transition of focus from student to teacher. Goldin and Neuman report on the individual student's meanings of mathematical concepts. Pirie and Clarke shift to a focus on the development of meaning within a social context, the former within a small group of students and the latter within the larger context of the whole classroom. Jaworski and Mousley et al. report on methods designed to characterize the classroom experience from the teacher's perspective. D'Ambrosio moves back to an individual focus, but one that is centered on the teacher. Finally, Pirie (Chapter 11) examines common themes running through the chapters that address important issues, including the role of theory and the establishment of criteria for judging the goodness of qualitative research.

Chapter Perspectives

To understand the contributions that the authors make, it is important to place the information reported in each chapter into its proper perspective. A useful analytical framework for reading the chapters includes identifying the specific goals of the research and the assumptions that underlie each work, the objects of study and their situated contexts, the nature of the primary data collected, the unit of analysis and the type of understanding sought by the analysis, and the applicability of the findings to educational practice. The following comparisons illustrate how this framework can illuminate the diverse perspectives of the reported research methods.

Goldin and Neuman provide contrasting purposes of research and objects of study within similar contexts. Both researchers use clinical interviews involving carefully constructed mathematical tasks. Although the primary data in each study consist of children's observed behavior, the objects of study are very different. Neuman's findings are framed in terms of descriptions of the variations in the ways that children experience a given mathematical phenomenon, whereas Goldin's findings relate to the growth of children's complex, internal representational capabilities. Each chapter presents a different aspect of a complete clinical study—Goldin discusses principles of interview design, and Neuman focuses on how a phenomenon is experienced and depicted in a model and on criteria for establishing the reliability and validity of this model.

The research of Pirie, Clarke, and Jaworski illustrate the ways in which choices of methodology and analysis are driven by the nature of the research question and the underlying theoretical perspective. The primary data in all three studies were collected in classrooms, yet the objects of each study and the goals of research were different. Pirie audiotaped the conversations of small groups of students to develop a theory explaining how classroom discussion facilitates students' mathematical understanding. Clarke used videotapes of classroom lessons and students' interpretations of episodes in these tapes to investigate how the process of "coming to know" was developed by classroom participants. Jaworski used an ethnographic approach to collect data centered on teachers' interactions with students to characterize an investigative approach to teaching.

The chapters by Jawarski and by Mousley, Sullivan, and Waywood illustrate the subjective, interpretive nature of qualitative analysis. Using descriptions of her interpretation processes, Jaworski helps the reader understand the meanings

she assigned to observed classroom behavior and her reasons for attributing significance to particular incidents. Mousley et al. emphasize the subjective nature
of the interpretations they made as they organized and categorized the survey
responses. They discuss the subjective role that language plays, both in their
respondents' descriptions of mathematics lessons and in the researchers' categorizations of these responses.

D'Ambrosio highlights the constructivist nature of the research act. As preservice students and in-service teachers participated in the design and implementation of small-scale studies, they constructed their own understandings of the
nature of reflective practice and, in the process, became more empowered,
autonomous decision makers.

Unlike the other authors who focus on aspects of research design, Neuman presents a partial description of her findings. This information illustrates the central
component of phenomenographic research—the development of a model depicting the variations in ways that a collection of individuals experiences a given
phenomenon. A discussion of a proposed set of criteria for claiming reliability
and descriptions of ways to establish validity are illustrated in the context of the
author's phenomenographic model.

Each chapter can also be comparatively positioned within a set of contexts
common to research in mathematics education. These contexts include the use of
mathematical tasks, the mathematics classroom and its participants, the study of
the construction of knowledge that is individually or socially derived, or both,
and the researcher's role in data collection.

The chapters differ on how mathematical topics are used—either as foreground
or as background for the investigation. Neuman's research and one of
D'Ambrosio's studies investigate students' understanding of specific mathematical content. In contrast, Goldin, Pirie, Clarke, and Jaworski study specific types
of mathematical behavior that exist across a range of mathematical situations.
Although not always the explicit object of study, the nature of the mathematical
task in these four chapters is an integral part of the context of each investigation.
Goldin, Neuman, and D'Ambrosio illustrate the importance of in-depth analysis
of mathematical structure in the design of research tasks. In contrast, Mousley et
al. use an implicit mathematical context. Respondents to their survey are asked to
imagine a quality mathematics lesson and then to list characteristics of this lesson.

Another theme running through each chapter is the way the classroom context
is used. At one extreme, Goldin and Neuman situate their research within clinical
interviews that use mathematical tasks designed specifically for the interviews.
The classroom context appears only implicitly in Goldin's recognition of the
experiences that his subjects bring to the interviews. In contrast, Pirie, Clarke,
Jaworski, and D'Ambrosio purposefully incorporate the realities of school mathematics into their research, studying mathematical behavior that is an integral part
and direct consequence of this context. Mousley et al. make the mathematics
classroom the explicit, but indirect, object of investigation, using others' impressions of this context rather than direct observations as their primary data.

The reported research also varies as to the authors' perspectives on the source of knowledge construction. Goldin situates knowledge and reasoning squarely in the head of each subject, regarding knowledge construction as the building of internal representations by the individuals through interaction with a structured environment. Neuman, while studying individual children, focuses her research on the experiential *relationship* between subject and object. D'Ambrosio describes the growth of understanding of the research process by preservice students as a constructive activity. In contrast, Pirie and Jaworski represent a social constructivist orientation investigating the ways in which students' knowledge is constituted in the process of classroom interactions. Jaworski presents both radical and social constructive perspectives with regards to students' learning as she discusses how her point of view changed from the former to the latter during the course of her research. Clarke, in his study of classroom interactions augmented by individual student interviews, considers a symbiotic relationship in which the two perspectives of individual and social construction are mutually dependent and supportive.

Several authors characterize the knowledge derived from their research activity in terms of social constructions. In the interpretation of her data, Jaworski describes the development of intersubjective meanings that occur between herself and the teachers involved in observed classroom incidents. Mousley et al. comment on how theory related to quality mathematics teaching developed from shared understanding within their group of researchers.

The chapters also illustrate the range of roles that the researchers assumed in the collection of their data. Pirie describes how her selection of an unobtrusive position in data collection was determined by the goals of her research—electing to audiotape interactions to capture students' discussions that were unaffected by any adult intervention. At the other extreme, Jaworski, as a participant observer, actively interacted with the teachers and students she studied. The clinical interviewers in Goldin's study also directly interacted with the children under study. They employed carefully established protocols, however, to minimize variation across the interviews.

D'Ambrosio's use of a teacher's voice to illustrate the development of teacher-researcher activities reinforces the vital role that research must play in the field of mathematics education. Qualitative research, with its ability to capture more of the reality and complexity of classroom experience, provides an appropriate vehicle for investigating important issues as well as for narrowing the gap between research and practice.

A common thread linking the chapters in this book is the interpretative nature of qualitative research methods. Interpretation is a necessary component of techniques that are designed to study, within complex learning environments, the meanings that participants make of their experiences and aspects of human cognition that can only be inferred from overt behavior. Qualitative methods lend themselves well to this type of inquiry.

The chapters also illustrate the aim of qualitative research discussed by Ernest, whereby the particular is used to illuminate the general. Each author presents concrete instances that "suggest, evoke, and illustrate" situations that exist beyond the immediate context of each study. The specifics of the different techniques also serve as exemplars, and through a look at the particulars of the research studies reported here, qualitative research methodology is illuminated more generally by this monograph.

It is recommended that this book be regarded as a whole. Instead of providing discrete descriptions of research techniques that can be taken separately, the chapters, taken together, enrich the reader's understanding of each individual contribution. Comparing and contrasting the reported information not only complement and extend one's understanding but provide new windows on the field of mathematics education. The chapters also show a glimpse of the power of qualitative methods, developed in other human sciences fields and modified to fit new needs, to uncover hitherto inaccessible, but important aspects of the complex reality of mathematics teaching and learning.

Chapter 2

Toward a Definition for Research

Susan Pirie

Before the reader plunges into the remaining chapters of this book, it is appo-
site to ask, *even* if initially the possible response might appear to be obvious,
"What does the title of this book, *Qualitative Research Methods in Mathematics
Education,* mean?" If we unpack the wording a little, two notions bear scrutiny:
"qualitative methods" and "research in mathematics education." The first is perhaps a predictable focus for an early chapter in a book such as this; the second,
however, is a more fundamental concern.

Mathematics education is congruent with neither mathematics nor education.
Mathematics education is an emerging discipline, no longer in its infancy yet not
fully adult. We are in the formative adolescent years when it behooves us to seek
to establish our identity as a legitimate, independent, academic community. To
do this we must, among many other tasks, address the notions of "research" and
"methods" as they apply to the field within which we work. It is time for us to
put aside the debate that tries to uphold or refute the supremacy of quantitative
over qualitative methods. Neither has merit *in itself.* The appropriateness of
methods and methodologies espoused by researchers can be considered only in
the light of the intentions of the specific research being undertaken.

As the discipline of mathematics education comes to be more clearly defined,
our prime concern should be the business of deciding what constitute the appropriate areas for inquiry. The process of defining the nature of acceptable research
in the field of mathematics education is not a task that can be undertaken light-
ly. The roots of such research lie below the surface of a whole spectrum of cultures. They are fed by the backgrounds of those who undertake the research and
the historical precedents of the environments from which they come. It is imperative that we, as a community, address the questions of what we consider legitimate research in the field of mathematics education and what we term acceptable
results of such research. If we do not do this for ourselves, we will continue to
be judged by the criteria of other disciplines.

It is certainly inappropriate for our research to be evaluated solely from the
standpoint of scientific proof. The appeal of the scientific paradigm lies both in
its appearance of certainty and in its common acceptability, which stem from a
long tradition of established practice. The methods devised within this paradigm
have evolved over time and have been shaped and mathematically developed so
that generally acceptable criteria for evaluation of the results exist. We must not

be seduced by this history. Blind application of scientific methods will not necessarily produce research results of interest or value to the mathematics education community. Notions of representativity, replicability, and generalizability
are fundamental to quantitative research but not necessarily to work in all areas
of mathematics-education. On the one hand, we cannot ignore the affective and
socially influential domains surrounding the teachers and students we study. On
the other hand, we are not engaged solely in anthropological or sociological
study. Our interests lie in the realm of *mathematics* education, and we cannot dis-
regard the influence and peculiar nature of the subject matter, namely, the mathematics, on the teaching and learning that concern us.

Teppo, in the introduction to this book, alludes to the numerous fields from
which mathematics education research has in the past drawn its techniques and
methods. It is right that we should have done so, but we need to be aware that we
are borrowing from another field of concern and, if necessary, adapt and make
these methods more precisely our own. Diversity is essential as we seek the
emergence of the discipline of mathematics education, and imagination and innovative approaches are needed as we attempt to explore the nature of the field
within which we work. Innovation, however, must not be at the expense of rigor;
a tension must be preserved between novelty and acceptability. If we are to have
external credibility and if our research is to be seen as of value to the larger community outside mathematics education, we need to begin to seriously consider
the closer definition of research acceptable to *our own* community.

As a prelude to this defining process, we need to articulate for one another the
ways in which we have come to adopt the methods we are individually using. We
need to clarify for the rest of our community the cultures from which we are
coming and to make explicit the perspectives from which we are viewing the
problems we tackle. We should not feel a need to define ourselves in terms
appropriate to some other discipline, but we must be clear to ourselves what it is
that we are and what it is that we do as researchers in mathematics education.
Only then can we expect those outside the field to recognize the legitimacy of
our work . Honesty and openness are needed in our disclosure of how we choose
our methods so that self-critical appraisal takes place alongside external scrutiny. We cannot, of course, be complaisant in our isolation, defining ourselves and
ignoring the concerns and perspectives of others. The external criticisms need to
be addressed, particularly the criticisms of our uses of qualitative methods. For
instance, consider the case-study method. The issues of validity and reliability
cannot be tossed aside as "irrelevant to case study" but must be examined for relevance in the particular circumstances and to the particular questions that we are
considering. Questions of concern to the academic community at large need to
be openly debated by mathematics educators—but from the perspective of their
own research paradigms.

Any discussion concerning itself with research methods needs first to examine
the questions that such research is expected to answer or illuminate. What are our
questions in mathematics education? What are the issues we wish to examine?

More fundamentally, what do we consider to be research in our discipline? We do not yet have any coherent response to these questions I have posed.

At this point the reader is invited to actively join in the debate. The list that follows presents various scenarios in which no attempt has been made to represent the wealth of current and past work in mathematics education. They are offered as a provocative starting place for discussion. Where would *you* draw the dividing lines between, say, research and personal interest? The question you need to answer is not "What are you interested in knowing more about?"; research should encompass a wider perspective than purely personal development, yet its effects need not be generalizable to the whole community. The question is not "What would be useful to you in your teaching?" I contend that writing textbooks and creating materials properly lie in the domain of curriculum development. However valuable and revolutionary these tools might be, their production does not constitute research, although they may, of course, evolve as a consequence of research findings. The question that you *are* asked to address here is "What should the mathematics education community as a whole accept as legitimate research?" As you attempt to grapple with this problem, examine your personal background and culture to trace the influences that they have on your decisions because here lies the crux of the matter. Our personal histories are unique, yet we must find and depict common ground for the acceptable basis of research within our discipline. Consider the following scenarios:

- A teacher reads a variety of journal articles on teaching fractions and, on the basis of this reading, carefully plans a sequence of lessons. From the teacher's perspective the lessons go well and the pupils seem to have a good grasp of the concept of fractions by the end of the set of lessons.

- A classroom teacher, unhappy with the lack of understanding of some of her pupils, records herself teaching a particular lesson, transcribes it, and carefully examines her interactions with various children with a view to improving her own communication skills. As a result of this examination, she changes her behavior in class and the pupils appear, to her, to have a better grasp of the concept being taught.

- A mathematics educator from outside the classroom takes a transcript of recorded classroom interactions and examines it against a background knowledge of existing, reported research findings in classroom communication with a view to siting the teacher's behavior in the wider perspective of classroom practice. The teacher has been chosen as the subject of study because the investigator has previously noticed particular mathematical practices among some of the pupils in this teacher's class.

- A large, international sample of children is tested on a particular range of topics with a view to ranking countries by the mathematical ability of their children.

- The data gathered above are examined with a view to exploring the impact of cultural environments on mathematics achievement.

- On the basis of existing findings relating to errors and difficulties that pupils have with a particular mathematical topic, a piece of computer software is written specifically to offer appropriate and precise remediation to pupils struggling with this topic. The software developed is used in a variety of class-rooms with a view to comparing the effects on pupils with different mathematical backgrounds and problems.

- The findings above relating to the software are compared with the achievement of similar pupils who have not been exposed to the computer with a view to determining the efficacy of the remediation.

- All these data relating to the software are taken as a base for theorizing on why the novel approach did (or did not) result in increased understanding of the targeted topic.

- On the basis of broad, accumulated, personal experience, a mathematics educator puts forward a theory about the structure of the learning of novice teachers with a view to influencing general teacher-training programs.

- … and so on….

Some of the previous scenarios you may have been able to categorize instantly as within or outside your acceptable boundary for legitimate mathematics education research. As suggested earlier, pause and reflect on why you could do this. Can you begin to define your boundaries with a degree of precision? It is precisely this defining process that we, as practitioners within the discipline of mathematics education, have to undertake. Answers will not be produced overnight, but without active debate they will also not evolve over time.

There is yet a further question to consider in our endeavor to define mathematics education research. Can the *results* of the inquiry, in fact, be used to determine the acceptability of the work as "research"? If so, then methodology and methods will play a very big part in the debate. My contention is that acceptable research lies somewhere on a continuum from "lying on one's back in the grass gazing at the sky while thinking about the general notion of arithmetic" to "testing all 8-year-old children in the world on their ability to compute accurately the answers to all possible addition problems involving two numbers with two digits." The acceptable interval between these extremes will be governed, as stated earlier in part, by the purpose of the inquiry, but not entirely. If as a result of my sky gazing, I conclude that arithmetic is all about understanding numbers, am I doing research? What if instead I produce a theoretical structure for the learning of number theory that will revolutionize how arithmetic is taught? Have I been doing research? If as a result of my two-digit addition test, I am able to confirm that there is a wide range of ability among 8-year-olds across the world, can I justify my work as research? But suppose that I also notice the unpredicted fact that a very high proportion of children in only one specific nation have very low accuracy scores on all computations involving the number 7. Does this justify my actions as research? No single person can dictate the answers to these questions for the whole community, but mathematics educators need to participate in a continuing, vigorous discussion of what constitutes research.

The choice of research methods is a very personal decision, although it will be on this choice that the acceptability of the results will largely depend. Unlike the questions posed earlier in this chapter for which there are as yet no definitive answers, those that follow must be, and can only be, answered by the individual. Responses are needed that apply to specific research questions. There are not, and can never be, prescriptive answers applicable to all mathematics education research. In this area, the researcher is personally responsible for providing appropriate answers.

- When is it appropriate to attempt to remain objective and approach our data through statistical methods? When is the researcher's personal knowledge of the social setting relevant?

- When do we want to take a broad overview, and when is in-depth interviewing more likely to yield the desired information? When is a representative sample and when is a specific individual the more valuable unit of scrutiny? Do we seek insight or do we want generalizability?

- When are we working with existing theory, and when are we hoping to build new theory? When can we predefine the coding of our data for analysis, and when do we prefer to allow a taxonomy to emerge from the data as they are gathered?

- When and how do we take account of the dependency of our study on notions, such as understanding and emotions, that are never directly accessible but must come to us mediated or filtered through language and behavior?

This book is not intended to be a how-to manual, nor is it a polemic advocating the use of qualitative research. The research questions must always come first. One does not set out to do qualitative research; one sets out to advance the knowledge or understanding of some portion of the field of mathematics education and then searches for the most effective way of achieving this goal. The remaining chapters in this book illuminate the ways that different researchers have addressed some of the previous questions and provide insights into their decision making.

Chapter 3

The Epistemological Basis of Qualitative Research in Mathematics Education: A Postmodern Perspective

Paul Ernest

In the past decade or so, a new paradigm widely referred to as the qualitative research paradigm has begun to dominate research in mathematics education. Although its roots go back a long way, in mathematics education this paradigm emerged in Piagetian-style research based on clinical interview methods. There were anticipations that fit with the qualitative research paradigm, such as William Brownell's studies of understanding and problem solving in the 1930s and 1940s (see Noddings, 1994). However, only lately has research of this type become widely accepted and commonplace in the leading journals in the field.

The emergence and growth of the qualitative research paradigm in mathematics education represent an important shift in style in a still young field of inquiry. This development raises a host of issues about the nature of significant research questions, research methods, styles of research reporting, and the possible impact of such research on the teaching and learning of mathematics. Many of these issues are difficult to address in the abstract and are best demonstrated through concrete exemplars, as consistency with the epistemology of the qualitative research paradigm also requires. This monograph presents many such examples.

The qualitative research paradigm has a deep philosophical significance. The aim of this chapter is to address some of the general epistemological and foundational issues and implications concerning qualitative research in mathematics education and to relate the paradigm to broader developments in 20th-century thought—especially postmodernist thought. In this chapter, I sketch the philosophical background of the qualitative research paradigm and relate it to current developments in the philosophy of mathematics. I survey the epistemological foundations of this paradigm and its relationship with constructivist and social theories of learning and their implications for mathematics education research. After elucidating some of the theoretical assumptions and characteristics of the qualitative paradigm, I contrast it with two other educational research perspectives: the scientific paradigm and the critical theoretic paradigm.

A central aim of the chapter is to distinguish research methodology from methods. The qualitative research paradigm provides a methodology, that is, a general theoretical perspective on knowledge and research, that allows specific methods, instruments, and techniques to be selected for particular projects. Maintaining this distinction is vital to ensure that qualitative research is conducted thoughtfully and to prevent it from becoming formulaic and recipe driven.

PHILOSOPHICAL BACKGROUND

From Modernism to Postmodernism

The beginnings of modernism are often attributed to Descartes's (1637/1955) seminal contributions to epistemology. He imagined a logical master plan that could provide indubitable foundations for all knowledge. This plan was modeled on the geometry of Euclid, "the only [true] science … bestow[ed] on [hu]mankind" (Hobbes, 1651/1962, p. 77). Descartes's epistemology came to be known as rationalism, and his powerful rational vision was to dominate many areas of knowledge, including philosophy, physics, and mathematics. The approach of rationalism (and modernism) is to recast knowledge by using the logical structure of axiomatic geometry as a model to demonstrate the indubitability of the knowledge claims involved. This model is central to what Lyotard (1984) terms the metanarrative of modernism: the style of narrative of the overarching philosophical discourse used to legitimate scientific knowledge.

Early 20th-century philosophy of mathematics also reapplied this model to mathematics itself in the quest for absolutely certain foundations for mathematical knowledge. However, the failure of the prescriptive programs of the logicist, intuitianist, and formalist schools in the philosophy of mathematics to achieve this certainty is well documented (Ernest, 1991, 1997; Kline, 1980; Tiles, 1991). The applications of the scientific and rationalist legacy of modernism in the physical sciences and social and management sciences have continued unabated despite technical setbacks like these. Science seeks to build unified abstract theories to explain the phenomena of the world and to predict future regularities and outcomes. The absolute space-time framework of Newtonian mechanics may have given way to relativistic and quantum models of the universe, but the laws of science continue to be used to make powerful and widespread predictions. For a while, the modernist perspective dominated other subjects, such as positivistic philosophy and behaviorist psychology. It also had an impact on research in mathematics education both through these human sciences and directly through the influence of mathematics itself. The rational planning model of management, itself a development of modernism, continues to be applied in the government of education despite radical critiques (Stenhouse, 1975).

However, there have been significant developments in the cultural and intellectual spheres that reject the assumptions of modernism. Modernism's legacy, the rigid barriers between adjacent fields of inquiry, is dissolving, and an increasing number of interdisciplinary fields of study are developing. The influence of logical positivism, logical empiricism, and linguistic analysis on anglophone philosophy is beginning to wane. Instead, contemporary philosophy is now making contact with those European traditions that regard knowledge as historically and culturally situated and not as objective and existing solely in some Platonic or other disembodied realm of pure ideas. Part of this move is the recognition that knowledge, money, and power do not circulate in different and non-intersecting realms, thus challenging the Cartesian dualism of mind and body. Instead, there is a growing acceptance among some, at least, that knowledge, money, and power are all materially embodied and that all form an interconnected part of the human world we inhabit. This insight is part of the emerging perspective of postmodernism in philosophy and cultural theory, according to which a number of knowledge fields are being simultaneously reconceptualized as distributed and concretely based practices. These fields include the following:

- Philosophical postmodernism (e.g., Lyotard, 1984; Rorty, 1979): Grand logical ("top-down") metanarratives, like Descartes's rationalism, are being replaced by locally distributed ("bottom-up") knowledge practices in which knowledge is produced, shared, and warranted in "local," institutionally grounded linguistic practices. The academic community of mathematics educators may be regarded as one or more "local" communities of this type.

- Poststructuralism: Self and knowledge are being reconceptualized as distributed over a number of different discursive practices (Foucault, 1972; Henriques, Urwin, Venn, & Walkerdine, 1984).

- Wittgensteinian epistemology: Meaning and knowledge are regarded as situated in habitually conducted or changing "language games" embedded in social "forms of life" (Wittengenstein 1953).

- Tacit and personal knowledge (e.g., Ryle, 1949; Polanyi, 1958): These forms play an essential role in human and scientific knowing but are not expressible in explicit propositional form, contrary to the ideals of logical, rational, scientific knowledge.

- Cognitive science and the philosophy of mind (e.g., Gardner, 1983, 1987; Minsky, 1986): Mind is understood to be modular, with local knowledges, skills, and agencies in place of a single controlling intelligence.

- Social psychology: New emphases on situated learning prioritize context over individual minds (Gergen, 1985; Harrè, 1979; Lave & Wenger, 1991) and stress the formative import of discourse (Harrè & Gillett, 1994; Shotter, 1993).

- Sociology and philosophy of science: There is a new emphasis on the historical, laboratory, and rhetorical practices of scientists instead of on overarching theories of method (Feyerabend, 1975; Kuhn, 1970; Simons, 1989; Woolgar, 1988).

- Philosophy of mathematics: This embodies a shift of emphasis onto the methodologies and practices of mathematicians away from the logical theories of mathematical knowledge and truth (Kitcher, 1984; Lakatos, 1976).

- Social epistemology (Fuller, 1988; Toulmin, 1972), semiotics (Eco, 1984), and feminist epistemology (Harding, 1991): Parallel "bottom-up" developments in epistemology have been taking place.

These examples illustrate the epistemological shift in which knowledge fields are reconceptualized as comprising multicentered human practices. Within these decentered practices, knowing cannot be divorced from the concrete particulars known. These range from exemplary problem solutions and a knowledge of laboratory practice in science (Kuhn, 1970; Woolgar, 1988) through a knowledge of particular linguistic practices and speech acts (Austin, 1962). This means that the nature of knowledge is being reconceptualized, which is important for education where the selection, recontextualization, and communication of knowledge, as well as the assessment of its acquisition, are central activities.

The Philosophy of Mathematics

Accompanying the emergence of these new of conceptions of knowledge and human knowing is a new tradition in the philosophy of mathematics that has been gaining momentum. This movement has variously been termed *postmodernist* (Tiles, 1991), *maverick* (Kitcher & Aspray, 1988), and *fallibilist* (Ernest, 1991, 1997; Lakatos, 1976). This tradition is primarily naturalistic and concerned to describe mathematics as an extant knowledge field, including the practices of mathematicians, past and present. It is quasi-empiricist and fallibilist in its epistemology (Kitcher, 1984; Lakatos, 1976). A number of additional philosophers and mathematicians can be identified as contributing to this tradition, including Wittgenstein (1953, 1978), Putnam (1975), Wang (1974), Davis and Hersh (1980, 1988), and Tymoczko (1986). Also, a growing number of researchers are drawing on other disciplines to account for mathematics in terms of social and cultural practices. Their aim is to document mathematics as a social institution in the past and present and as an element of all human cultures, both urban and tribal. The outcome is an overlapping set of vistas that illustrate the various human aspects of mathematics and that together challenge the traditional modernist conception of mathematics as objective, superhuman, and value-free. These researchers and their disciplinary perspectives include Bloor (1976) and Restivo (1992) in sociology; Wilder (1981) and Livingston (1986) in cultural studies and ethnomethodology; Rotman (1993) in semiotics; Aspray and Kitcher (1988), Joseph (1991), Kline (1980), and Gillies (1992) in the history of mathematics; and Ascher (1991), D'Ambrosio (1985), Gerdes (1996), and Zaslavsky (1973) in ethnomathematics. Thus the fallibilist, postmodernist tradition in the philosophy of mathematics represents the convergence of several multidisciplinary perspectives (see Ernest, 1994a).

Within the philosophy of mathematics and within other fields that theorize about mathematics is a move to reconceptualize accounts of mathematics to accommodate greater plurality and diversity, including external, social dimensions of mathematics—its history, applications, and uses. There is also a widely shared commitment to a multidisciplinary account of mathematics that accommodates ethnomathematics, mathematics-education studies, and feminist and multicultural critiques. This commitment is important because if mathematics is conceived as inseparable from human contexts and practices, then social implications for mathematics education follow, enabling notions of accessibility, equity, and social accountability to be applied to the discipline of mathematics. The outcome is a demystification of mathematics, to the benefit of the discipline and mathematicians and also to students, teachers, and other users of mathematics in society.

Postmodernism and the Qualitative Research Paradigm

Postmodernism is a portmanteau term used to denote a variety of perspectives of different strengths and persuasions. Most mathematics educators would not wish to subscribe to all variants and formulations and could not because of inconsistencies between different versions. However, the shared feature of different versions of philosophical postmodernism is the rejection both of foundationalism (the quest for indubitable foundations for knowledge) and of the associated logical metanarratives of certainty for mathematical, scientific, and other forms of knowledge.

The philosophical postmodernism of Rorty (1979) and others rejects the grand design of modernism, which is based on one big idea of a logical order, built up from clear and simple ideas and explicitly stated postulates. It rejects the Cartesian epistemology with its overconfident logic-centered metanarrative. Postmodernism is instead polycentric, pluralistic, and more connected to tradition. It values the concrete, the local, what is given in, and shared through, local practices. This postmodernist decentering of knowledge has a powerful affinity with the qualitative research paradigm, with its emphasis on the concrete, the particular, the case study, and human-based knowing. Thus postmodernism provides an epistemological foundation for the qualitative research paradigm. But note that it is just one of many possible supporting narratives. It is not another unique metanarrative invoked to justify a knowledge field.

The essential function of a research paradigm is to support and facilitate the generation of knowledge, and, of course, one of its components is epistemology. From the epistemological point of view, two standpoints can be distinguished: the absolutist and fallibilist perspectives (Ernest, 1991). The difference between these standpoints is profound. An absolutist epistemology views "truth" as something that can be attained—that aspects of the world or thought can be understood completely or at least known with certainty. Such a view is associated with philosophical modernism and with some versions of the scientific paradigm. Fallibilist approaches to research, which include the qualitative research paradigm, fit with postmodernism and do not regard the world as something that can be known with any certainty. Followers of this approach see the relationship between the knower and the known as problematic and accept that no certain knowledge is attainable by humans (e.g., Guba & Lincoln, 1989). This humility with regard to epistemology, knowledge, and the results of the methods employed in the research process resonates with developments in philosophy, the humanities, and social sciences. It means that neither the qualitative research paradigm nor its methodology can be employed mechanically in the quest for knowledge. Every such approach is fraught with epistemological difficulties and stands in need of justification. Such an approach can result in only a partial and imperfect knowledge of events—the boundaries and claims of that knowledge stand in need of qualification and justification. Perhaps it is only because the scientific research paradigm has been the dominant paradigm in educational research, whereas positivism was the dominant paradigm in scientific research, that it has not had to justify its methodological approaches to the same extent as has the qualitative research paradigm.

EPISTEMOLOGY

Epistemological Foundations

The qualitative research paradigm is the product of a number of significant epistemological shifts for which postmodernism provides a philosophical foundation and support. These include shifting emphasis to human knowing from disembodied knowledge and to knowledge of concrete practices and particulars from universal generalizations and laws. I now expand on these important shifts and delineate the basis and sources of this paradigm. Historically, the qualitative research paradigm has epistemological foundations that are at least as old as those of modernism. Where one locates the beginnings of a tradition is almost arbitrary. I could start with the pre-Socratic Greek philosopher Protagoras of the 5th century BCE, who wrote, "Of all things the measure is Man, of the things that are, that they are, of the things that are not, that they are not" (Freeman, 1956, p. 125). This emphasizes the human features and limitations of knowing that are central to the qualitative research paradigm.

A more recent starting point, not long after Descartes's seminal contribution to modernism, is in the work of Vico. Vico (1710/1858) argues that we can know *rationally* only what we ourselves have made and that other forms of knowing, such as knowledge of persons, are of a different, more human kind. For these latter forms of knowledge, "we must seek aid from our imagination to explain them and, like painters, form human images of them" (Vico, 1744/1961, p. 168). Thus, Vico claims that there are two forms of knowing. The first emphasizes the rational. In the second, the emphasis is on the concrete, analogical, and particular aspects of knowing that are typical of the qualitative research paradigm.

The notion that there are two fundamentally different ways of knowing was further and seminally elaborated by Dilthey, one of the chief founders of modern hermeneutics (the study of interpretation, which originated with biblical exegesis). He distinguished the method of understanding for the human sciences (*Verstehen*) from that of the physical sciences (*Erklären*). Verstehen is the method of understanding necessary to grasp the subjective consciousness of participants in some meaningful activity or context. Erklären, in contrast, is the method of seeking causal explanations in studying natural phenomena.

This distinction was developed in the hermeneutic tradition as a means to extend knowledge and understanding beyond the limits of the scientific research paradigm and to recognize the essential role of interpretation (Blaikie, 1993). Verstehen has been further elaborated as an epistemological concept by Weber, Sch₂tz, and others this century in the social sciences: "Its goal is to find out what the actor 'means' in his action, in contrast to the meaning which this action has for the actor's partner or a neutral observer" (Schütz, 1970, p. 9). This is the central epistemological concept of the qualitative research paradigm.

Perhaps the most important critical contribution to hermeneutics and the philosophical foundations of social theory is that of Habermas (1971). Habermas is the leading exponent of the Critical Theory of the Frankfurt School, and his distinction among three knowledge-constituting interests is often taken as providing the basic distinction between educational research paradigms (Bassey, 1990-91; Carr & Kemmis, 1986; Schubert, 1986). He distinguishes the scientific ("quantitative") paradigm and the qualitative ("interpretative") paradigm; in addition to these two manifestations of traditional ways of knowing, he distinguishes the critical theoretic research paradigm, which some theorists subsume under the qualitative paradigm.

Thus in the history of epistemology and the human sciences, two different ways of knowing have long been distinguished. These correspond to the scientific perspective and that of the qualitative paradigm.

CONSTRUCTIVIST THEORIES OF LEARNING

One of the central components of the qualitative research paradigm is the constructivist perspective on learning. This is taken to include the different variants of constructivism, although radical and social constructivism will be distinguished later. It is primarily the influence of Jean Piaget that has established constructivism as a central theoretical perspective on learning in mathematics education. However, constructivism offers more than an account of learning and includes a fully fledged epistemology and a research methodology. (An epistemology includes a theory of public knowledge and its justification as well as a theory of individual knowing. Note that some proponents of constructivism regard the position as postepistemological because they reject foundationalism and epistemology as they are traditionally formulated [Noddings, 1990].) The constructivist perspective has had a profound impact on research on the psychology of mathematics education in the past decade or two and also underpins many recent developments in teaching.

Piaget's methodology centers on the use of the clinical interview. In this procedure, an individual subject is required to perform certain carefully designed tasks in front of, and with prompting and probing from, an interviewer. A series of sessions are likely to be needed for the researcher to develop and test his or her model of the subject's understanding concerning even the narrowest of mathematical topics. Piaget's clinical interview method is a seminal contribution to qualitative research methodology in mathematics education because it supplies in-depth information on which to construe an individual's thinking and cognitive processing. With its accompanying methodological assumptions, it is among the most widely used approaches of today (Steffe, 1991b; Steffe & Gale, 1995).

Piaget's epistemology has its roots in a biological metaphor, according to which the evolving organism must adapt to its environment in order to survive. Likewise, the developing human intelligence also undergoes a process of adaptation in order to fit with its circumstances and remain viable. Indeed, Piaget claims that the human intelligence is ordering the very world it experiences in organizing its own cognitive structures. "L'intelligence organise le monde en s'organisant elle-meme" (Piaget, 1937, cited in von Glasersfeld, 1989, p. 162).

Ernst von Glasersfeld (1989, 1995) and colleagues have extended Piaget's epistemology significantly in developing radical constructivism based on two principles: (a) knowledge is not passively received but is actively built up by the cognizing subject, and (b) the function of cognition is adaptive and serves the organization of the experiential world, not the discovery of ontological reality.

According to the first principle, knowledge is not transferred directly from the environment or other persons into the mind of the knower or learner. Instead, any new knowledge has to be actively constructed from pre-existing mental objects within the mind of the learner in response to stimuli or triggers in the knower's experiential (or psychic) world to satisfy the needs and wants of the learner herself or himself. As Kieren and Pirie (1991) argue, knowledge construction is based on a recursive restructuring of personal knowledge in the light of the knower's construings of mathematical experiences. Consequently, individual learners construct unique and idiosyncratic personal knowledge even when exposed to identical stimuli. As Kilpatrick (1987) and others have made clear, the acceptance of this principle or variants of it is very widespread among mathematics educators, psychologists, and cognitive scientists.

The second principle states that all knowledge is constructed and can reveal nothing certain about the world nor any other domain. This includes mathematical knowledge and parallels developments in fallibilist philosophies of mathematics. This assumption is much more radical because it amounts to a rejection of scientific realism. It implies not only that all our constructions will fall short in attempting to describe aspects of external reality, whether this be the physical world or learners' understandings of it, but that this reality is essentially unknowable. As Kilpatrick (1987) points out, this is an unpalatable consequence to many researchers who believe both that learners construct their own meanings and that we inhabit a knowable external reality, thus accepting the first but rejecting the second principle of radical constructivism.

Constructivism has introduced an important sense of awareness of epistemological limitations into research in mathematics education. As the postmodernist philosopher Rorty (1979) puts it, human knowledge can never mirror nature.

Von Glasersfeld's (1989, 1995) radical constructivist formulation is that our knowing can at best pragmatically fit the world and can never epistemologically match or mirror it.

Constructivism has had a profound impact on research in mathematics education and probably constitutes the major impetus for the recent shift toward more qualitative research. However, the constructivist epistemology requires that the methodology be used with humility and caution. Although we may tentatively come to know the knowledge of others by interpreting their language and actions through our own conceptual constructs, we must acknowledge that the others have realities that are independent of ours. Indeed, these realities of others along with our own realities are what we strive to understand in qualitative research, but we may never take these realities as fixed (Steffe & Gale, 1995).

The researcher as constructor of knowledge has to be included in the discussion of research. The researcher cannot be viewed as external to the object known in this type of research in mathematics education. "When we speak of cognition, education, problem solving, mathematics or learning and teaching, we must take care to recognize the role of the observer in the description and analysis of the problem" (Confrey, 1995a, p. 196).

Contributions From Social Perspectives

A number of other traditions and developments have helped introduce the qualitative research paradigm to social science research and, subsequently, to research in mathematics education. In particular, these include theoretical developments in sociology, symbolic interactionism, ethnomethodology, and social theory (see, e.g., Garfinkel, 1967; Goffman,1971; Mead, 1934; Schütz, 1972). These perspectives are centrally concerned with the social construction of persons, interpersonal relationships, and the types of interpersonal negotiation that underpin everyday roles and functionings, such as those of the teacher in the classroom. Berger and Luckmann (1966), building on these theoretical perspectives, elaborated the theory that our knowledge and perceptions of reality are socially constructed and that we are socialized in our upbringing to share aspects of the conventional view. Applications of these theories have a direct impact on research in mathematics education including research with a constructivist flavor (e.g., Bauersfeld, 1994) and without one (e.g., Bishop, 1985, 1988; Eisenhart, 1988). This impact is both theoretical, in terms of the underpinning epistemology and overall framework, and methodological.

Research in mathematics education is also drawing on other socially orientated traditions within psychology (Ernest, 1994b). Some of these use the theories of Vygotsky (1978) and other more recent activity of sociocultural theorists, such as Lave and Wenger (1991). For example, Bartolini-Bussi (1994) draws on activity theory, whereas Saxe (1991) combines anthropological and sociocultural perspectives. There are also influences from more radical social theoretic developments, such as the poststructuralist psychology of Henriques et al. (1984), founded on the work of Foucault (1972) and applied to mathematics education by Walkerdine (1988, 1989) and others.

One outcome of the impact of socially orientated perspectives has been the emergence of various forms of social constructivism in mathematics education. This includes the anthropologically derived position of Bishop (1985, 1988), Bauersfeld's (1992) interactionist version of constructivism, and Ernest's (1991, 1997) coordination of the social growth of collective mathematical knowledge with the individual's construction of personal knowledge. What these social constructivist ideas share is the notion that the social domain affects the developing individual in some crucial formative way and that the individual constructs or appropriates her or his meanings in response to her or his experiences in social contexts.

Some recent research in mathematics education that incorporates a constructivist perspective also commonly attempts to coordinate a social dimension with the constructivist perspective on learning (Cobb, 1989; Richards, 1991; Steffe & Tzur, 1994). Currently a controversy exists among supporters of various forms of constructivism and sociocultural learning perspectives (Ernest, 1994b; Lerman, 1996; Steffe & Gale, 1995). Cobb (1994) reviews contributions to sociocultural and constructivist perspectives and suggests that the main differences between them are over the location of mind, whether in the head or in the individual-in-social-action, and the concomitant view of mathematical learning, whether constituted by active cognitive reorganization or by enculturation into a community of practice. The associated published dialogue elucidates some of the key terms and ideas involved but also reveals unresolved tensions between competing perspectives. (The dialogue is published in *Educational Researcher* 1994, 23(7), pp. 4–23 and 1995, 24(7), pp. 23–28.)

Implications for Mathematics-Education Research

The emergence of constructivism in research in mathematics education has foregrounded a new set of research emphases that are central to the qualitative research paradigm. It is important at this stage to recognize some of them. These include attaching importance to—

- attending to the previous constructions that learners bring with them;
- attending to the social contexts of learning;
- questioning the status of knowledge, including mathematical knowledge and logic, and the learner's subjective knowledge;
- proceeding cautiously with regard to methodological approaches, since there is no "royal road" to knowledge or "truth";
- attending to the beliefs and conceptions of knowledge of the learner, teacher, and researcher, as well as their cognitions, goals, metacognitions, and strategic self-regulative activity;
- attending to language, discussion, collaboration, negotiation, and shared meanings in the personal construction of knowledge.

These emphases combine to indicate that constructivist research in mathematics education needs to consider the learner as a whole person—the complex social context of the learner, teacher, and researcher—and the constitutive and self-implicated role of the researcher in research, whatever the focus. These are all important features of the qualitative research paradigm in action in mathematics education.

However, a note of caution should be sounded in attributing these emphases to constructivism. If constructivism had never emerged in psychology or mathematics education research, it is likely that all these emphases and the qualitative research paradigm in education would still have emerged from anthropology and sociology. Although constructivism is important in research in mathematics education, especially for those with a background in psychology, it is by no means the sole source of the insights we gain from it. Most of the same insights are equally available to those drawing on anthropology, sociology, and ethnomethodology. We must therefore reject any myth of origins that promotes constructivism as an essential part of the qualitative research paradigm.

EDUCATIONAL RESEARCH PARADIGMS

I have been using the term *paradigm* to describe the overall framework within which qualitative research takes place. This draws on Kuhn's (1970) philosophical analysis of science as having normal and revolutionary phases. During normal phases, there is a single accepted paradigm within the scientific community (e.g., Newton's mechanics or Darwin's theory of evolution). During a revolutionary phase, several paradigms compete, and their supporters are usually so immersed in their own paradigm that they find it difficult to relocate themselves within another even when their own has been refuted. Kuhn's claim is stronger, namely, that competing paradigms are incommensurable, that is, mutually incomprehensible. But there is controversy in the philosophy of science literature over this claim (Lakatos & Musgrave, 1970).

With Kuhn's conception, research is usually understood to take place within a recognized or unconsciously assumed overall theoretical research perspective or paradigm. In education, and in the social sciences in general, are found multiple research paradigms, each with its own assumptions about knowledge and coming to know (epistemology), about the world and existence (ontology), and about how knowledge is obtained (methodology). Following the work of Habermas (1971), a number of educational researchers distinguish three main educational research paradigms: the qualitative (or interpretative), the scientific, and the critical-theoretic research paradigm (Bassey, 1990–91; Schubert, 1986). It should be mentioned that there is some controversy over whether Habermas's distinction between the interpretative (i.e., qualitative) and critical theoretic research paradigms is as strong as he contends (this controversy is discussed later).

Habermas argues that underpinning every knowledge-seeking enterprise is a particular type of interest or desire at work, even in the case of science. He

distinguishes three types of interest that underlie the quest for knowledge: to predict and control the phenomena under study (the technical interest), to understand and make sense of them (the practical interest), and to achieve social justice through this understanding (the emancipatory interest). These correspond to
the interests underlying three educational research paradigms: the desire to predict and control educational processes through knowledge (the scientific paradigm); the desire to understand educational phenomena, including individual
sense making (the qualitative paradigm); and the desire to change education—
and through it, society—for the better (the critical theoretic paradigm).
Corresponding to these interests are the intended outcomes of the three paradigms, respectively: objective knowledge, scientific generalizations, and truths;
subjective understanding, personal truths, and illuminating studies of unique
individuals; social changes and improved social institutions and conditions.

Bassey (1990–91), Ernest (1994c), and Schubert (1986) offer a discussion of
these paradigms from an educational perspective. They have been discussed
specifically in the context of mathematics education by Dunne and Johnston
(1992), Ernest (1994d), and Galbraith (1991). An outline of the qualitative
research paradigm is now given, followed by brief descriptions of the two other
paradigms.

The Qualitative Research Paradigm

The qualitative research paradigm developed from the methodology of sociology and social science research, including anthropology and ethnomethodology. It
is primarily concerned with human understanding, interpretation, intersubjectivity,
lived truth (i.e., truth in human terms), and so on. It takes from ethnomethodology
a concern to record phenomena in terms of participant understandings. It uses various ethnographic, case study, and largely qualitative methods and forms of
inquiry, and it attempts to overcome the weaknesses of subjectivity through triangulating multiple viewpoints. Much attention has been paid in the literature to the
problem of how qualitative research findings can be validated (e.g., Lincoln &
Guba, 1985).

In mathematics education research, the qualitative research paradigm can be
seen in the work of many researchers. A seminal early use of the research paradigm is that of Erlwanger (1973) in his celebrated case study of a single child's
learning (Benny). In the two decades since, a wide variety of qualitative research
has been published that presents, for example, in-depth knowledge of student
learning of mathematical topics, problem-solving procedures and strategies, and
teachers' beliefs.

One of the special features of the qualitative research paradigm is its use of
the case study. Traditionally, scientific inquiry has been concerned with repeat-
able (replicable) circumstances that can be described by general laws. All the
particulars of the world are unique, but shared features and resemblances allow
generalizations to be made, although always with a degree of uncertainty and

unreliability (Popper, 1959). Once general laws have been derived, the scientific research paradigm adopts a top-down perspective, using the general to deduce predictions about particular instances or observations.

The qualitative research paradigm works in an opposite direction and explores the unique features and circumstances surrounding a particular case. However, the aim is not to celebrate the uniqueness and oddity of a case. It is to explore the richness of a particular that may serve as an exemplar of something more general. Kuhn (1970) has argued that even in the physical sciences, much use is made of particular, exemplary problem solutions that serve as general models of reasoning and problem solving.

Research in the qualitative paradigm builds up a rich description of the case under study. Geertz (1973) calls it a thick description. Since a case typically concerns human beings and their interrelationships and contexts, this description allow a reader to understand the case through identification, empathy, or a sense of entry into the lived reality. Thus the kind of truth involved can be regarded as akin to that of the novelist: the truth derived from identification with, and living through, a story with the richness and complex interrelationships of social, human life.

However, a case is meant to be illustrative and generative. The particular is intended to illustrate the general—not with the precision of the exact sciences, but suggestively as an illustration of a more general and complex truth. The aim is, as Blake wrote in his *Auguries of Innocence,* "to see a world in a grain of sand"—to illuminate the general through the particular. Thus research in the qualitative paradigm adopts a bottom-up perspective, using a particular and concrete instance to suggest, evoke, and illustrate, if not describe, the general case.

Because of its renunciation of certainty, the issue of reflexivity arises for the qualitative research paradigm. The paradigm incorporates an epistemology that rejects the disembodied viewpoint of positivism that takes for granted the assumption that it gazes on a fully knowable and separate objective reality. Instead, in the qualitative research paradigm, the researcher uses herself or himself (and her or his conceptual framework) as a research instrument and should incorporate reflections on the implications of using this "instrument," with its limitations, in any account of the research.

The qualitative research paradigm is referred to under a wide variety of names, including interpretative (and interpretive), naturalistic, and alternative paradigms research. Some researchers prefer to avoid the name "qualitative research paradigm" because although it is in widespread use, there is a risk of confusion with qualitative research methods. In fact, the qualitative research paradigm can use quantitative as well as qualitative methods and data, just as the scientific research paradigm in education can also use qualitative methods as well as quantitative. Quantitative data and methods can be used within the qualitative research paradigm, as and when appropriate (paradoxical as this might seem), because of the important difference between *method* and *methodology* in educational research. Methods are particular data-gathering or analysis techniques. For example, mathematics achievement tests or Likert-type attitude questionnaires provide data that are typically analyzed by statistical or quantitative methods. In contrast, the transcripts of "think aloud" protocols during problem solving or videos of classrooms or videos of personal interviews provide data that are typically analyzed by qualitative research methods. Educational-research *methods* are specific and concrete approaches. In contrast, educational-research *methodology* is a *theory* of methods—the underlying theoretical framework and the set of epistemological (and ontological) assumptions that determine a way of viewing the world and, hence, that underpin the choice of research methods. In this broad sense, an educational-research methodology with all its assumptions corresponds to an educational-research paradigm.

Despite the theoretical possibility of other pairings, the qualitative and scientific research paradigms do generally tend to use qualitative and quantitative methods, respectively. Typically, during research in the qualitative research paradigm, the categories of analysis are generated, at least in part, during the analysis of qualitative data, whereas prechosen categories are applied in the analysis of data in the scientific research paradigm (Strauss, 1987). This is one of the major operational differences between the research methodologies.

One reason for qualitative research methods to be employed within the scientific research paradigm arises when researchers in mathematics education find themselves in transition between the paradigms. Mathematical training often implants the assumptions of the scientific research paradigm. Thus, the first use of qualitative methods can be against the hidden backdrop of some or all of the assumptions of the scientific research paradigm.

The Scientific Research Paradigm

The scientific research paradigm is also called the positivistic, neo-positivist, or experimental research paradigm in education. It originates with the scientific method as employed in the physical sciences, in experimental psychology, and so on. It is concerned with objectivity, prediction, replicability, and the discovery of scientific generalizations describing the class of phenomena in question. The forms of inquiry used include survey, comparative experimental, quasi-experimental, and so on. There is often an emphasis on quantitative data, but qualitative data can also be used, as and when appropriate. What is central to the scientific research paradigm is the search for generalizations predicting future educational outcomes. Thus process-product research in mathematics teaching is typical work in the scientific paradigm. It examines correlations between teaching practices and student learning outcomes and seeks to empirically validate relationships between them (e.g., Good, Grouws, & Ebmeier, 1983). Similarly, the construction of empirical learning hierarchies by the CSMS project (Hart, 1981), the comparison of instructional programs (e.g., Charles & Lester, 1984), the quantification of teaching behaviors (e.g., Cooney & Henderson, 1972), and the evaluation of aptitude-treatment interactions (e.g., McLeod, Carpenter,

McCornack, & Skvarcius, 1978) fall within the scientific research paradigm. Although it may be controversial to make this claim, in my view Piaget also used qualitative research methods (clinical interviews) to advance his theory of cognitive stages. This latter use, with its age-stage measures and predictions, lies squarely within the scientific research paradigm.

The scientific research paradigm has many of the advantages associated with the physical and biological sciences. When successful, it results in replicable and objective generalizations. These have the strengths of being rigorously scientifically tested. The paradigm also has the strengths of clarity, precision, rigor, standardization, and generalizability. It is also, in theory, universally applicable. However, the weakness of this paradigm is that it involves simplifying the phenomena described, and its application is too often based on unquestioned assumptions. All persons and human situations and contexts are unique and individual, but the scientific research paradigm treats whole classes of individuals or events as identical, or at least indistinguishable, except in terms of a range of selected variables. Thus, this approach can often be insensitive to contextual variations and individual differences, although in theory it can always be refined to accommodate omitted aspects. Some of the epistemological assumptions associated with this paradigm are questionable, too. For often it is associated with an absolutist epistemology and a Newtonian-scientific ontology. However, these are defensible perspectives, even if they are sometimes uncongenial to those working in the qualitative research paradigm.

The Critical Theoretic Research Paradigm

The critical theoretic paradigm has developed out of the Critical Theory of the Frankfurt School, especially the work of Jurgen Habermas (1971). The central feature of this position is the desire not just to understand or to find out, but to engage in social critique and to promote social and institutional change to improve or reform aspects of social life. In education, this often involves working on social justice issues, such as redressing gender, class, or racial inequalities. To this end, it often involves participant engagement and validation. One of the best known discussions of this approach applied to educational research is that of Carr and Kemmis (1986). As in this reference, the critical theoretic paradigm is often closely associated with action research, which is popular among the "teacher-as-researcher" movement, with teachers working to change their teaching or school situations to improve classroom learning. In my view, action research, however, too often balks at addressing oppression in society to fit comfortably under the critical theoretic paradigm. Such projects as Paolo Freire's (1972) work emancipating Brazilian peasants through literacy, although not explicitly critical theoretic, serves as an excellent example of this type of research. Likewise, in mathematics education, the paradigm is reflected in the work of Gerdes (1985) in Mozambique and such researchers as Mellin-Olsen (1987) and Skovsmose (1985, 1994) in Scandinavia.

The critical theoretic research paradigm is explicitly concerned with improving some context, situation, or institution. Most other educational research is also concerned with improving schooling in some way or other, but this improvement is usually more of an indirect consequence of the inquiry. The paradigm has the advantage of specifying this goal explicitly and not being concerned with trying to leave undisturbed the situation being investigated. The disadvantage of this paradigm is that hidden institutional sources of resistance to change, such as teacher and pupil ideologies, institutional structures, and so on, may often prevent progress. If there is no progress and there is little of the knowledge that the other two educational research paradigms seek to establish, then the danger is that there may be no worthwhile outcome for the energy and time invested.

A philosophical criticism of the critical theoretic research paradigm is that its intended outcome (emancipatory social change) is of a different category from the intended knowledge outcomes of the scientific and qualitative research paradigm (Blaikie, 1993). The rational basis for emancipatory knowledge qua knowledge has not been made explicit (Carr & Kemmis, 1986). However, Habermas's (1981) project in recent years has been to meet this challenge by developing a theory of communicative action that unifies knowledge with emancipatory action.

Comparing the Research Paradigms

Given that multiple educational research paradigms exist, it is worth comparing them briefly. Table 3.1 shows a simplified summary and comparison of the three major research paradigms by using some of the factors previously mentioned (based on Bassey, 1990–91; Ernest, 1994c; and Schubert, 1986).

Table 3.1
Simplified Summary and Comparison of the Three Main Paradigms

Component	Paradigm		
	Scientific	Qualitative	Critical theoretic
Ontology	Scientific realism (objects in physical space)	Subjective reality (personal meanings)	Persons in society and social institutions
Epistemology	Absolutist, objective knowledge	Personal, constructed or socially constructed knowledge	Socially constructed knowledge
Methodology	Mainly quantitative and experimental, involving many subjects and contexts	Mainly qualitative case studies of particular individuals and contexts	Mainly critical action research on social institutions
Intended outcome	Applicable knowledge and generalizations	Illuminative subjective understandings	Intervention for social reform, social justice
Interest	To comprehend and improve (through prediction and control) the world	To understand and make sense of the world	Social justice, emancipation

One of the major epistemological differences among the paradigms concerns what is problematized. The scientific research paradigm locates uncertainty exclusively in the immediate object of inquiry, such as the teaching and learning of mathematics in a particular classroom. This paradigm does not require any reflexivity concerning the researcher's constitutive role in knowledge and meaning making. There are of course objectified requirements to attempt to remove distortions introduced by the researcher in the process of inquiry, such as the concern to establish the validity and reliability of the research instruments used. In contrast, the other two paradigms do not regard the world and its events as something that can be known with any certainty. They problematize the relationship between the knower and the known and adopt a position of humility with regard to epistemology, knowledge, and the results of the methods employed in research. This means that neither of these two research paradigms or methodologies should be employed mechanically in the quest for knowledge but that every application stands in need of justification. A fallibilist epistemology requires the recognition of the limits of knowledge claims at every level of educational research. A note of caution should be added. Sometimes, critical theoretic research presupposes that it has a privileged viewpoint delivering reliable knowledge about the social situation it seeks to change.

The three paradigms represent clusters or general styles of approach to educational research, characterized in terms of their types of basic assumptions. Within each paradigm (and the fit may be loose in parts), it is possible to have a wide variety of approaches. Some of the disciplined approaches that fit more or less within the qualitative research paradigm are the phenomenological, ethnomethodological, psychoanalytic, and hermeneutic approaches. Perhaps in either the qualitative or the critical theoretic paradigms (and perhaps overlapping with both) are the social constructivist, poststructuralist, and feminist standpoints (Harding, 1987). Dunne and Johnston (1992) relate all three educational research paradigms to gender issues in research in mathematics and science education. Ernest (1994a, 1994b) includes contributions representing many of these approaches to research in mathematics education.

It has been suggested by some scholars that the distinction between the qualitative and the critical theoretic research paradigms is not as clear-cut as the preceding account suggests. After all, it is largely based on Habermas's distinction in defining a third research paradigm, namely the critical theoretic one. Certainly the possibility of overlap between the qualitative and the critical theoretic paradigms should be countenanced, and indeed some examples of research in mathematics education are hard to locate within just one of the paradigms (e.g., Walkerdine's [1988] poststructuralist approach). Some other researchers sometimes distinguish only two major paradigms, the scientific and the interpretative (i.e., qualitative) research paradigms (e.g., Lincoln & Guba, 1985), with the latter incorporating the critical theoretic paradigm. HarrÈ and Gillett (1994) also contrast only two research paradigms in contemporary psychology, the Newtonian (scientific) and the discursive (qualitative) paradigms, thus reducing the distinction to a dichotomy.

Finally, it should be acknowledged that issues of philosophy and epistemology concerning educational research paradigms are controversial. For rather than acknowledging that multiple valid paradigms and sets of assumptions underpin research, each with different strengths and aims, some researchers have preferred to fight for their own paradigm as the sole valid one. Scientific research paradigm supporters have argued that they own the sole route to objectivity and truth. Supporters of the qualitative research paradigm have argued that the quest for objectivity and truth is futile and that only they can offer valid understanding. Critical theoretic research paradigm supporters have argued that the others are victims of "false consciousness" and that only they can reveal the ideologically induced distortions in education and society.

Thus there is no consensus about which educational research paradigm is "true" or "correct." There are only proponents of one or another paradigm and those who argue that all have some validity, as I do here. From the point of view of the fallibilist epistemology underpinning the qualitative research paradigm, "correctness" is not possible, anyway. Instead, it is important to be aware of the strengths and weaknesses of scientific, qualitative, and critical approaches and to be able to question the epistemological assumptions that are made in each of them. Gage (1989) has written of the paradigm wars waged among supporters of the three paradigms in the educational research community in the United States. His recommendation is that educational research paradigms are tools that should serve our practical ends in education and that the best policy is to acknowledge their multiplicity while judging them by their fruits.

Chapter 4

Observing Mathematical Problem Solving through Task-Based Interviews

Gerald A. Goldin

Over a period of 2 decades, mathematics education has evolved to stress conceptual understanding, higher-level problem-solving processes, and children's internal constructions of mathematical meanings in place of, or in addition to, procedural and algorithmic learning (Davis, Maher, & Noddings, 1990; von Glasersfeld, 1991). With this trend, the structured clinical interview has found greater acceptance as a research method. It lends itself well to the qualitative study and description of mathematical learning and problem solving without the exclusive reliance on counts of correct answers associated with pencil-and-paper tests.

In general, such structured interviews are used in research for the twin purposes of (a) observing the mathematical behavior of children or adults, usually in an exploratory problem-solving context, and (b) drawing inferences from the observations to allow something to be said about the problem solver's possible meanings, knowledge structures, cognitive processes, affect, or changes in these in the course of the interview.

For me, structured interviews are especially attractive as a means of joining research with educational practice. Reforms in school mathematics in the United States endeavor (among other goals) to foster the discovery of patterns and ways of reasoning about them and to develop skill in constructing original, nonstandard solution methods. Guided explorations by children and small-group problem solving are encouraged. These goals supplement (if they do not actually supplant) more "traditional" teacher-centered, direct instruction emphasizing mastery of standardized mathematical representations, rules, and procedures. In the

This chapter expands on talks presented at the 16th Annual Conference of the Mathematics Education Research Group of Australasia (MERGA-16, July 1993, Brisbane, Australia), and at the 17th Annual Conference of the International Group for the Psychology of Mathematics Education (PME-17, August 1993, Tsukuba, Japan). The research described was partially supported by a grant from the U.S. National Science Foundation (NSF), "A Three-Year Longitudinal Study of Children's Development of Mathematical Knowledge," directed by Robert B. Davis and Carolyn A. Maher at Rutgers University. Opinions and conclusions expressed are those of the author and do not necessarily reflect the views of the NSF or the project directors.

reformed context it becomes increasingly important to be able to describe and assess the longitudinal mathematical development of individual children. We need to find ways of observing that permit valid inferences about the deeper understandings that the new emphases try to develop (Lesh & Lamon, 1992). Thus, task-based interviews have importance both as research instruments and as potential research-based tools for assessment and evaluation. They offer the possibility of obtaining information from students that bears directly on classroom goals and can help answer research questions central to the educational reform process: What long-term consequences are innovative teaching methods having for children's mathematical development? What powerful problem-solving processes (if any) are students learning in "reform" classrooms? What cognitive representational structures are they developing? Are all children developing these, or only some? What are the affective consequences of reform? What beliefs about mathematics are children acquiring?

The main purpose of the chapter is to discuss some of the scientific underpinnings of task-based interview methodology in the study of mathematical problem solving. I touch on a set of issues having to do with the reproducibility, comparability, and generalizability of research findings. The importance of having an explicit theoretical perspective when structuring an interview is discussed, as well as the fact that choices made during interview design can result in foreseeable consequences—for instance, obtaining some information at the expense of other information. I try to be aware throughout the chapter of constraints and limitations imposed by the social and psychological contexts of interviews as well as of the interplay among task variables, contextual factors, observed behaviors, and cognitions inferred by the researcher.

The main points are illustrated with reference to five structured, individual interviews, designed around mathematical problem-solving tasks for the purposes of a longitudinal study. These provide concrete examples related to the central questions. The views described here helped shape the development of the scripts for these interviews and were in their turn considerably influenced by that process. What we learned in developing the interview scripts, carrying out the interviews, and interpreting the results influenced some principles of interview design and construction that are suggested for consideration by the mathematics education research community.

QUESTIONS RAISED BY TASK-BASED INTERVIEW RESEARCH

Whether we regard task-based interviews as research instruments or as assessment tools, their use to observe and draw inferences from mathematical behavior raises fundamental questions. It is my view that future research studies involving clinical interviews would benefit greatly by giving explicit, advance consideration to the following questions:

1. In what sense do the interviews permit genuinely scientific investigations? By this I mean to inquire about the implications of the task-based interview

methodology employed for (a) the examination, analysis, and communication to others of the measurement process, (b) the replicability of results (from one interview to another with the same subject, from one population to another with similar characteristics, from the current study to other studies, and so forth), (c) the comparability of outcomes across studies that may employ different interview instruments, and most important, (d) the eventual *generalizability of the findings* that are obtained from the observations made.

2. What role does theory play in structuring the interviews? To what extent are the observations made during an interview contingent on the tacit or explicit theoretical assumptions that underlie the interview questions and procedures? How does theory guide the choice of questions in the interview? How does it guide the contingencies that are planned for? How does it allow for unplanned contingencies? How are we to draw inferences about cognition, affect, or both, from our observations? What is the interplay among task variables (the characteristics of the problems on which task-based interviews are based), observed behaviors, and the inferences we can draw? How should we come to modify, substantially revise, or even discard our theories on the basis of the empirical outcomes of the interviews?

3. What constraints or limitations are imposed by the social, cultural, and psychological contexts of the interviews? How may the student's expectations, presumptions, apprehensions, and intentions interact with mathematical cognitions and affect (and with task variables) to influence the interview outcomes?

The intent in raising these questions is to begin the discussion from a scientific perspective, offering illustrative examples from the current study, and to propose some preliminary and partial answers—in the context of that study—that may be more generally applicable. My goal is to frame some general principles of interview design and construction that may be appropriate for the mathematics education research community to adopt. For example, it may be possible to characterize the trade-offs that take place as questions are selected for incorporation in an interview script and, through explicit principles, to optimize the information gathered in a task-based interview.

The ideas advanced here have their origins in earlier studies of mathematical problem solving and in discussions about observation, measurement, and assessment (Bodner & Goldin, 1991a, 1991b; Cobb, 1986; DeBellis & Goldin, 1991; Goldin, 1982, 1985, 1986, 1992a; Goldin & Landis, 1985, 1986; Goldin & McClintock, 1980; Hart, 1986). But they are immediately instigated by a series of task-based interviews that a group of us at Rutgers University created in the context of a longitudinal study of individual elementary school children's mathematical development. Five scripts were written, and used from 1992 to 1994, as the basis for a series of individual problem-solving interviews with children. The next section describes these briefly. I then return to explore aspects of the scientific nature of task-based interviews and address the role of theory and the role of context. The chapter concludes with comments concerning principles of interview design and construction.

AN EXPLORATORY LONGITUDINAL STUDY

In a study whose outcomes are still being analyzed, the mathematical development of an initial group of 22 children was observed for approximately 3 years. At the outset, in the 1991–92 school year, subjects were 8 to 10 years old. They were then in the third and fourth grades in a cross-section of New Jersey's public schools: two urban schools (5 third graders and 4 fourth graders); one school in a predominantly blue-collar, "working class" community (7 fourth graders); and one school in a suburban, "upper middle class" district (6 third graders). These schools, and the children's teachers, were participating in an intensive, constructivist-oriented mathematics teacher development–mathematics education reform partnership called MaPS (Mathematics Projects in Schools), sponsored by the Rutgers Center for Mathematics, Science, and Computer Education and the Graduate School of Education and directed by Carolyn A. Maher and Robert B. Davis. In fact, one reason for initiating the longitudinal study—for which data sources included videotapes of the children's individual problem solving, as well as their small-group mathematical activity inside and outside class—was to be able to assess some of the project's outcomes in relation to individual children's mathematical understandings as they grew over time.

One component of this study consisted of a series of task-based, individual interviews with each child over a part of the 3 years, conducted under the direction of the author (DeBellis & Goldin, 1993; Goldin, 1993; Goldin, DeBellis, DeWindt-King, Passantino, & Zang, 1993). Five interviews were designed and administered between spring 1992 and Spring 1994, with the goals of observing complex, individual mathematical problem-solving behavior in detail and drawing inferences from the observations about the children's thinking and development. Thus, this component of the study was, from a scientific standpoint, mainly exploratory and descriptive—subjects were not a random sample from a larger population, and no general hypotheses were being explicitly tested. Rather, we hoped to describe individual mathematical development in as much detail as possible, focusing not on standard, discrete skills or algorithmic problem solving, but on the growth of complex, internal representational capabilities. Tied to these goals, the interview design included several steps: (a) planning in relation to mathematical content and structure, anticipated observations, and inferences—discussed further in the next two sections; (b) creating an interview script, and its critique by the research group in a graduate seminar; (c) pilot testing the script in a different school, with children not part of the longitudinal study, and revising it on the basis of the pilot test; and (d) training and rehearsing with clinicians, including practice sessions. Initially we hoped that half or more of the 22 children would remain in the study for the full term; originally six interviews were planned, but funding constraints limited us to five. As it turned out, 19 of the original group of children participated in all five interviews.

The interviews themselves were designed to take less than one class period. In every interview, alternative embodiments for external representation were given to the child: paper and pencil, markers, cards, chips or other manipulatives, paper cutouts, a hand calculator, and so on, in accordance with the task. The questions within an interview tended to increase in difficulty, so that each child began with a level of comfort, but even mathematically advanced children encountered some questions that were challenging before the interview ended. Free problem solving was encouraged wherever possible, with (specified) hints given or suggestions made only after the child had the opportunity to respond spontaneously. All responses were accepted by the clinician (with occasional exceptions, specified in advance); thus "wrong" and "correct" answers were treated similarly. Follow-up questions by the clinician were asked without an overt indication of the correctness of earlier responses. Two video cameras operated simultaneously during each interview—one focusing on the clinician and the child or the child's face, the second focusing on the work the student was doing (working with paper and pencil or handling manipulatives); in Interview 3, a third camera also provided a close-up of the child's facial expressions. An observer made notes during the interview. Subsequently the videotapes were transcribed, viewed, and analyzed. What follows is a capsule description of each interview script. The full texts of the interviews are available for research purposes from the Rutgers Center.

Task-Based Interview 1

The first interview script (55 pages, about 45 minutes) was written during 1991–92 and administered in May and June 1992. The task, based on a high school–level problem of the National Assessment of Educational Progress, involves laying out for the child three cards, one at a time (see Figure 4.1): "Here is the first card, here is the second card, and here is the third card."

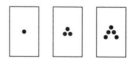

Figure 4.1. The first three cards presented in Task-Based Interview 1.

The cards are drawn from a stack in an envelope, so the child may infer from the context that there is a deck larger than the few cards shown and (possibly, tacitly) may also infer that there is a pattern present. After a brief pause to allow a spontaneous response, the child is asked,

• "What do you think would be on the next card?"

The materials placed ahead of time on the table are blank index cards (the same size as those with dots), felt-tipped markers of different colors, round red and black chips (checkers), a pad of paper, and a pencil. The child can use any items.

A series of exploratory questions follows, with contingencies based on the nature of the responses and special emphasis on exploring the child's pattern construction and use of external representations. After a complete, coherent response to the first question has been elicited, the child is similarly asked the following questions in slow succession:

- "What card do you think would follow that one?"
- "Do you think this pattern keeps going?"
- "How would you figure out what the 10th card would look like?"
- "Here's a card [showing 17 dots in the chevron, or inverted V, pattern]. Can you make the card that comes *before* it?"
- "How many dots would be on the 50th card?"

The script is written so that for each main question, exploration proceeds in four stages: (a) posing the question ("free" problem solving) with sufficient time for the child to respond and only nondirective follow-up questions (e.g., "Can you tell me more about that?); (b) heuristic suggestions if the response is not spontaneous (e.g., "Can you show me by using some of these materials?"); (c) guided use of heuristic suggestions, again to the extent that the requested description or behavior does not occur spontaneously (e.g., "Do you see a pattern in the cards?"); and (d) exploratory (metacognitive) questions (e.g., "Do you think you could explain how you thought about the problem?"). The clinician's goal is always to elicit (a) a complete, coherent verbal reason for the child's response and (b) a coherent external representation constructed by the child, before going to the next question (for the question about the 50th card, an external representation is not required). A complete, coherent reason means one based on a described or modeled pattern, but this pattern is *not* required to be "canonical" (i.e., to have the 4th card drawn with 7 dots in the chevron pattern) for the response or external representation to be considered complete and coherent.

This "nonroutine" task embodies an additive structure in an arithmetic sequence represented through a geometric arrangement of dots. It provides opportunities for the child to detect numerical or visual patterns, or both; to use visual, manipulative, and symbolic representations; and to demonstrate reversibility of thinking.

Task-Based Interview 2

The design for the second interview script (38 pages, up to about 55 minutes) was completed in fall 1992. The script was used in individual interviews administered during winter 1993 with the same children (then in fourth and fifth grades). As in the first interview, materials (a pad, a pencil, markers, and checkers) are placed ahead of time on the table in front of the child. First some preliminary questions are asked with the intent of exploring the child's imaginative and visual processes: The child describes whether she or he is right- or left-hand-ed. Then the child is asked to imagine a pumpkin, to describe it, to manipulate the image in various ways (including cutting the pumpkin in half), to spell the word *pumpkin,* to spell it backward, and to talk about these activities. A series of mathematical questions follows. For each, the follow-up includes (where appropriate): "Can you help me understand that better?" or "Are there any other ways to take (one half) (one third)?" or both questions.

- "When you think of one half, what comes to mind?"
- "When you think of one third, what comes to mind?"
- "Suppose you had 12 apples. How would you take (one half) (one third)?"
- [Next cutouts are presented in succession: a square, a circle, and a 6-petal flower. For each, the child is asked] "How would you take (one half) (one third)?"
- [Circle cutouts are presented to the child, first with (one half) (one third) (one sixth) represented conventionally (as in a pie graph), then with the same fractions represented unconventionally (the part representing the fraction at the center of the circle). In each case the child is asked] "Can this card be understood to represent (one half) (one third)? (Why?) (Why not?)"
- [A 3-by-4 array consisting of 12 circles and 6-petal flowers is now presented.] "How would you take (one half) (one third)?"
- The child is also asked to write and interpret the usual notation for the fractions one half and one third.

Next a solid wooden cube is shown. Some preliminary questions are asked about its characteristics (number of faces, edges, and corners). The child, guided as necessary toward understanding what these mean, is then asked to think about cutting the cube in various ways:

- "Now think about cutting this cube in half. What would the two halves look like?"
- "Suppose we painted the cube red and then cut it the same way. How many faces are painted red, for the smaller pieces you told me about?"

Similar questions follow about cutting a series of up to five additional cubes, depending on the time available. These cubes are marked with lines at designated vertical or horizontal positions, or both, which results in mutually congruent pieces that are respectively $1/3$, $1/4$, $1/8$, $1/9$, and $1/27$ the volume of the original cube. The script contains numerous suggested exploratory questions and a series of retrospective questions at two different points. This interview thus provides opportunities for the children to express a variety of conceptual understandings related to one half and one third, in many different embodiments in both two- and three-space dimensions. A multiplicative structure is embodied in cutting the solid wooden cube across different dimensions, and special emphasis is placed on exploring visualization by the child.

Task-Based Interview #3

The third interview script (28 pages, about 50 minutes) was completed in May 1993 and administered during May and June of that year. It begins with some introductory questions designed to elicit some of the child's affect in relation to mathematical problem solving: "Could you think back to the first time you remember doing mathematics? What do you remember?" "What is the earliest you remember doing math in school?" "Did your (parents) (brothers or sisters) ever do mathematics with you? Did they like to do mathematics?" "Do you remember doing puzzles or playing games at home? What games did you play?" "Did you ever see or do mathematics on TV?" "Do you remember doing mathematics with friends?" Each question is followed up at the clinician's option; for example, "When did that happen? How old were you then? Could you tell me more about what happened?" In all instances, the child is asked, "How did you feel about that?" or "How did you feel when that happened?" and, if not yet described, "Did you enjoy it? Was there anything you didn't like about it? How do you feel about mathematics now? Do you think this ... has anything to do with how you feel about mathematics now?"

The child is also asked, "Do you think you are good at solving problems?" "What do you think makes someone a good problem solver?" "Who do you think solves problems best in your class? Why do you think (name) is a good problem solver?"

Two different sets of problems are then presented successively: (a) cutting a birthday cake (without or with frosting) to share equally among two or three children and (b) moving colored jelly beans back and forth between two jars. Both problems embody symmetry and coordination of conditions—the first in the context of volume and area, the second in a numerical context. Emphasis is on exploring the child's affect as well as his or her metacognitions about the two tasks. Materials on the table are a ruler; markers; pencils; a pad of blank paper; scissors; sheets of graph paper; a spool of string and a length of cut string; construction paper, Styrofoam shapes with rectangular, circular, and triangular bases; and jelly beans.

The main birthday cake questions were the following:

- "Which would be easier, to cut a birthday cake into three equal pieces or four equal pieces? Why? Could you explain that to me?"
- "Does the shape of the cake matter?"
- "Suppose the cake has icing on the top and on the sides. (Four) (three) people are at the birthday party. How would you cut the cake so that each person gets an equal amount of cake and an equal amount of icing?"

After various explorations, brought to a close when 25 minutes have passed since the start of the interview, the child is encouraged to retrospect with additional questions. Then two transparent glass baby-food jars with twist-off lids, each filled nearly to the top with jelly beans, are presented to the child. One has

100 orange jelly beans and is labeled "ORANGE"; the other has 100 green jelly beans, and is labeled "GREEN."

- "The next problem is about jelly beans. This jar has 100 green jelly beans [points to the green jar], and this jar has 100 orange jelly beans" [points]. Suppose you take 10 green jelly beans from the green jar and put them into the orange jar [points] and mix them up [pretends to transfer the jelly beans, but does not do it]. Then suppose you take 10 jelly beans from this mixture and put them back into the green jar [pretends]. Which jar would have more of the other color jelly beans in it? Would there be more green jelly beans in the orange jar, or would there be more orange jelly beans in the green jar?"

If the child does not do so spontaneously, he or she is first encouraged to try the experiment and, if necessary, is guided to do so as follows:

- "Could you show me how to do it with the jelly beans? Let's try the experiment ..."
- "Will it always come out that way? Why do you think so?"

After the student has expressed a firm conclusion, the clinician asks follow-up questions and a final set of retrospective questions focusing on affect as well as on cognition.

Task-Based Interview 4

Interviews 4 and 5 return to selected mathematical ideas from the first two interviews. Interview 4 (41 pages, up to about 55 minutes) again explores the child's strategic and heuristic thinking in the context of sequences of cards, in close parallel with Interview 1. Materials this time include a hand calculator. Four problems, depicted in Figures 4.2a–d, are presented in succession, in the format of Interview 1: "Here is the first card, here is the second card, and here is the third card." After a brief pause to allow a spontaneous response or detection of a pattern in Problem 1, the child is asked, "What do you think would be on the next card?" and questions are posed as in Interview 1. After several questions, or after 15 minutes, Problem 2 is presented (see Figure 4.2b), without the clinician removing the cards of Problem 1 that were discussed. After further exploratory questions, Problem 3 is posed (Figure 4.2c), and after additional questions the child is given Problem 4 (Figure 4.2d).

The key follow-up questions in all four problems are similar to those in Interview 1. Once the child has given both an external representation (for Problem 1 only, a good verbal description is accepted) and a coherent reason, the clinician moves to the next problem. As usual, suggestions are made only when the child reaches an impasse. If the child does not spontaneously detect relationships between problems, the clinician asks about this after Problem 2. During the final retrospective, the first 3 cards of Interview 1 (Figure 4.1), with which the children engaged a year and a half earlier, are laid out. Gesturing to

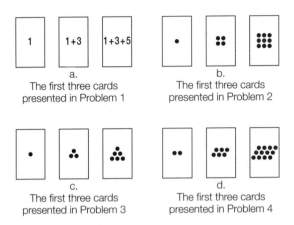

Figure 4.2. The sequence of tasks in Task-Based Interview 4.

all the cards, the clinician asks if the child sees any way to relate today's cards to the previous cards.

Task-Based Interview 5

Interview 5 (27 pages, up to about 55 minutes) also returns to selected mathematical ideas from the earlier interviews, particularly fractions related to ^{1}/2, ^{1}/3, and 1/4 as explored in Interviews 2 and 3. Materials given to the student include scissors; a 12-inch ruler marked in both inches and centimeters; an 18-inch length of white curling ribbon; paper circles, squares, and triangles; a pile of red and white plastic chips; a calculator; paper and pencils; and a solid piece of wood the approximate shape and size of a stick of butter, measuring 1" × 1" × 5". The interview begins with open-ended questions about fractions: "When you think of a fraction, what comes to mind?" "Can you tell me more about that?" "Can you show me what you mean?" "Have you studied fractions in school yet?" "What (else) have you studied about them?" "Do you like fractions?" "What do (don't) you like about them?"

The child is then given a sheet of pink paper with five fractions written on it and is asked a series of questions; as always, spontaneous problem solving is allowed before the next question:

$$\frac{1}{2} \quad \frac{1}{3} \quad \frac{2}{3} \quad \frac{3}{4} \quad \frac{4}{6}$$

- "What fractions do you see here?" "Can you explain …what one of these fractions means?" "Why is it written this way?" "Could you show me [using] the materials?"
- "Which fraction is the (smallest) (largest) fraction in the group?" "Why?" "Could you show me what you mean?" "Are there any fractions in this group

that are the same size?" "(Why?) (Why not?)" "Could you show me what you mean?"

Next some pictorial representations on a sheet of yellow paper and new questions are given (see Figure 4.3):

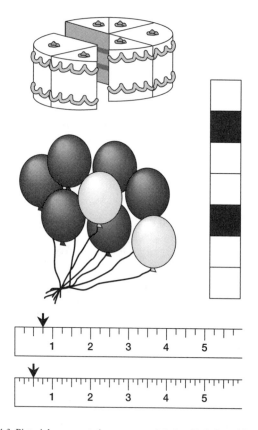

Figure 4.3. Pictorial representations presented during Task-Based Interview 5.

- "Could you use a fraction to describe any of these pictures?" "What fraction or fractions would you use?" "Why?" "Could you show me what you mean?"

All spontaneous answers are accepted, after which the clinician asks about the pictures the child may have omitted and whether the pictures on the yellow sheet of paper go with each other or with the fractions on the pink sheet.

The child is next given a sheet of blue paper with five new fractions written on it.

$$\frac{5}{5} \quad \frac{3}{1} \quad \frac{5}{4} \quad \frac{11}{8} \quad \frac{10}{8}$$

For the balance of the interview, the child solves up to four problem tasks, one at a time), each accompanied by exploratory, nondirective questions. It is not expected that all problems will be completed. When 5 minutes remain, the clinician skips to the final retrospective:

- [A circular shape is presented.] "How could you show one third of this shape?" "Why is that one third?" "Is there any other way to show one third?" "How could you show one fourth of this shape?" "Why is that one fourth?" "Is there any other way to show one fourth?"

- [The 1" × 1" × 5" piece of wood is presented.] "Pretend this is a stick of butter. You need a tablespoon of butter to make a cake. You don't have a measuring spoon, but you know that there are 8 tablespoons in a stick of butter. Here is the butter. How could you find exactly one tablespoon?" [If the answer is imprecise, ask once] "Is there any way to find out more exactly?"

- "Imagine a big birthday cake shaped like a rectangle. Can you imagine what it looks like?" "Describe what it looks like." "Now imagine that there are 12 people coming to the birthday party and they each want a piece of cake. Your job is to cut the cake so that each person gets the same-size piece. How will you cut the cake?" "Could you show me what you mean?" "Are there any other ways to cut it?" [The clinician continues to explore cutting the cake, including the situation of icing on the cake.]

- "A toymaker found some wooden shapes in the corner of her workshop. Some were squares, and some were triangles. She decided to put them together to make little houses [demonstrates using a square and a triangle). The squares looked like this [gestures to the pile of squares]. The triangles looked like this [(gestures to the pile of triangles]. The houses looked like this [places the triangle on top of the square to make a figure that looks like that shown in Figure 4.4]. After a while, she noticed that she had matched exactly $3/5$ of the squares with exactly $2/3$ of the triangles. How many squares and triangles were there to start with?" "Using these materials, could you show me how she did that?" [If time permits:] "Could there be a different number that works?" ...

Figure 4.4. House composed of a square and a triangle.

After each of these four problems, the child is asked, "Have you ever done a problem like this before?" (If yes) "When? What do you remember about it?" and so on. Interview 5 ends, like the others, with a retrospective discussion.

Selected interviews with the children form the basis of a number of studies. The thesis of Zang (1994) examines the development of strategic thinking in four of the children, comparing Interview 1 and Interview 4; the thesis of DeBellis (1996) studies affect in four of the children, using Interviews 1, 3, and 5; and the thesis of Passantino (1997) looks at the development of fraction representations for all of the children, comparing Interviews 2 and 5 (see also DeBellis & Goldin, 1997; Goldin & Passantino, 1996; Zang, 1995). With these scripts as examples, we now consider some general perspectives on structured, task-based interviews of this sort as a research technique in mathematics education.

ON THE SCIENTIFIC NATURE OF TASK-BASED INTERVIEWS

The longitudinal study, like many that use task-based interviews, is exploratory. Consisting as it does of a collection of individual case studies, its outcomes are not in a strict sense scientifically reproducible, and it might seem at first that this is all that can be said. Nevertheless, there are certain respects in which methods of scientific inquiry have been carefully regarded in the creation and administration of the interview scripts. I believe aspects such as these to be essential if we are to make real progress in understanding the nature of mathematical learning and problem solving through empirical observation. Thus, it is possible to envision the research being extended in a direction that permits replicability.

First, it is crucial to maintain carefully the scientific distinction between that which is observed and inferences that are drawn from observations. In this study we (at best) are able to *observe* children's verbal and nonverbal behavior, as captured on videotape during the sessions. From these observations, we (and others who use similar methods) seek to *infer* something about the children's internal representations, thought processes, problem-solving methods, or mathematical understandings. We cannot "observe" any of the latter constructs.

Second, our inferences are going to depend on (often tacit) models and preconceptions about the nature of what we are trying to infer and its relation to observable behavior. A scientific goal of the theory of mathematics education must be to make such models as explicit as possible. As we do this, we move away from depending on the ad hoc design of task-based interviews toward constructing them more consciously on the basis of explicit theoretical considerations. The task-based interview is like an instrument of scientific experimentation, and it is theory that describes how such an instrument is expected to interact with the system observed (in this case, the child as problem solver) so as to permit the drawing of valid inferences from the observations and measurements made. This point is discussed further in the next section.

Third, inferences from task-based interviews are likely to be unreliable, in that different observers may disagree about what inferences they would make after observing the same videotape—even when they agree on the theoretical constructs for which they are looking. The process of drawing inferences about children's thinking is fraught with uncertainty. At least at the outset, then, another scientific goal must be to describe the *criteria* that are to be used when inferences are drawn, so that the inferencing process itself becomes open to discussion.

For these issues to be addressed meaningfully, there must be a sense in which the task-based interviews are themselves explicitly characterizable as research instruments, subject to reuse, refinement, and improvement by different researchers. Thus in the study described here, we devoted great effort to structuring the interview scripts—ahead of their actual administration—to achieve two features: (a) flexibility and (b) reproducibility. Let us consider these twin goals.

Flexibility by the clinician in a task-based interview means being able to pursue a variety of avenues of inquiry with the learner or problem solver, depending on what takes place during the interview. Such flexibility is essential for our investigations to allow for the enormous differences that we know occur in individual problem-solving behaviors and that we infer exist in individual children's meaning-making activity. Because a major goal is to elicit and identify processes the children use spontaneously (i.e., without direct hints or coaching), flexibility is necessary to avoid "leading" the child in a predetermined direction in the problem solving.

Reproducibility in contrast means that the clinician is not merely inventing questions extemporaneously as the child responds. It permits, to a certain imperfect but improvable degree, "the same interview" to be administered by different clinicians to different children in different contexts. The degree to which this is possible increases as the research experience base with each particular interview accumulates. In asserting reproducibility as a fundamental goal, I am fully aware that I take a position at variance with the version of radical constructivism that asserts on a priori grounds its impossibility. The argument is sometimes made that since no two individuals ever solve "the same" problem, reproducibility is a fiction. The mistake of those asserting this position is confusing the problem instrument (the task, or task-based interview instrument, as structured by the researcher apart from the child) with the *interaction* being observed or measured (the problem solving that occurs when the child participates with the clinician in the actual interview). Of course, no two sequences of *interactions* are identical. From a scientific perspective, however, the wide differences that are observed to occur from interview to interview can be better understood and attributed when variables that are in principle subject to control (i.e., the task variables) are, in fact, controlled. Thus, the creation of reproducible task-based clinical interviews is an essential scientific step.

To accomplish this step, sufficiently many problem-solving contingencies must be anticipated. The criteria for the clinician's choices of questions or suggestions must be made as explicit as possible *in advance* for each contingency, with the balance covered by general instructions. This is what we have sought to do in the process of interview design.

For example, in Interview 1, three cards are presented. After a brief pause (to allow any spontaneous responses to the presented cards), the child is asked, "What do you think would be on the next card?" Contingencies then include "response" and "don't know." If the child responds, the next contingencies include "offers a complete, coherent reason" or "has not yet given a complete, coherent reason," with or without having constructed a "coherent external representation." The definitions (from the directions in the Interview 1 script) are as follows:

> A complete and coherent verbal reason means one based on a described pattern. A coherent external representation means a drawing, picture, or chip model. It is not required that the "canonical" fourth card (with 7 dots) be drawn, or the canonical pattern described, for a response to be considered a complete and coherent reason and a coherent external representation. An answer such as "7, because it's 2 more" is a coherent verbal reason, but it is not considered complete because it refers only to finding the next card and not to the basis for the pattern. An answer such as "7, because this card has 2 more than that one, so the next one has 2 more also" would be considered coherent and complete. If there is a discrepancy between the number of dots stated and the number in an external representation, the verbal reason is not considered "coherent." This [describes] the "boundary" between responses that are and are not accepted as complete and coherent....

The clinician's next question or suggestion (e.g., "Why do you think so?" or "Can you show me what you mean?" that leads, if necessary, to "Can you show me using some of these materials?") depends on the contingency that best describes the child's response. This is the level of detail at which many (although not all) contingencies are considered in the script design. We thus seek to make *explicit* the usually *tacit* conditions that ordinarily influence a skilled clinician. But this level of detail demands much preparation and rehearsal by the clinicians.

In principle, such detailed structured interview descriptions lead to several desirable features: (a) increased *replicability* of the interview itself, although contextual and other factors will still vary widely from occasion to occasion, and, of course, the knowledge structures of individual children are highly variable; (b) a degree of *comparability* of interview outcomes between different children, across different populations of children, across different conditions of school learning, and so forth; (c) subsequent experiments to investigate the *generalizability* of observations made in individual case studies; (d) explicit *discussion and critique* of the contingencies built into the interview, which permits the criteria for the clinician's responses to be analyzed and improved; and (e) an explicit basis for discussing the analysis of outcomes, that is, the process of drawing inferences from observations. For earlier perspectives on these ideas, see Cobb (1986), Goldin and McClintock (1980), Hart (1986), and Steffe (1991a).

THE ROLE OF THEORY

One purpose of clinical task-based interviews in mathematics education is to permit us to characterize children's strategies, knowledge structures, or competencies—perhaps to be able to look at the effectiveness of instruction, to understand developmental processes better, or to explore problem-solving behavior. However we choose to define our inferential goals, a theoretical framework for describing or characterizing what we seek to infer is necessary. But the role of theory is not limited to this. Theory must also tell us something about how the characteristics of the task in the task-based interview (e.g., its language, its mathematical content and structure, its appropriateness for particular cognitive processes, the interview context) are expected to interact with the cognitions we are trying to infer, so that the interview can be designed to elicit processes of the desired nature. To say that the problems in the task-based interviews described here are of a level of complexity thought to permit a variety of strategies to be employed, or internal representations to be constructed, already presupposes major theoretical assumptions.

The questions asked and the observations made during any scientific investigation, including investigations using task-based, clinical interviews, depend heavily on the theory we bring to it. Thus, in my view, the main question is not whether theory *should* influence us in this enterprise. I maintain, in agreement with R. B. Davis (1984), that it always, inevitably does:

> Perhaps the attempts to use the methods of science [in education] have failed because science has been misunderstood.
>
> In these attempts it had been assumed that science was primarily factual, that indeed it dealt almost solely in facts, that theory had no role in science. Careful observation of science reveals this to be false. It might be closer to the truth to say that "facts"—at least interesting facts—are almost unable to *exist except in the presence of an appropriate theory* [emphasis in original]. Without an appropriate theory, one cannot even state what the "facts" are. (p. 22)

The question pertaining to clinical interviews is the extent to which the influence of theory remains tacit, taking place through *unconscious* assumptions of clinicians, researchers, and/or teachers, or becomes explicit and thus open to discussion and challenge. Our goal in the present study is to be as explicit as possible.

The theoretical underpinning of this series of interviews includes the concept of (internal) *competencies* and structures of such competencies. These are envisioned as developing over time in the child and as being capable of being *inferred* from observable behavior—when the appropriate conditions exist for the individual to take certain cognitive steps and some corresponding behaviors are seen. Another fundamental theoretical assumption is the idea that competencies are encoded in several different kinds of internal representations and that these *interact* with one another and with observable, external representations during problem solving. A third assumption is that *representational acts* occur in which representational configurations (internal or external) are taken to symbolize or stand for other representational configurations.

The model that most strongly influenced the development of the scripts is one that I have been developing for some time as a way of characterizing mathematical problem-solving competency. It includes five kinds of mutually interacting systems of internal, cognitive representation (Goldin, 1987, 1992b): (a) a verbal/syntactic system (use of language); (b) imagistic systems (visual/spatial, auditory, kinesthetic encoding); (c) formal notational systems (use of mathematical notation); (d) planning, monitoring, and executive control (use of heuristic strategies); and (e) affective representation (changing moods and emotions during problem solving). The interplay between the children's internal representations and external representations that they use or construct during the interviews provides one of the most important means of drawing inferences.

For example, from children's descriptive statements about what a birthday cake looks like (Interview 5, Problem 3) we infer internal visual/spatial representations. From their gestures as they describe how they would cut a birthday cake into 2 or 3 pieces (Interview 3) or 12 pieces (Interview 5), with accompanying drawings, we infer simultaneous internal, kinesthetic representations. Children's explanations of the fractions written symbolically in Interview 5 permit inferences concerning their internal representations of this formal mathematical notation. Steps they take relating one sequence of cards to another in Interview 4 permit inferences concerning internal executive control (heuristic or strategic representations). Affective representation is inferred not only from the child's statements in response to questions, but also from facial expressions and spontaneous comments and gestures. I would stress again that the whole process of inferencing is, at this stage in the research, of limited reliability, but that strengthening the degree of reliability is an important goal.

Since the study is longitudinal, a major focus is how systems of representation *develop* in the child over a period of time. In this respect, the theoretical model incorporates three main stages: (a) an inventive/semiotic stage, in which internal configurations are first assigned "meaning," (b) a period of structural development, driven by the meanings first assigned, and (c) an autonomous stage, in which the representational system functions flexibly and in new contexts. We hope to be able to infer representational acts associated with each of these stages.

The distinction between external and internal representation means that we must attend carefully to both. We regard the tasks posed as *external* to individual children, embodying syntax, content, context, and structure variables that we select when we design the interviews. In particular, the mathematical structures of the tasks (semantic structures and formal structures—additive, multiplicative, and so forth) are consciously chosen. The behaviors observed result from *interactions* between the task environment and the child's internal representations.

To posit interactions between internal and external representational systems thus requires a great deal of analysis of mathematical structures associated with the tasks. Parallel but not identical structures—in some instances, homomorphic structures, in other instances, structures less directly related—were intentionally included in the different interviews. For example, a certain additive structure is embodied in the (canonical) sequence in Interview 1. Other additive and multiplicative structures relate to the sequences in Interview 4, which are also structurally related to each other. The card sequences are all presented in parallel ways to the children. A certain multiplicative structure underlies the cube-cutting task in Interview 2. Reflection symmetries are embodied in the cards in Interviews 1 and 4, in the cutout and cube-cutting tasks in Interview 2, and in the birthday cake task in Interview 3. More subtle, hidden symmetry is present in the jellybean problem in Interview 3. Rational number structures occur in Interviews 2 and 5. The analysis of all these relationships is theory based, and many assumptions are being made just in asserting that a structural relationship between tasks exists.

Another key theoretical distinction is between the child's *spontaneous* bringing to bear of any particular competency, or the child's doing so only when *prompted*. This is a subtle but crucial distinction, which involves the child's exercise of planning competencies to call on other competencies (verbal, imagistic, formal notational). For example, from a child's spontaneous response to the task in Interview 1 that each card is two more than the previous card can be inferred the implementation of at least part of a problem-solving plan. Should the child make the same observation only after being asked by the clinician, inference of such a planning representation would be unwarranted. These ideas have influenced the task-based interview development as follows: We pose tasks that permit the children to perform at each step *spontaneously*. We explore not only the child's overt behavior, but the *reason* the child states for taking each step. Recognizing that competency structures may be partially developed, we do provide hints or heuristic suggestions when blockage occurs. This often permits the child to demonstrate competencies that otherwise he or she would never "get to" during the problem solving, which adds to the information gained. There is always a trade-off entailed here, in that the more specific the hint or suggestion provided by the clinician, the less extensive the information gained about the child's representation of planning and executive control in problem solving.

We seek information about each kind of internal representational system; thus, not satisfied with a coherent verbal explanation only, we nearly always encourage the child to construct a concrete, external representation. We include a cross section of questions exploring visualization, affect, and strategic thinking. In particular, Interview 2 is designed especially to detect and explore in greater depth imagistic systems (visual/spatial and tactile/kinesthetic) in problem solving while attending to affect and to other kinds of internal representation; Interview 3 focuses on affect in greater depth (see also McLeod and Adams, 1989), whereas Interview 4 returns to tasks selected for the possibility of eliciting certain planning or strategic representational capabilities.

It is my view that the characteristics of the task-based interviews are variables that are *inevitably* built into clinical interview designs. Considerations of task structure in these interviews are sufficiently complex to form the basis themselves of several articles, yet task structure is an essential component to understanding and making inferences from observed problem-solving behavior. It needs to be examined independently of the individual children as a part of the process of drawing inferences from children's interactions with the tasks. My main point is that there is no way to avoid this interplay between theory and observation. It is not a sufficient answer to respond, as some do, that task structures do not "exist" apart from individual problem solvers. *We simply have the choice of proceeding unscientifically, choosing tasks that seem interesting and just "seeing what happens," or trying to proceed systematically with tasks explicitly described and designed to elicit behaviors that are to some degree anticipated.*

Although the analysis of outcomes in these interviews is theoretically based, we seek not only to observe and draw inferences from *expected* processes but also to search for unanticipated occurrences. The hoped-for results include the further refinement and development of the theoretical model for problem solving, including the identification of inadequacies and progress toward an assessment framework, as well as conjectures for further investigation through future experimental studies.

THE ROLE OF CONTEXT

Task-based interviews do not take place outside of a social and psychological *context*. That context influences and places constraints on the interactions that occur during an interview and puts limitations on the inferences that can be drawn. It is one of the components that theory must address, if we are to validly interpret interview outcomes.

The view taken here is that "social and psychological context" affects the interview interactions through internal representations that the child has constructed, which are in principle subject to description. These are considered "contextual" because the semantic content of the representational systems involved is not, at least initially, mainly derived from, or related to, intended mathematical representations associated with the tasks posed in the interviews.

We observe, for example, that the child's expectations in an interview may be influenced by the fact that it is conducted by a relative stranger, the clinician. The interview takes place in school and thus might be assumed by the child to involve some kind of test that "counts" toward an evaluation. Children often seem to think, especially at the outset, that the tasks are likely to have "right" and "wrong" answers and that certain methods will meet with the clinician's approval, whereas others will not. The interview itself may be taking place at a moment when the child is alert, tired, hungry, distracted, or excited. On the one hand, the child might prefer to be back in his or her regular class with friends or might, on the other hand, be looking forward to an interesting break from the classroom routine. The fact of being videotaped was for the children in our study a familiar experience (owing to the project in which their teachers were participating); the context of their experience would be different were the video cameras a complete novelty.

It seems to be an almost inevitable feature of task-based, clinical interview methodology that the tasks are unrelated, at least initially, to a goal or purpose generated by the child. For example, the butter problem and the toymaker problem (Problems 2 and 4 in Interview 5) are both posed in a *stated* context. The butter problem (or one like it) is a problem that could conceivably arise as a practical need in a variety of real-life situations not too different from the stated context. It would very likely be experienced differently if the child were actually *in* one of those situations and had generated the problem goal (as opposed to solving the problem as part of a clinical interview). The toymaker problem, in contrast, is a rewrite of a rather well known mathematical problem involving married couples in a village. We rewrote the problem to present a concrete, external representation with which the child could experiment if desired. Although the context of making toys is one the child can easily imagine, the problem goal is not one that occurs "authentically" in that context. It is posed as an almost whimsical question, arising perhaps as a curiosity (curiosity-based problem solving is, of course, an essential aspect of mathematical inquiry) but not as a practical question that needs to be answered for the toymaking to proceed. Thus, the contexts of these two problems are different in an important respect. Such contextual factors could influence, for example, the importance that the child ascribes to the problem goal and, in turn, the child's persistence, enthusiasm, choice of strategy, and so forth.

Another meaning of context, one that might be called "mathematical context," refers to unstated aspects of the tasks themselves as they are presented during the interview—aspects that although seemingly small may have important effects. For example, in presenting the three cards in Interview 1 and again (several times) in Interview 4, we permit the child to see the cards being drawn from a stack of cards in a manila envelope. From this minor contextual feature (which was intentionally included), the child may infer that there is a deck of cards larger than the three that are shown and, possibly, that there is a pattern in the cards. Three cards presented wholly out of context might not so readily elicit this expectation. Evidently, certain contextual influences are undesirable (e.g., those that might mask our ability to observe competencies that are present in the child), whereas others are helpful (e.g., those that would facilitate the child's "thinking mathematically").

Since so much that may occur during a task-based interview is context dependent, how can we consider what we observe to be more than accidental, one-time events? One important condition is to require that *the constructs we infer from our observations be reasonably stable against contextual variations*. For example, suppose we infer, in Interview 2, a child's ability to represent imagistically (visually, kinesthetically, or both) the cutting of a cube across two perpendicular directions. The inference may be drawn from the child's coherent description of the component pieces of the cube, with appropriate gestures indicating how the cube was imagined to be cut. Although it is indeed the case that this child's behavior may vary considerably from one context to another, when we infer such particular competencies or structures of competencies from that behavior, we are inferring aspects of the child's cognition that we expect to be fairly stable. If the inferred competency were to disappear in short order, it would not be useful in a theory of mathematical learning.

Understanding the contextual dependence of the interviews also means recognizing how very difficult it is to establish advance criteria for all the inferences about each child's cognition and affect that we want to draw from our observations. When observations are interpreted in context, new likelihoods occur. The plan we have been following is to make the best conjectures possible and to try to be explicit about the reasons for conjectures, including relevant contextual factors, as these occur (Zang, 1994).

Such discussions of contextual issues barely scratch the surface. For task-based interview methodology to be pursued seriously, a deeper understanding—indeed, a theory of how social, psychological, and mathematical contextual factors may influence mathematical problem solving during a task-based interview—is essential to the interview design process.

PRINCIPLES OF INTERVIEW DESIGN

I conclude this chapter by summarizing what, in my opinion, are some of the most important underlying characteristics of the five interviews described here and try to abstract from these the most salient general principles behind their design. Although each interview has its own particular focus, certain broad characteristics are maintained in all of them:

1. Each interview is based on particular mathematical ideas appropriate for the age group of the children (grades 3–6) and on mathematical topics with associated meaningful, semantic structures, as well as formal, symbolic structures, for example, additive or multiplicative structures, sequences, schemata underlying rational number concepts, and so forth. We want the mathematical content to be based on topics that can be studied in depth and are flexible enough to allow evidence of widely differing capabilities on the part of the students.

2. Each interview consists of a series of questions posed in one or more task contexts. These begin at a level that all the children are expected to understand (of course, in differing ways). They become increasingly difficult, culminating in questions that can still be attempted by all the children but that will pose major challenges even to the most mathematically astute students.

3. The children engage in *free problem solving* to the maximum extent possible. This prioritizes exploring the strategies that the children use spontaneously—whatever method or methods seem most appropriate to them as they work on the task. They are reminded occasionally to talk aloud about what they are doing and to describe what they are thinking. Hints and prompts, or new questions, are offered *only after* the opportunity for free problem solving and are then followed by a further period of observing how the child responds without directive intervention. This rule is (in view of time constraints) occasionally broken because of our desire to ensure reaching a subsequent section of the interview in the allotted time, but it is broken with the recognition that possibly important information is necessarily being lost.

4. All student productions are "accepted" during the interview; the clinician does not impose preconceived notions about appropriate ways to solve the problem but does treat "wrong" answers similarly to "correct" answers (with occasional,

specified exceptions). Responses elicit follow-up questions without an indication of correctness. The rare exceptions, involving guiding the students toward particular understandings, are decided in advance and occur only where the understandings are essential for subsequent interview questions to be meaningful.

5. Materials for constructing a variety of external representations are available for student use and vary from task to task: paper and pencil, markers, cards, chips and other manipulatives, paper cutouts, hand calculators. A major task goal is always the construction of representations by the children—ideally, a multiplicity of them.

6. Each interview includes reflective questions, typically posed retrospectively, that address the child's problem-solving processes and the child's affect.

7. Because the interviews are designed for use in a longitudinal study, there is a conscious effort to incorporate into later interviews some tasks that are similar in context, mathematical content, structure, or all three, to those posed earlier.

Building on these specific characteristics and the issues discussed in this chapter, I propose to formulate the following tentative and partial principles of interview design and construction with the goal of trying to establish the strongest possible scientific foundation and maximizing the information gathered through a task-based interview.

1. *Accessibility.* Interview tasks should embody mathematical ideas and structures appropriate for the subjects being interviewed. Subjects must be are able to represent task configurations, conditions, and goals internally and, where appropriate, externally.

2. *Rich representational structure.* Mathematical tasks should embody meaningful semantic structures capable of being represented imagistically, formal symbolic structures capable of notational representation, and opportunities to connect these. Tasks should also suggest or entail strategies of some complexity and involve planning and executive-control–level representation. Opportunities should be included for self-reflection and retrospection.

3. *Free problem solving.* Subjects should engage in free problem solving wherever possible to allow an observation of spontaneous behaviors and reasons for spontaneous choices. Providing premature guidance results in a loss of information. This principle may mean some sacrifice of the speed with which the subject understands the problem or progresses through it.

4. *Explicit criteria.* Major contingencies should be addressed in the interview design as explicitly and clearly as possible. These contingencies should distinguish "correct" and "incorrect" responses (but rarely) with structured questions designed to give subjects opportunities to self-correct in any contingency. This is an important key to the replicability and generalizability of task-based interview methodology.

5. *Interaction with the learning environment.* Various external representational capabilities should be provided, which permits interaction with a rich, observable learning or problem-solving environment and allows inferences about problem solvers' internal representations.

It is hoped that the discussion in this chapter furthers the goal of understanding mathematical learning and problem solving scientifically through the use of task-based interviews as research or assessment instruments.

Chapter 5

Phenomenography: Exploring the Roots of Numeracy

Dagmar Neuman

This chapter uses the findings of a study of beginning school children's experiences of subtraction to illustrate various aspects of phenomenographic research. The focus of the chapter is placed on the model, developed from the data, that pictures the phenomenon being studied. A detailed analysis is presented of the phenomenon as it is experienced by the researcher, together with the research problem that the phenomenon gave rise to. Later, in the description of the categories related to the model, an account is made of the ways the phenomenon seemed to appear to the subjects in the study This information provides the foundation for a discussion of the criteria of "interpretative awareness," proposed as a means for establishing reliability in phenomenographic research, and also for a discussion of two aspects of validity—the coherence and intelligibility of the model and the possibility of demonstrating its pragmatic validity.

The study reported here had its origin in two conflicting observations (Neuman, 1987). On the one hand, pupils with difficulties in mathematics, who were interviewed at the end of their school career, were found who did not know all the subtraction facts within the number range 1–10. On the other hand, informal observations of 25 first-grade classes found that in all these classes, one or more children already seemed to know these facts on their first day of school. Both observations were contradictory to the commonly held view that all children, when they do sums and drill tables during their early school years, sooner or later learn the basic facts by heart.

Findings from Swedish research (e.g., Kilborn, 1979) and from my early pilot studies indicated that subtraction within the range 1–10 was an interesting area for investigation. These findings revealed that children who displayed difficulties in mathematics knew the addition facts. They also revealed that children who

I wish to thank Ference Marton, who was my advisor in this first attempt to carry out phenomenographic research; Shirley Booth and Jörgen Sandberg, who patiently read versions of this paper and provided constructive criticism that has helped to shape the final product; and Anne Teppo, who made the most competent effort to bring the chapter into a reasonably comprehensible form. I also wish to thank Anne Teppo for her thorough work on the language used in the article. The studies that form the basis for the chapter were funded by the Swedish Board of Education, the Swedish Ministry of Education, and the Solna Local Education Authority, who are acknowledged with gratitude.

could subtract within this range in due time learned to add and subtract within higher number ranges, whereas those who could not never seemed to develop mental calculation skills.

Four pilot studies that I carried out revealed that pupils with difficulties in mathematics used a counting approach, counting forward or backward in ones, in their attempts to calculate. Other children used what I called a structuring approach that helped them avoid counting. Instead of counting four steps backward to solve the task $9 - 4$, for instance, they answered 5 instantly, with the younger children explaining, if asked, that they knew because $4 + 4 = 8$ or because $5 + 5 = 10$. Those explanations illustrate that their basic facts were anchored in a sense of number and in a conceptual understanding of the inverse relation between addition and subtraction.

I searched for a suitable method for studying both the cause of the difficulties some pupils experienced and the ways other children, prior to entering school, had begun to create a more viable sense of number. At Göteborg University, I became acquainted with the INOM group (INlärning och OMvärldsuppfattning, or "Learning and ways of experiencing our world"), whose research and educational aims fit my intentions. The professor in the center of the group was Ference Marton, who later coined the word *phenomenography* (Marton, 1981; Marton & Booth, 1997) for the kind of research group carried out. I use examples from the study I conducted to describe certain aspects of phenomenographic research.

PHENOMENOGRAPHY

To fully understand a qualitative research methodology, we must place it in the context of an ontology, concerning the nature of the world we live in, and an epistemology, concerning how we acquire knowledge about this world. Therefore, in this part of the chapter, I discuss some of the fundamental philosophical assumptions underlying phenomenographic research.

Phenomenography is a theoretical and methodological research specialization, anchored in a nondualistic ontology, akin to a phenomenological philosophy. According to this ontological position, our world is a real world that is experienced by all our senses but interpreted and understood in different ways by different human beings, depending on our earlier experiences. This world, however, is seen as one world only, not as one subjective world represented in the mind of the individual and one objective external world. It is one world that is

> objective and subjective at the same time. An experience is a relationship between object and subject, encompassing both; the experience is as much an aspect of the object as it is of the subject.... The expression "how the subject experiences the object" is synonymous with the expression "how the object appears to the subject" (Marton & Neuman, 1996, p. 317).

Yet phenomenography is not phenomenology. Even if it definitely shares some of the phenomenological philosophy, it must be seen as an approach with its own fundamental assumptions, methods, and goals.

The word *phenomenon* is a key concept in phenomenography. It is used in the sense it has in phenomenology—"the thing as it appears to us"—opposed to the Kantian *nuomenon*—"the thing as such." A phenomenon is not identical with one of the ways in which it can be experienced but with the whole complex of intertwined ways it has appeared to all people, both historically and in the present. Whereas the goal of phenomenology is to describe the *essence* of all the ways in which a phenomenon can be experienced, the goal of phenomenography is to explore and identify the *variation* in the ways in which it can appear.

A phenomenon appears, as a rule, in a limited number of ways. This is a central assumption in phenomenography, where findings are mainly grounded in empirical analyses. It has also been empirically shown that if 20 to 30 individuals are interviewed, and other people from the same population are interviewed later, there rarely appears any new way of experiencing the phenomenon that is studied (e. g., Giorgi, 1986; Marton, Beaty, & Dal'Alba, 1993; Säljö, 1979, 1982).

If there are only a limited number of ways in which a phenomenon can be experienced, it must be of educational value to try to reveal these ways. Marton and Booth (1997) suggest that the models depicting the outcomes of phenomenographic research have educational value in helping teachers and curriculum designers identify "a notional path of developmental foci for instruction" (p. 81).

PHENOMENOGRAPHIC RESEARCH

To think of research with a fallibilist epistemology—and with results that are interpretations of other peoples' ways of experiencing something—in terms of reliability and validity may be seen as a contradiction. The crucial thing for establishing reliability in phenomenographic research is the use of phenomenological reduction (Sandberg, 1996) or, in Ihde's (1997) words "to circumvent certain kinds of predefinition" (p. 31). Sandberg sees the researcher's interpretive awarness as one possible criterion of reliability. Following Ihde, he gives five guidelines for how to maintain such an awareness throughout the research process. The first criterion is that the researcher must be continuously oriented to the phenomenon being studied throughout the research process. To be oriented to the phenomenon also means to be oriented to the formulation of the research question. Referring to Kvale (1994), Sandberg points out that a weakness in many qualitative studies "is the lack of a clear definition of the research question" (p. 157). This, rather than the variation in possible interpretations of the data, often makes the presented results difficult to understand. Second, the analysis and presentation of the outcomes should consist of a description of the ways of experiencing the phenomenon, not of explanations of why these experiences appear the way they do. (Researchers are often tempted to use their arsenal of theories and models to explain things outside the experiences reported by the interviewees.) Third, all aspects of the experiences that are observed should, at the beginning of the analysis, be seen as equally important in order to faithfully interpret the essential aspects of the interviewees' ways of experiencing the phenomenon. Fourth, the researcher must continually adapt the different possible interpretations that appear when he or she reads through the data until the basic meaning structure has been stabilized. Finally, the researcher should not only identify *what* the interviewees experience but also *how* they experience this "what." The concluding model of the descriptions should relate the interviewees' expressions of what they seem to experience to how they seem to experience it. This chapter focuses on the first, second, and fifth criteria by using the phenomenographic model developed in the School Starter Study to illustrate the implementation of interpretative awareness.

Study Design

The assumption of educational benefits related to phenomenographic research influenced the design of my study and made it rather embracing. I decided to interview all children in two new beginner classes during their first weeks at school before they received any formal teaching in mathematics. I then followed these children for 2 years in a teaching experiment based on the knowledge obtained in the interview study. After these 2 years, I carried out a new interview study with those children who had not been able to solve any of the subtraction problems in the interviews conducted when they began school. I also interviewed children in a control group both when they began school and 2 years later. As in the research classes, only those control children who had not been able to solve any of the subtraction problems in the interviews at the start of school were interviewed later. I also regularly visited the two classes using the teaching experiment and met the teachers at least once every fortnight to listen to their experiences and to plan the new work.

One important goal for me in the interview study was to reveal maximum variation in the ways the phenomenon I studied could appear to all pupils in a typical Swedish school beginner class before formal instruction in mathematics had begun. A goal of similar importance was to reveal the maximum number of ways that pupils in "the risk zone" might experience the phenomenon. To have at least 20 pupils in this zone, I also carried out one extra interview study with two school beginner classes 1 year after the first interview. This latter study also enabled me to determine that no new categories could be identified.

To be able to study a dynamic learning process during an extended period of time, I also decided to follow in more depth two children in the research classes. I used the results of the interviews carried out at the start of school to select two children who had displayed the earliest, that is, the least developed, ways of experiencing the studied phenomenon. I then met with them twice a week for 2 years in clinical interview lessons that were tape recorded and transcribed (Neuman, 1994).

Thus, three kinds of methods were used: clinical interviews, a quasi-teaching experiment, and a longitudinal case study using recorded clinical interview lessons. The teaching experiment and the case study were mainly undertaken to deepen the understanding acquired through the interview study. They also provided validity through technical triangulation (Larson, 1993), in which different forms of data are assembled concerning the same phenomenon, and pragmatic validity (Kvale, 1989) through putting the results of the interview study into practice. This chapter focuses on information developed from the initial clinical interviews.

The Definition of the Phenomenon

A clear definition of the phenomenon to be studied, as experienced by the researcher, is of great importance in phenomenographic research. If the phenomenon is not well defined, it is impossible to formulate appropriate interview questions or to present the outcomes of the study as representing the variations in the ways in which this phenomenon has appeared to the interviewees. The definition of the phenomenon is closely related to the formulation of the research problem that the researcher has set out to study.

My research problem concerned subtraction within the range 1–10. I had already observed that for pupils displaying mathematical difficulties, subtraction problems could be hard or easy depending on the numbers used. For instance, Problem A "Andy had two pencils, but nine children wanted to make drawings; how many more did he need?" could be hard, whereas the same problem with seven pencils (Problem B) seemed easy. In the same way, Problem C, "Andy had nine pencils and lost seven of them; how many are left?" could be hard, whereas the same problem with two pencils lost Problem D could be easy.

An analysis of the strategies used by the pupils in the pilot study who displayed mathematics difficulties revealed why Problems A and C could be considered difficult. For these pupils, exactly as for very young children, the semantic structure of the problems, not numerical factors, seemed to be the focus of attention when they solved word problems (Carpenter & Moser, 1984). They seemed to experience missing addends (A and B) as addition, thinking of addition as counting forward, and "take away" problems (C and D) as subtraction, with subtraction as counting backward. Thus, the pupils solving Problem A had to count seven steps forward and in Problem C, seven steps backward, whereas they had to count only two steps forward in Problem B and two steps backward in problem D.

In his research, Fischer (1992) has illustrated that there is an enormous difference between how children experience three and four visually presented objects. Whereas nearly all 3- to 4-year-olds immediately denoted a collection of three objects as "three" without counting or grouping, hardly any of these children could denote a collection of four objects correctly without counting the objects or grouping them into two groups of two.

Figure 5.1 is a picture similar to those I used to communicate the phenomenon I wanted to study. Children in my pilot studies sometimes solved problems through these kinds of drawings. They depicted, as I saw it, the one-to-one correspondence between number symbols and counted objects that, according to research on early numerical thinking (e.g., Gelman & Gallistel, 1978; Steffe, von Glasersfeld, Richards, & Cobb, 1983), represents an important aspect in the child's early conception of number.

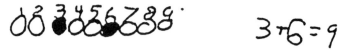

Figure 5.1. Child's drawing of "nine stones" (Skolverket, 1995).

In Figure 5.2, I have transformed Figure 1 to fit Problems A and C as they seemed to appear to those children who focused their attention on the situated aspects more than on the numerical aspects of the problems. (In the following discussion, "number" is considered a part-part-whole pattern.) In Problem A, the part of the number experienced as "the missing part" appears as the last part, since it is thought of as added to the known part "two." Similarly in Problem C, the part of the number that is experienced as lost appears as the last part, since it is thought of backward from 9.

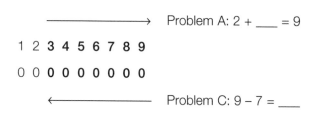

Figure 5.2. Depiction of situated aspects of Problems A and C.

To perceive the numerosity of the last part of a number can be extremely difficult, since it can never be experienced in an ordinal way, through what Fuson (1992) has called "count-to-cardinal" (p. 134). The counting word related to the last object of this part never tells you anything about its cardinality. Neither in the missing addend, 2 + _ = 9, nor in the take-away subtraction, 9 − 7 = _, does the word *nine* tell you about the numerosity of the last part, seven, in Figure 5.2. In Problem C, *nine* is actually the first word the pupils experience if the subtracted part is counted backward, and the second word in the problem (*seven*) does not tell them anything about where to stop the backward numeration to find the word at the limit of this part. If the numerosity of the last part is outside the subitizing range, it also cannot be subitized as a cardinality or experienced intuitively in any way at all. We have to invent some idea or some method to be able to know about it.

In the pilot study, the pupils who displayed mathematics difficulties had invented a method of "double counting" to deal with the numerosity of the last part. They put up one finger for each enumerated word when they counted this part. Finally they "read off" the finger configuration, for instance in Problems A and C, as "one hand + 2 = 7." This double counting helped children perceive the numerosity of the last part in Problem A and told them where to stop the backward enumeration in Problem B. Yet it was a solution strategy that seemed to stay concrete and procedural, never being transformed into objects that could be operated on in thought. (See Grey and Tall [1994] for later reports on this neverending procedural behavior.)

The preceding analysis enabled me to define the phenomenon I wanted to study. It concerned *the variation of ways in which to experience a numerosity larger than three when the numerosity is presented in a subtraction problem as the part of the whole number that constitutes the missing or lost part.*

I will subsequently denote this missing part "the puzzling part," since to me it was very confusing that preschoolers could become aware of the numerosity of this part without any need of the laborious double counting that seemed to be necessary for the pupils with mathematics difficulties. How children became aware of the numerosity of the puzzling part was the research question that I wanted to answer through my study.

To present this phenomenon to children, I needed to develop interview questions that involved subtractions of the missing addend kind and of the take-away kind. The puzzling part in these questions should be larger than 3 and thus be difficult to perceive intuitively. The whole number should not be larger than 10 or smaller than 7, preferably close to 10. (If the whole is too small, it might even be possible to subitize the numerosity of the puzzling part.)

Four subtraction problems of this kind were formulated:

1. Your teacher has 3 pencils, but there are 7 children who all want to write. How many more pencils does she have to fetch?

2. If you have 10 pencils in your rucksack and lose 7 of them, how many do you have left?

3. Your teacher has 2 pencils, but there are 9 children who all want to write. How many more pencils does she have to fetch?

4. Your teacher has 4 pencils, but there are 10 children who all want to write. How many more pencils does she have to fetch?

Two addition problems for which the added part was the larger one were also given to compare ways of experiencing addition and subtraction among the school beginners.

I also decided to let the children take part in a guessing game in which they could make five guesses of how nine buttons were hidden in two boxes. They counted the buttons themselves and gave them to me before I hid them. The guessing game was given first in the interview, and it was primarily intended to catch the children's interest. It did not always confront them with the phenomenon, but it was still a good problem because five answers were given to the one question.

The Contextual Analysis

The phenomenographic analysis is seen as a process of exploration. It is "contextual" (Svensson, 1989), going back and forth in a sort of hermeneutic spiral, where the parts are interpreted from an understanding of the whole and the whole from a closer analysis of the parts. The analysis in my study began in the interview situation and then continued as one after another, the tape-recorded interviews were listened to, transcribed, and read several times. A diffuse, global idea about the phenomenon began to take form during this process. That global idea was subsequently differentiated into its constituent parts, and a more detailed analysis was begun when enough transcribed interviews were at hand. This analysis was carried out through two coinciding interpretative procedures. In one of them, all the answers to one question at a time were analyzed, and the individuals to whom they were related were disregarded. The intention was to identify different ways of experiencing the phenomenon. In mutual interplay with this procedure, a second procedure was carried out whereby the ways of experiencing were related to each individual in an attempt to observe whether answers to several questions expressed one and the same way of experiencing the phenomenon within a single interview. Tentative categories were formed and given tentative names. The characteristics of each category were described in a summary in which excerpts from the transcripts were included. The intertwined procedures were carried out several times. At the beginning, the interpretations often were overlapping or were suddenly seen as wrong. Thus, one interpretation gradually succeeded another, with the summaries changing accordingly. An interpretative analysis of this kind can never be said to be definitely finished. Still, at some point, the categories are seen as satisfactorily stable, and the researcher decides that they can be presented.

THE MODEL REPRESENTING THE OUTCOMES

After the analysis is completed, an attempt is made to let the categories form a model that, according to the researcher's interpretations, depicts the phenomenon as experienced in the collective awareness of the individuals who took part in the study. These categories reflect *what* the phenomenon seems to be to those interviewed as well as *how* this "what" seems to be experienced by them. It is often possible to relate the categories hierarchically, ordered according to their gradually greater inclusiveness. Categories describing more inclusive ways of experiencing the phenomenon include well-integrated, still functional aspects of less inclusive ways. The model, thus, often pictures a kind of evolution. Yet this does not mean that it envisions the order in which children's mental development of some cognitive competence occurs. It is *the phenomenon* appearing in its variation of ways that is pictured in the model.

The model as pictured in Figure 5.3 presents my interpretation of the ways in which the interview children experienced the phenomenon under study. The prenumerical categories in the original model have been omitted from Figure 5.3 because the purpose of this chapter is to illustrate phenomenographic methods rather than to present complete research findings. In Figure 5.3 the four categories (written in lower-case bold letters), *extents, finger numbers, word numbers,* and *abstract numbers,* depict *what* the whole numbers, including the puzzling part, seemed to be to these children. The two superordinate categories (written in upper-case bold letters), numerically *unstructured* and numerically *structured,* depict *how* the whole numbers in the interview problems were experienced.

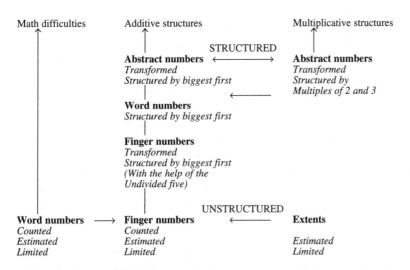

Figure 5.3. Ways of experiencing the phenomenon among the 7-year-old Swedish school beginners.

The categories written in lower-case italics depict more specifically *how* the numerosity within the puzzling part was experienced. When the whole number was numerically unstructured, the children seemed to experience this numerosity as *limited, estimated,* or *counted.* The answers to the interview questions in these situations were hardly ever correct. However, when the whole number was perceived as numerically structured, the answers were correct, and the numerosity of the puzzling part of the number appeared to be perceived intuitively. In these situations the part-part-whole pattern of the number appeared numerically restructured by a *biggest first* structure, *transformations,* or *multiples of 2 and 3.*

It is not the purpose here to describe the model in detail but rather to present information to illustrate the nature of a phenomenographic model and the use of the criteria for intuitive awareness mentioned by Sandberg (1996) in reporting this model. The following discussion provides more information of the "what" and "how" aspects of the categories given in the unstructured and structured sections of the model. The information describes the variation in the way the phenomenon is experienced rather than presents an explanation of why these experiences appear the way they do.

The Four "Whats"

An analogue experience of number akin to the one pictured in Figure 5.1, or its concrete counterpart in the form of finger configurations that I have called "finger numbers," always seemed to be a part of the interpretation frame through which the children saw the problems. When numbers appeared as *extents,* the children did not seem to pay attention to the single units in this "picture." The size of the whole extent could only be experienced ordinally with the help of the counting word related to its last object. *Word numbers* were also experienced through the position of the last counting word. Yet, here the children illustrated that they paid attention to each single unit—to each counting word they enumerated.

Children paid attention to each single unit also when finger numbers were used. A finger configuration categorized as a finger *number* began with one hand and continued with the thumb, forefinger, middle finger, and so forth, on the other hand. Thus, a finger number could be simultaneously experienced in an ordinal way by the position and name of the finger where it ended and in a cardinal way by the "5 + some number" configuration. Mostly, but not always, finger numbers were put up by the children without any need of counting. Several children did not use their fingers in a concrete way but, *after* an immediately given correct answer, illustrated how they had "thought with their hands."

For children experiencing numbers as *abstract numbers,* the numerosities of both parts within the number were immediately experienced in an abstract way, each part and also the whole related to one single symbol. Yet some kind of analogue experience of number akin to the one pictured in Figure 5.1 still seemed to constitute the background of the words they used to communicate their thoughts.

The Three "Hows" When the Numbers Appeared as Numerically Unstructured

When, according to my interpretation, the situation described in the problem was of focal attention in the children's awareness, the part-part-whole pattern of the number appeared numerically unstructured. The puzzling part was the last one (as in Figure 5.2)—the part that never can be experienced ordinally through the counting word related to its last object.

The earliest identified way of experiencing and communicating the numerosity of the puzzling part I have called *limited.* Here, the children used the number word at the end of this part when they communicated its numerosity—probably to tell me where the part ended. They did not yet seem to be aware of any contradiction in the use of the same counting word for whole and part. They could, for instance in the guessing game, repeatedly guess that there were 9 buttons in one of the boxes, but still some buttons in the other box, or say that there were 7 pencils missing in Problem 1 (3 pencils and 7 children) and 6 left in Problem 2 (10 pencils, 7 of them lost). In Problem 2, they seemed to think of the lost pencils as the ones related to the words *ten, nine, eight,* and *seven.* Thought of backward, the word *seven* denoted the limit of the part that should be taken away; thought of forward, the word *six* denoted the limit of the part left. Mary and Joan exemplify this early ordinal way of experiencing Problem 2:

Mary: Seven ... six, five, four, three, two, one ... *six* left.
Joan: Then I've got one, two, three, four, five, *six* left.

The puzzling part here mainly seemed to be experienced in an early ordinal way; the focus was put on the point in the counting-word sequence where it ended.

In the category I have called *estimated,* on the contrary, the puzzling part seemed to be experienced in an early *cardinal* way. It was still an experience of an extent or of a manifold, but now it was the extension in between the limit words that seemed to be of focal attention, not the limit words per se. Emma, for instance, solves Problem 2 (10 pencils, 7 of them lost) in the following way:

E: Then I've got four left ... or two ... four or two ... you can't be sure....
I: No ... can't you work out in some way if you've got four or two left...?
E: Maybe three ... I think it's two.
I: But isn't there any way of working out how...
E: No.
I: Couldn't there be eight left?
E: Eight left!!??
I: Why isn't that possible?
E: Well, because I've dropped ... well if you lose that much, it can't be that much!

Emma seems to be well aware of the relation between the two parts, but as she explains, there is no way for her to work out the exact number of pencils left— something that does not seem to bother her much.

One type of answer was categorized as a *counted* finger number. This way of experiencing number was displayed by only one child in one of his answers (to Problem 3). After the finger number was displayed, this boy counted the last part of it with the word *one* related to the third finger, the word *two* related to the fourth, and so on. Thus, the fingers were what constituted the analogue experience of the whole number, and the words were used to count the last part of the finger number.

Another type of answer was categorized as a *counted* word number. Here, the words constituted the analogue experience, and the fingers were used to count the last part of the word number. This way of experiencing numbers was the one observed in practically all the answers given by the pupils displaying mathematics difficulties.

Numerically unstructured word and finger numbers appeared rarely, and when they did, their puzzling part was only rarely counted. I interpreted these "counted" ways of experiencing numbers as being transitional between numerically unstructured and numerically structured ways of experiencing numbers. These ways seemed to be invented when children began to understand that adults expected exact answers to mathematical problems, but when they still did not know about any, or only about some, of the ways in which numbers can be structured.

The Three "Hows" When the Numbers Appeared as Numerically Structured

The three ways of experiencing numbers as numerically structured helped me understand how children could avoid double counting, even when they understood that the problems could, and should, have "exact answers." These ways of experiencing numbers were qualitatively different from the unstructured ways of experiencing them.

Two of the numerically structured ways of experiencing numbers—the ones categorized as *biggest first* and *transformations*—could be observed when the solution was concretely formed by finger numbers. The "biggest first" idea was then formed when children focused their attention on the first hand as constituting one single object—an "undivided five"—instead of seeing it as five single unit items. When the first hand was kept undivided, the biggest part had to be related to this hand. Thus, as soon as the biggest part was five or larger, it became the first part.

To solve Problem 2, for instance, the children put up all fingers and then folded seven before answering three. To solve Problem 3, nine fingers were put up and the ninth and the eighth fingers were folded. Susie, solving Problem 3 (two pencils and nine children), exemplifies how the "undivided five" could appear in the children's responses while they formed a finger number:

Susie: First I sort of counted five ... then I put up two ... then I put up two more ... then I put them down [the last two fingers].

We can see how the two parts in the analogue experience pictured in Figure 5.2 become swapped when the numbers get the biggest first structure. Then there is no "puzzling part" any more.

Peter, Caroline, and Charles illustrate the biggest first structure as related to word numbers and abstract numbers when solving Problem 2 (10 pencils, 7 of them lost). All three children had answered "three," just before they explained their thinking:

Peter: [Quietly and rapidly] One, two, three, four, five (inaudible) ... and then eight, nine, ten.

Caroline: Seven ... eight, nine, ten.

Charles: 'Cause if you have ten and drop seven ... then ... you have ten ... drop seven ... well ... you can count seven plus three ... then it's ten.

Instead of counting seven steps backward, or subtracting 7 from 10, Peter counts all and Caroline counts on while they easily subitize the words *eight, nine, ten* as a "threeness." Charles thinks of abstract numbers and just adds 3 to 7.

Whereas these three children illustrate how problems experienced as subtractive sometimes have to be thought of forward, when the problem becomes numerically structured by the biggest first experience, Ann and Andy illustrate how additively experienced problems, such as Problem 3 (two pencils and nine children), sometimes have to be thought of backward. Both children had answered "seven" before they explained their thinking:

Ann: One, two, three, four, five, six, seven, eight, nine, ... and then I thought ... count to nine ... seven ... and then I said it!

Andy: I thought like this ... nine ... and then I took away two from the nine children who had got those pencils ... and then there were seven left.

Andy seems to use some kind of egocentric speech in his explanation, but it is evident that he has subtracted 2 from 9. No double counting of the last part is necessary when the number has this biggest first structure.

Transformations of one number combination to another resulted in this same intuitive and immediate experience of parts and whole of the number. Transformations were also identified when they were concretely formed by finger numbers. In Problem 3 (three pencils and seven children), for instance, none of the parts was as large as five; the first hand, thus, could not be undivided. For this problem, the children often moved the thumb from the first to the second hand—or sometimes the thumb plus the forefinger—to transform 5 + 2 into 4 + (1 + 2) or into 3 + (2 + 2). Transformations of finger numbers were also common in the guessing game and in Problem 4 (four pencils and ten children). Often the answers to these problems were given directly. The children did not illustrate, before they were asked to explain their immediate answer, that it was related to their imagining a transformed finger number.

Transformed number combinations were also frequently displayed when the numbers appeared as abstract. For instance, the most frequently used correct way to solve Problem 4 (four children and ten pencils) was to perceive the number combination 6 + 4 as transformed from 5 + 5.

Numbers structured by multiples of 2 and 3 were expressed in guesses like "Four in this box and five in that," with the explanation " 'cause four and four's eight." After the immediately given answer "four" to Problem 1 (three pencils and seven children), the children gave explanations of this kind: "I know... 'cause three and three's six."

Validity of the Model

In phenomenographic research, validity is related to the *intelligibility* of the outcomes. These outcomes are judged partly with respect to the collected data and partly with respect to the model depicting the outcomes. On the one hand, if the categories describing different ways of experiencing a phenomenon cannot be understood as parts of a structured whole constituting the phenomenon, the model is not intelligible. On the other hand, if the seed of later categories can be found in earlier ones, and if it is possible to see transformational forms between the categories, then the structure is considered to be intelligible.

If the model can be used to interpret data presented by other researchers' findings or to interpret phenomena identified historically or in other cultures, not only the phenomenographic model but also the other observations appear more intelligible. For example, some of the categories I found have also been identified by other researchers. The idea to choose the most convenient way—counting forward or backward in subtraction of all kinds—has been observed being used by most primary school children (Resnick, 1983). Resnick named this way of handling subtraction "the choice model" (p. 119). Interestingly enough, Resnick (personal conversation) had mainly observed this model in a Swedish study carried out by Svensson, Hedenborg, and Lingman (1976). Unstructured word numbers had also been described previously by Steffe, von Glasersfeld, Richards, and Cobb (1983), who referred to them as "verbal unit items." Further, Russell and Ginsburgh (1984) had shown that the prime distinction between children who find mathematics difficult and those who do not is that the former group of children seem to know fewer basic number facts.

The importance of the "undivided five" had been reported long before I found it in my study, but related not to finger numbers but to the tiles that young Japanese children use in the first grades (Hatano, 1982). Brissiaud (1992), studying his son, has pointed out the importance of finger numbers structured by the hand (five) in children's early acquisition of number sense. These "finger symbol sets" (p. 41), he underlines, function as an analogue numerical reference system of an ordinal-cardinal kind that can be used without any need of counting. Brissiaud sees an analogue system of some kind as being "a necessary underpinning for the construction of a logico-mathematical system, such as number" (p. 65). Werner (1973) put forward a similar idea more than 50 years earlier, stating that the hand seems to represent a natural number area. His research indicated "a definite relationship between the ability to articulate the fingers and the early development of number concept" (p. 296).

A phenomenographic model can also be validated through historical comparisons. The early Chinese people, for instance, placed a single horizontal rod, picturing the undivided hand, above vertically placed rods, picturing the fingers. Similarly the Roman numeral V pictured the hand. If the left line in V is thought of as representing the four fingers, and the right line, the thumb, all part-part-whole relations within the number range VI–X (VIIII) (with the exception of 3|3|6) can be experienced intuitively by using two of the ways of structuring displayed by the school beginners—the biggest first structure, created by the undivided five, and transformations carried out by moving one thumb between the hands (Figure 5.4).

Pragmatic Validity

Pragmatic validity, as described by Kvale (1989), provides another way to defend the outcomes of qualitative research. This type of validity can be

V I	VI I	VII I	VIII I	VIIII I
V I	V II	VI II	VII II	VIII II
3+3	V II	V III	VI III	VII III
		V III	V IIII	VI IIII
				V IIIII

Figure 5.4. Roman numerals VI–X structured by the undivided five and transformations.

obtained, for instance, through putting the results of an interview study into practice. For example, see the teaching experiments of the phenomenographic
researchers Ahlberg (1992), Lybeck (1981), Neuman (1987, 1993, 1994, 1997),
and Pramling (1991, 1994). I finish my discussion of phenomenographic methods by briefly describing how I used pragmatic validity to test the validity of the
outcomes of my study.

   The interview study gave me several useful ideas for my teaching experiment.
Since experiencing numbers as extents was the most frequently reported way of
experiencing numbers in my study, one idea was to introduce mathematics through
measuring instead of through counting. The intent here was to help all children see
the extents as being divided into units. A second idea was to avoid the use of the
counting words to begin with, since these words seemed to be used in ways that
would not be taken as shared by all pupils. A third idea was to introduce subtraction before addition, since in subtraction, children know about the whole number
and have, especially if they form finger numbers, the possibility to become aware
of the two parts within this whole without any need of double counting.

   To create situations in which the children could get these kinds of experiences,
the mathematics classroom became a fantasy land—the Long Ago Land. In this
land there were no counting words, no measures, no coins, no mathematics at
all—but problems continually appeared for which mathematics was needed.
Thus, the children were required, bit by bit, to create together the mathematics
they needed for the moment. As they invented measures of different kinds, for
instance, to compare two quantities of liquid, pouring one after the other of the
units into a bucket, they quickly discovered that they needed tallies of some kind
to remember how many units had been poured. The fingers were proposed as
useful tools by most children, but some thought that strokes drawn in the sand
(that is, on the chalkboard) could also be suitable. When discrete quantities later
were recorded, the strokes soon became too many to subitize or represent by fingers. At this, we told the children that the people in the Long Ago Land recorded hands and fingers as well as just fingers, and the symbol V was introduced for
the hand. Thus, analogue number representation became structured by the "undivided 5" before the children had a reason to invent the counting words.

   This is not the place for describing the teaching experiment in detail. It might
be said, however, that in the interview study carried out after the second year, all

children in the two research classes could add and subtract within the range 1–10 over the 10 limits without any need to count or keep track. This was very different from the ways the children in the control group solved these kinds of problems. The outcomes of the interview study could, as suggested by Marton and Booth (1997, p. 81), be used as "a notational path of development foci for instruction."

CONCLUSION

The methods presented in this monograph are different, as are the goals and underlying perspectives of each author's research. This variation makes the picture of what mathematics teaching and learning mean and of how they can be researched rich and detailed. However, it also creates difficulties in our attempts to formulate criteria for what counts as acceptable qualitative research. For instance, at the ICME-8 conference in 1996, suggestions were made to formulate a set of research guidelines. Many participants, however, saw this as placing a straight jacket upon the researcher, preventing creativity and excluding certain kinds of research.

To describe fundamental assumptions, goals, methods, and knowledge (validity) claims for a given research study, as was done in this chapter, would help us judge individual studies from within their respective methodological frameworks. I hope that such descriptions can serve as a step toward creating a consensus for judging the quality and acceptability of qualitative research in mathematics education.

Chapter 6

Working Toward a Design for Qualitative Research

Susan Pirie

This chapter can be considered a response to the call by Merton (1968)

for the practice of incorporating in publications a detailed account of the ways in which qualitative analyses actually developed. Only when a considerable body of such reports are available will it be possible to codify methods of qualitative analysis with something of the clarity with which quantitative methods have been articulated. (p. 444)

If this is true for the sociologist, how much more important it is within mathematics education, where many of the practitioners of research originate in the enumerative discipline of mathematics.

Quantitative and qualitative methods are not alternative paradigms for the same research activities. Each has much to offer, but what is offered and what constitutes the goals of any project must together guide the choice of methodology. Is the intention to build or to test theory? To survey an issue or look at it in depth? To look at large quantities of data for similarities and to abstract these because of their general applicability and hence assumed essentiality, or to look at individual cases and abstract essential features, generalizing them because of their perceived vital nature? It is not my intention to argue here for one paradigm over the other in a variety of given situations. Rather, I set out my reasons for the methodologies I have espoused in my own research and the processes by which the decisions on method and methodology were made.

I am offering not a textbook on a particular mode of conducting research but an account of the reality of selecting methodology and method for one specific project. The reader will be taken through the decision making that must accompany any research and be shown the need for a robust research design that will accommodate the slings and arrows that outrageous fortune throws at intrepid researchers, be they novice or not. Experience offers insight into potential problems, but care and a secure theoretical base for the design of the research offer the surest way to bring the undertaking to a satisfactory close. The structure of

---

This account of the exploration of discussion between pupils in the mathematics classroom would not be complete without my expression of loss and gratitude for the work done by Rolph Schwarzenberger, whose illness and death tragically curtailed the invaluable contribution he made to the project.

this chapter is based on the questions that must be asked of any research and the illumination of these questions through discussion of how they were tackled and answered within one specific research project.

The research topic comes first, and the methodology and methods must be not just "taken, ready made, off the shelf" but be chosen and adapted carefully to best access the answers sought (Burgess, 1984, p. 4). My research exemplifies the philosophy of theory as process: theory changing, evolving and being construct-ed to fit or explain new cases. One focus of my interest—and it is this that I examine in detail in this chapter—is the phenomenon of discussion between pupils in the mathematics classroom. My intention is to discuss the processes of selecting the appropriate research methodology and methods. I then illustrate how, through the examination of purposefully gathered data, we sought features, properties, and categories within the phenomenon that would enable or enhance the positing of theories relating to the effects of discussion on pupils' mathemat-ical understanding.

RESEARCH QUESTIONS

What Provoked the Original Research Question?

The research project titled "Discussion: Is it an aid to mathematical under-standing?" was initiated by Rolph Schwarzenberger and me as a result of a report by a British government committee of inquiry into the teaching of mathematics in schools (Cockcroft, 1982) and the general reaction of teachers to that report. The report claimed in paragraph 243 that "discussion between teacher and pupils themselves" was one of the six elements that should be included in mathematics teaching at all levels. As a result of this highly readable report, teachers in great numbers took this to mean that discussion was per se a good thing, without either questioning the meaning of discussion or querying what it could achieve *in the mathematics classroom.* The report gave the following reason for the recom-mendation:

> The ability to "say what you mean and mean what you say" should be one of the out-comes of good mathematics teaching. (p. 72)

This implies that mathematics trains one to talk clearly (which may be a wor-thy general educational goal) but not that discussion aids the understanding of mathematics.

In fact, the Committee itself had been unable to find much evidence of the existence of discussion. There existed at that time considerable research into the effects of discussion on learning (Barnes & Todd, 1977; Edwards & Furlong, 1978; Mehan, 1979), and more particularly, discussion between teachers and pupils (Barnes, Britton, & Torbe, 1986; Mehan, 1985), but nowhere could we find any specific research to support the value of discussion between pupils themselves (Pirie & Schwarzenberger, 1988a). It was, therefore, on this latter area that the research project focused. Schwarzenberger and I wanted to explore the notion and nature of discussion between pupils in mathematics classrooms without the influence of the teacher's presence. We intended to look for links between such discussion and the growth of pupils' mathematical understanding. In other words, we hoped to answer this question: "How does pupil-pupil discussion influence understanding *of mathematics?*"

The recommendations of the Cockcroft Committee were based on the notion that *in general* talking to others helps to clarify one's ideas and focus one's thinking. We believed, however, that there was reason to perhaps question the generalizability of this notion to mathematics. Our concern was that a mismatch, unique to mathematics, exists between the written and the spoken languages used. One of the strengths of mathematics is that the symbolic language in which it is written is brief, precise, and unambiguous—for the initiated! For learners, one problem is that the language used to verbalize these symbols can be lengthy, multiple, and ambiguous (Pirie, 1991a, 1996a, forthcoming). Our contention was that the imprecision of talk in a subject dependent for its power on the precision of its symbolic language might radically alter the effect of discussion on learning in mathematics from the effect expected in other disciplines.

What Secondary Questions Are Raised?

Initial areas of research interest are generally broad and in need of sharper focusing, both in terms of questions asked and of intended outcomes.

It became abundantly clear from our first exploratory classroom visits that there would be no simple answer to the research question we had posed, nor indeed had we expected one. We observed incidents where discussion appeared to advance the understanding of the pupils involved and where it quite definitely confused and misinformed the participants and inhibited progress toward the solution of their problems. Our tasks, therefore, became first, attempting to understand the nature of pupils' mathematical discussion, and second, finding a way to assess its effect on their mathematical understanding (Pirie & Schwarzenberger, 1988a). It is with the first of these, the wish to understand better the phenomenon of pupil-pupil discussion before commenting on its value, that this chapter is concerned. To this end, we were interested in the whole range of forms that such discussion could take, rather than, at this stage, in the typicality or frequency of aspects of the phenomenon.

For reasons of time and scale the project focused mainly on secondary pupils. Two questions faced us:

1. Given our purpose, what methodological strategies would enable us to fulfill our aims?

2. How could we obtain relevant data—data that would aid us in our specific task?

We were concerned about producing adequate descriptions of the ways that pupils talk to one another. We needed to explore ways of analyzing such discourse and its contexts—ways that would offer insights into those processes inherent in pupil-pupil talking that might influence the growth of the mathematical understanding. We wished to generalize, that is, to produce a general picture of the phenomenon of pupil-pupil discussion, by abstracting from specifically gathered data those features that recur and appear to characterize this particular form of classroom interaction. More precisely, we were interested in the general features that seemed to affect the growth of mathematical understanding.

APPROPRIATE METHODOLOGIES AND METHODS

Ethnography

Several general research paradigms offered us potential methodological stances, which I lay out briefly and examine for their possible applicability to our project. The first is the ethnographic paradigm, the interpretation of which has taken various forms over the last few decades (Burgess, 1984; Wolcott 1975). Ethnography, in its broadest sense, is concerned with the sociocultural features of an environment; with how people interact with each other; and with the rules, the structures, and the processes of these interactions. In general, it borrows methods of operation—data collection and analysis—from the discipline of anthropology and applies them to specific subgroupings of people within a larger defined group. We can talk of the "culture of the classroom" and investigate how, within this particular closed environment, a culture develops that differs in many respects from the normal lived experiences of its participants. Ethnography as defined by Wolcott (1975, 1982) involves the suspension of one's own judgement that is based in one's own cultural assumptions and demands that one look through the eyes of those who are themselves the members of the culture under scrutiny. The intention is to illuminate an understanding of the culture, not to predict future behaviors.

The notion of ethnography was seductive. At first sight it seemed that it would yield the in-depth exploration that we sought. On closer inspection, however, two crucial aspects made the adoption of this paradigm, as our unadulterated methodological choice, unsuitable.

The first concerned the method of data collection. Participant observation, so often associated with ethnography, would in all probability prevent the phenomenon that we wished to observe from coming into existence! It was talk away from the presence of the teacher, but still within the culture of the mathematics classroom, that we wished to focus on, and it seemed highly likely that a knowledgeable adult observer would by her or his very presence alter the pupils' verbal interactions with one another. Interviewing the pupils after a lesson on how they had talked among themselves would also not be appropriate because it was their initial discussion, not their reflective reporting on it, colored by their expectations of what an adult would deem important, that we wished to capture. The second problem related to the suspension of the researchers' cultural view. The assessment of the effect of the discussion on the growth of pupil understanding had to be from an external, mathematically influenced viewpoint. It was dependent on detailed knowledge of the nature of the mathematical topic under consideration. We did not wish to investigate what the *pupils* thought they had learned, but what, from our observations of their current and subsequent actions and talk, *we* judged them to have learned.

Notwithstanding these criticisms, the general idea of the long-term gathering of in-depth data was an appropriate one. We were going to need to listen to specific groups of pupils discussing their mathematics, over the length of time they devoted to learning several particular mathematical topics, to come to know the ways they interacted verbally and the effects these interactions had on their learning. We were also going to need to catch this talk in a way that would not be influenced by the listener. After much deliberation, we decided against videotaping as the method of data gathering because at that time we considered it too intrusive. We settled for audiotaping, and we explained to those pupils whom we wished to record that they were not being tested in any way, that their teachers would not hear the tapes, and that we were just interested in how pupils talked about mathematics. We focused on three or four small groups in each class, and we recorded every lesson on each particular topic, which meant that we would usually be with the class for two or three weeks at a time. An audio recorder was placed on the table for each group of pupils, and the researcher, sitting across the room so that the pupils would not feel that they were being watched, took field notes on the lesson in general. These notes—on what was written on the chalkboard, for instance, or on the relevant activities of other pupils or the ostensibly important actions of the pupils being audiorecorded—were made on time sheets that could be later coordinated with the tape recordings.

Ethnomethodology

The focus of our interest was thus talk—a specific kind of talk it is true, but talk nonetheless—and the ways in which such talk was constructed, the language that was used, and the types of verbal interactions that took place. In fact, we were looking for some method of categorizing the specific pupil-pupil discussion that we hoped to trace. Other research focused on the analysis of talk was, therefore, a likely place to look for methodological strategies. Ethnomethodologists and those working through conversational analysis concern themselves with talk, treating it not as a resource for information on some other topic but considering it the object of study itself.

This emphasis on the talk itself appeared to come close to some of our thinking. To understand teaching and learning, of which talk is a natural, integral part, we must understand the talk, its coherence, its structure, and its context. "Conversational analysis has developed a conceptual machinery for unraveling the organization of conversation so that it may be described and analyzed" (Hitchcock & Hughes, 1992, p. 162). Part of our aim was to describe the nature of pupil-pupil discussion in the mathematics lesson, but we wanted to do more than this. We were, ultimately, still concerned with the results of particular verbal interactions in terms of the understanding gained. Jacob (1987) describes the more specific "ethnology of communication," but although talk among pupils can be the focus within such a paradigm, the aim of the research is again to examine speaking as an activity in its own right, not as a process of conveying meaning. There is no significance placed on the, say, mathematical, meaning of talk. One is looking at pupils' speaking as a cultural, social construct.

Sociolinguistics

Having, with some profit, surveyed the field of anthropology-related methodologies, we turned to that of linguistics. The narrow dissection of words and meanings was not of relevance to us, but a sociolinguistic approach might be appropriate to our quest within the field of educational research. Sociolinguists concern themselves with the wide diversity of linguistic forms and speech patterns that occur within communication through language. Their aim is to unpick the features of these patterns, to discover how social factors affect the development of such patterns, and to explore the effects of specific speakers and hearers and contexts on such patterns. Their interest lies in how these social environments affect verbal interactions (for examples of this approach, see Barnes, 1982; Sinclair & Coulthard, 1975). Here, too, lay our interests. What was the effect of the classroom context on the language the pupils used when talking with their peers? But more than that, what was the effect of the interaction on their understanding of mathematics?

Sociolinguistic and ethnographic approaches can both be used to investigate a concern with what people are doing when they are making sense of verbal interactions. Both approaches can be concerned with looking at patterns and regularities in the interactions or, indeed, with searching for the irregular. By examining the possibilities offered by research methods drawn from both paradigms, we hoped to be able to construct methods of data collection and analysis that allowed us to look not so much for patterns in the speech itself as for categories of verbal interactions revealed by the speech.

DATA COLLECTION AND ANALYSIS

What Will Constitute the Data?

Before proceeding further, we needed to be more precise about what would form our primary data. Given the way we were intending to work in the classrooms, we would be dealing both with a complete audio record of each lesson as it applied to each group we were considering and with field notes that could be collated with the recordings. What we chose to do with all this raw information would directly affect the methods of analysis available to us. Two considerations stood out as important. First, it was clear that we were not interested in analyzing in detail every utterance of every child throughout the entire period of data collection! Our focus was discussion—a task that we had not previously undertaken. We needed to produce a definition that fit with the ideas implied in the Cockcroft report, but was precise enough to use for identification purposes when we listened to verbal interactions between the pupils. We produced the following working definition, which in fact remained unchanged throughout the rest of the research.

Discussion is—
• *purposeful talk.* There are well defined goals even if not every participant is aware of them. These goals may have been set up by the group or by the teacher but they are, implicitly or explicitly, accepted by the group as a whole.
• *on a mathematical subject.* Either the goals themselves, or subsidiary [goals that] emerge during the course of the talking, are expressed in terms of mathematical content or process.
• *in which there are genuine pupil contributions.* [There is] input from at least some of the pupils that assists the talking or thinking to move forward. We are attempting here to distinguish between the introduction of new elements to the discussion and mere passive responses, such as factual answers to a teacher's questions.
• *and interaction.* [There is indication] that the movement within the talk has been picked up by other participants. This may be evidenced by changes of attitude within the group, by linguistic clues of mental acknowledgement, or by physical reactions that show that critical listening has taken place (Pirie & Schwarzenberger, 1988a, p. 460).

The second consideration we took into account was that much of the meaning of a live interaction can be lost when the talk is reduced to a transcript. Take, for example, the utterance "It's four over three." As written, it appears to be simply a statement of the improper fraction four-thirds as the solution to some given problem. With an emphasis on the word *over,* however, the implication might be a contradiction of some previous action or expression; in other words, that division by three is the correct process, not, say, multiplication as previously thought. Alternatively, spoken with a rising inflection and a suitably astonished facial expression, it could be expressing total incredulity that someone would think that "four over three" could possibly be the answer!

At the end of each lesson, therefore, the observer listened to the tape recordings and amalgamated the field notes with a detailed summary of the pupil-pupil interactions. All occasions of pupil-pupil talk that fit our definition of discussion were noted, and for these and other central incidents, both the time of occurrence and the tape-counter number were recorded. We did not at this point transcribe the tapes because intonation, pauses, and other audible activities were considered important to the categorization of the talk. In fact, we decided that these notes and recordings would form the data from which we would perform all our subsequent analyses. We transcribed portions of the tapes only for the purpose of writing about the research for an outside audience. We did, however, make a second copy of every tape in case of accident! It is important to make overt this explicit decision about the nature of the data used because it is from this perspective that results must be judged.

What Are Appropriate Methods of Analysis?

A method of analysis was needed that would look at all the incidents of discussion that occurred within the data. We were thus not attracted to any system of categorization that depended on a time-controlled sampling of the data. The method of "systematic observation," or "interactional analysis," seemed to offer one obvious way of dealing with the data. Basically, in these approaches, responses or episodes are coded with a set of preselected categories (Flanders, 1970; Galton, Simon, & Croll, 1980). The choice of categories is inevitably subjective, although it can have its basis in theory or previous research. The effect of this method is normally that the observer returns from the classroom with only a numerical record of the frequency of the occurrence of incidents in each category. We had a far richer primary data source—the entire recordings—but we could have applied some form of interactional analysis to it. Our reason for rejecting this method of working was, however, not due to potential loss of data. We were undertaking the research precisely because we did not know what those categories might be. We wished to extract the categories from the data, not to impose them on the data (Glaser & Strauss, 1967).

A proven, powerful method whereby every episode of classroom interaction can be categorized is that of discourse analysis (Sinclair & Coultard, 1975; Stubbs, 1981). Under such a scheme, the whole lesson is broken down into a hierarchy of episodes, and the individual episodes can be further coded as to the type of interaction that they typify. In its original inception, the method was used to deal with the form of the interactions, not the content, but it was a method that held appeal for us and seemed to be adaptable to our needs.

We were able to allocate all the episodes of talk in our entire primary data collection to three broad categories:

(i)   Talk clearly related to mathematics

(ii)   Verbal exchanges that were incomprehensible

(iii)   Social chat

Category (i) was then subdivided into episodes that fit our definition of discussion and those that did not, and category (ii) was subsequently reanalyzed to draw out those episodes that, although at first pass seemed incoherent to us, clearly held meaning for the pupils (Pirie, 1991b). We were still faced with the problem of how to categorize the episodes of discussion, and some element of subjectivity seemed inevitable. Our goal was to be as open as possible to all interpretations of the episodes.

Barnes (1982) has done much to open up discourse in the secondary classroom to the scrutiny of others. His snapshot observations of individual lessons, and his analysis by means of personal insightful comments, have laid his work open to criticism from purists who deplore his overt subjectivity. What such detractors miss, however, is the very real value of his reflective interpretations and the necessity of just such an exploratory approach to point the way to fruitful areas for further, more rigorous investigation. His focus is largely on the role and the effect of the teacher and on teacher-pupil interactions, however, and offers little insight into the possible categorizations of the phenomenon in which we were interested. Personal insight and reflection were, indeed, the only ways in which we were going to be able to start to come to grips with our data. Our aim was to be as systematic and theoretically guided as was possible in our choices of categories.

We looked to sociology for guidance. Our categories would be grounded in our data. Rather than spring from our own preconceptions, they would evolve from the data we gathered by the process known as "systematic theoretical sampling" and be stabilized through a procedure of constant comparison. Theoretical sampling is the process whereby data are repeatedly gathered and analyzed, with each subsequent data-collection decision dependent on the analysis of the previous data collected. The "process of data collection is *controlled* [*sic*] by the emerging theory" and the "initial decisions are not based on a preconceived theoretical framework" (Glaser & Strauss, 1967, p. 45). Through a constant comparison of episodes, initial data are examined for features, trends, and properties and are explicitly coded according to these categories; new data are gathered specifically to illuminate or contradict these categories and are systematically compared against all previous data; further data are collected and analyzed until the emerging theory or categorization appears to be stable. This method of analysis is inductive—it moves from data to tentative theory, to new data, to refined theory. As a method of data collection and analysis within the field of sociology, it is well documented in Glaser and Strauss (1967) and seemed ideally suited to our intentions. Its strengths are revealed by the ways we were able to deal with practical issues as they arose.

How Are Data to Be Gathered?

Turning to questions of practicality, how then should we set about gathering the necessary data? We needed a system that was both flexible and systematic. (See Burgess [1982] for a discussion of some of the issues related to sampling that arise in qualitative research.) Random sampling of schools and classes made no sense in our situation; we needed to observe classes where we had the maximum chance of encountering pupil-pupil discussion. We were looking to talk about neither "frequency of occurrence" nor "typical categories" but about the range of interactions that can be present. We had to collect examples of pupil-pupil discussion to be able to categorize them; we already knew that these were hard to find.

Various methods were available whereby we could observe the phenomenon of mathematical discussion between pupils and its effects on understanding. One technique open to us was to take any group of pupils, deliberately provoke mathematical discussion among them, and record the event for subsequent analysis. We had no doubt that this would be both possible and interesting and would filter out some of the complexity and wealth of uncontrollable factors inherent in a classroom. We should, however, then be wary of the gap between how we would idealistically like children to learn and how they did learn in the realities of the classroom. Our concern was pupil discussion within a normal classroom setting, in particular, discussion unaffected by the participation of a teacher. Hence, this method was discarded.

We focused the initial observation phase on the classrooms of four secondary teachers who consciously and deliberately used discussion as a part of their teaching style (Pirie & Schwarzenberger, 1988a). These teachers were, in fact, hard to find, and their classes must be considered atypical. Were our observations, therefore, in danger of being biased by the sample we were taking? On the contrary, we intended to base our theorizing on the essential features of the phenomenon as they emerged from the data. Edwards and Mercer (1987, p. 26) refer to this biased sampling as "an intentional consequence of [the] research design." We were interested not in counting or comparing cases, but in examining and categorizing incidents of discussion. The selection of our sample was based on theoretical, not statistical, grounds; the validity of our findings flowed from the evolution of the categories rather than from the representativeness of the study population.

The selection of the pupils whom we would observe was also done to maximize our ability to observe pupil-pupil discussion. The teachers identified children who were in the habit of discussing their work with their neighbors, and we explained to them that we wished to audio record their interactions during the next few lessons. The teachers identified a variety of mathematical experiences and topics from the normal teaching schedules that were likely to provoke discussion among the pupils, and these we observed.

One of the crucial features of theoretical sampling is that further data collection is guided repeatedly by the analysis of existing data until saturation is achieved, that is, until the emergent categories remain unchanged. For this reason, although it is likely that any research project will have one main method of data collection, there are "no limits to the techniques of data collection, the way they are used, or the types of data acquired" for the end purpose of illuminating the phenomenon under examination (Glaser & Strauss, 1967, p. 65). Several weeks after the initial classroom visits, with a view to gaining deeper insight into the effect of discussion, we interviewed the pupils we had observed in their working groups to elicit their understanding of the topics they had been working on. We used a loosely structured clinical interviewing technique (Ginsburg, 1981, 1983) whereby pupils talked their way through a task and the interviewer followed their paths of thinking, sometimes returning later to probe more deeply into relevant key ideas (Pirie, 1988).

How Is the Analysis to Be Performed?

A precise, systematic method of analysis was followed throughout this first data-gathering phase. The two researchers initially observed the same classes. Then, after the visit, they individually correlated their own tapes and personal field notes and categorized the data under the three headings previously discussed (mathematical, incomprehensible, and chat). Still without consulting each other, we next identified episodes of discussion according to our agreed definition. Finally, we came together to compare the kinds of things we had deemed important to record in our field notes, our individual categorizations, and our interpretations of the definition when we applied it to specific classroom incidents. The purpose of this duplication of observation was to consolidate the methods of recording and the focus of the field notes to ensure as far as possible that there was a common understanding of the method of observing and analyzing. Subsequently, we visited separate classrooms, following one teaching topic through from initiation to close. At regular meetings, each observer presented identified incidents of discussion for joint analysis, and each incident was then coded both by the mathematical topic it concerned and by any notable features it presented. Theoretical sampling lends itself well to collaborative working, since it depends on drawing features and potentially meaningful categories out of the data gathered. What can be seen as a problem within a research design, namely, different interpretations of the data, can be turned into a strength, since interpretation by more than one person can lead to a richer first analysis.

The category labels for features that seemed pertinent during that first analysis included "using mathematical language," "about their lack of understanding," "about how to do it," "reflection on their mathematics," "proof," and "focus on the meaning of the mathematical problem." None of these categories was intended to be exclusive, and indeed we found episodes in which we were using multiple categorization, such as "about the task," "recording," and "using nonmathematical language" as the following example illustrates.

Four 12-year-old girls were tackling an investigation (Frogs) in which black-and-white cubes are moved by slides and jumps. Their task was to exchange the places occupied by black cubes for those occupied by the white ones and to record this in some way. They decided to count and record the number of moves made.

Susanne: I know how it works—you have the whites on one side.

Tracy: OK. You have to have the whites a certain side, don't you?

Ann-Marie: I know!

Joanne: How do you reckon we are going to record this?

Susanne: So that we can remember it.

Tracy: I'll count how many moves you make.

Joanne: Come on—watch her.

Ann-Marie: Can't I jump that one? Can't I do that?

Joanne: Do it again and I'll count how many moves you make.

What we were beginning to see during our discussions was the emergence of three *groups* of categories. The first of these was *what it was* that gave the speakers something to talk about. Within this group the episodes could be classified as to whether (a) they had a task or concrete object as the focus of their talk; (b) they did not have an understanding of something, but knew this and thus had something to talk about; (c) they did have some understanding, which gave them something to talk about.

The second group was concerned with *the kind of language* used—the focus being on the language in which the discussion was conducted and not on the content of the statements made.

Again three classifications suggested themselves. Those were (f) the speakers lacked appropriate language—they did not have the correct or useful words, (g) the speakers used ordinary language, (h) the speakers used mathematical language.

It could be conjectured that the categorization of language as "ordinary" or "mathematical" would be somewhat arbitrary, since "mathematical" language for young children might be "ordinary" language for them a few years later. In practice, however, viewing the discussion in the context in which the pupils were working enabled us to make decisions with little difficulty or disagreement.

The third group that emerged was *the kind of statements* the pupils were making. A variety of statements could exist within any one episode. These were classified as (p) incoherent—that is to say, interactions that fit all our criteria for discussion but contained statements that were incoherent to us, the observers; (q) operational, or in other words, about specific (frequently numerical) examples of mathematics; (r) reflective, which we subsequently renamed "abstractive" as its nature became evident more in terms of statements of generalizations of mathematics than in terms of statements reflecting on mathematics.

We reviewed all the data collected and categorized each episode on each of the three groups. The example given above was categorized (a,g,q). The pupils were talking about the task of recording, using ordinary language, and making operational statements. Further examples of the use of this categorization can be seen in Pirie and Schwarzenberger (1988a) and Pirie and Schwarzenberger (1988b).

The essence of the method of constant comparison is the repeated reanalysis of existing data. Even before the decision was made to codify all the episodes in terms of the three groups above, when any new, interesting feature was observed, all the tapes previously discussed were rescrutinized for signs of that new feature. Although we were happy to agree with Glaser and Strauss (1967, p. 30) that "a single case can indicate a general conceptual category or property," we also wanted to capture the richness of each of the categories that we were identifying, and so we looked for further examples to round out our descriptions.

An emerging problem was how to identify the growth of understanding and relate it to the examples of discussion we were observing. Although the ability to talk purposefully about mathematics is—as are also the abilities to write mathematics and to solve problems—*prima faci* evidence of mathematical understanding, it is not necessarily the cause of, or even an aid to, such understanding. At this stage we based our judgement about the growth of mathematical understanding on the interview data, noted it, but did not do much in the way of theorizing on the effects of the discussion for the following important reason. It rapidly became apparent that the paucity of examples of discussion seen by the Cockcroft

Committee was no accident—the incidence of discussion was rare even in the classrooms of teachers working to promote it. Although pupils talked about the mathematics they were doing, this was more in the nature of working aloud than with the intention of initiating an interaction with the hearer. Less commonly, the goals were not well defined and the talk had a scattershot nature, going in no particular direction. It took the form of disconnected brainstorming. Although this may be a very valuable activity, it is not discussion within our definition.

To give us a wider, and at the same time deeper, base for categorization, our second round of data was gathered in the same way as the first, with the same teachers and pupils we already knew. At this stage we also defined more precisely our definition of "pupil-pupil" as opposed to "pupil-teacher" discussion, and we agreed that we would consider discussion that was provoked by a comment by the teacher but not discussions in which the teacher took any further part. Given the nature of our data and our method of analysis, this change in definition caused no problems for the research. We were simply able to review all existing data from this new perspective.

How Is the Design Adapted in the Face of Emerging Questions and Unforeseen Events?

In our aim to preserve an open mind to the possible emerging categories of interaction, we had deliberately not intended to start from any explicit hypotheses. We could not avoid, however, having some initial, generative questions that we believed could be fundamental, although we realized that as features of the phenomenon were revealed, we might revise our emphases. Hammersley and Atkinson (1990) refer to this as a "shopping list of issues" that "clearly draws on the authors' prior knowledge" but does "not constitute a research hypothesis or set of hypotheses, nor ... provide a research design as such" (p. 35). Our original list included questions like the following:

- Are there categories of pupil-pupil discussion that appear to be of more value for the growth of mathematical understanding than are others?
- Are there specific topic areas for which pupil-pupil discussion is appropriate or valuable?
- Are there special benefits to be derived from such discussion?
- What are the effects of leaving pupils with the misconceptions they take from their private discussions?
- Do pupils need to be immersed in this style of working for some length of time before any benefits become evident?
- Does making the aims of the discussion explicit to pupils enhance their learning?

This original "shopping list" was concerned with mathematical topics and the influences of discussion on understanding. Our inclination had been to watch for the effects of spoken language, but we had a growing feeling that we were ignoring a whole area of possible interest, the behaviors of the pupils—both their mathematical behavior and the roles they verbally adopted within their small groups. This generation of new questions in the course of the examination of the data is one of the hallmarks of theoretical sampling, and we approached the second analysis, therefore, from a different frame of reference. This time, using the second round of data and using the same systematic individual and then joint method of interpretation, we deliberately categorized the incidents of discussion from the point of view of verbal behavior. Among others, the following headings crystallized as relevant: "defining," "into algebra," "verbalizing for approval (frequently their own)," "confusing each other," and "collaborative checking."

This last category is worth a comment here because it illustrates how categories evolved through an examination of data from a new perspective, both at this point and at a later stage in the analysis. Up until now, we had not seen episodes in which pupils checked their work as fitting our definition of discussion. It was quite common for one pupil to check the working of the group, but we had not seen it as more than an aside to the general discussion about a task in hand. The following episode, however, suggested a new category of discussion was called for.

Janie and Meg were working with the image of balancing-scale pans as a representation of linear equations. For example, they had worked with the picture shown in Figure 6.1.

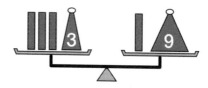

Figure 6.1. Balancing scale-pan picture for the equation $3t + 3 = t + 9$.

| *Janie:* | So, you've got to take the same off both sides. The same number of tins, or weights off this side and off there so you can get rid of them. |

They later progressed to writing the picture versions with "t" for tins. (The foregoing example would have been written $3t + 3 = t + 9$.) Later still they were faced with $8t - 9 = t + 12$.

| *Janie:* | Eight tins take away nine . . . |
| *Meg:* | Take nine off both sides [she crosses out the 9 and crosses out the 12 and replaces it by 3]. |

$$8t - 9 = \cancel{t} + \cancel{12}^{3}$$

| *Janie:* | And take off a "t," so $7t = 3$ and t equals [uses a calculator; pause] ... That can't be right. Let me do it again. Write it out again. |

Meg: [Writes 8t − 9 = t + 12, does the canceling again, writes 8t − 0 = t + 3] But take away nothing is just nothing. Take the "t" off each side [writes 7t = 3, takes the calculator away from Janie, and does 3 ÷ 7]. It doesn't work. A tin can't be [reading calculator] 0.42853. It must be a whole number. Try four.

Janie: [Using the calculator] 8 times 4 equals 32, take away 9 equals 23. 4 add 12 equals 16. No, that doesn't work. [They call the teacher over.]

We believed that this piece of discussion merited a category of its own; it was more than just an adjunct to the preceding conversation. We called it "collaborative checking."

The third analysis consisted of looking at the first batch of data gathered through the lens of the second categorization and looking at the second batch of data through the lens of the first analysis. When reviewing the first batch of data, we noted two other instances of "collaborative checking" that we had not previously extracted as separately categorizable episodes. Thus the intentions of systematicity and constant comparison between and among items of data can clearly be seen to be intentions adhered to.

Theoretical Sampling

The guiding questions at each stage in theoretical sampling are What groups do I turn to for data this next time? and For what theoretical reasons? The criteria must be goal directed and those of theoretical relevance. They can arise from new questions being generated by the data already collected. One option open to those working within this methodology is, according to Strauss (1987), to widen the field within which data are sought. An obvious choice for us would have been to look at discussion in other fields—not with the purpose of creating a more encompassing theory but to "stimulate theoretical sensitivity in the service of generating theory" (Strauss, 1987, p. 17) in the area of mathematical discussion. For the reasons outlined at the beginning of this chapter—the possible non-generalizability of work on discussion in other disciplines to the field of mathematics—we did not choose to do this.

An alternative approach we considered, before collecting further data at this stage, was to look at the types of mathematical environments we were observing to see whether these could be significant. One particular area in which discussion was evident (although we had only two examples) was when the pupils were working in small groups at a computer. We made the decision that this situation was very different from the ordinary classroom because the pupils moved en masse to another room for these lessons, which is typical of many schools' use of computers. Also, since we knew that a research project at the London Institute was looking exclusively at this environment (Hoyles, Healey, & Sutherland, 1990), we decided to exclude these episodes from future observation.

One of our teachers had the practice of teaching most of the mathematics syllabus through investigations with backup from time to time delivered through routine practice. This seemed to be a good environment to explore further, because he made it plain to his classes that he expected them to work together in threes or fours on all the investigations and totally alone on the practice days. Classes familiar with his methods automatically worked in this way. The advantage of observing overt problem solving of this nature was that the solution of the problem could be seen as a growth in understanding within the group, although not necessarily for individuals. We became interested in the question Does problem solving benefit from pupil-pupil discussion? To get a wider perspective on the effects on problem solving, we identified another teacher who, by contrast, used investigative group work as non-topic-specific relaxation between more orthodox spells of teaching through exposition.

Most of the discussion that we observed took place in small groups, but one of our original teachers espoused a philosophy of learning based on whole-class discussion, which frequently splintered to heated small-group discussion in which all the pupils had to be able to justify the arguments they put forward. At the beginning of the year, it was common to hear him say, in response to a question from a pupil, "Don't ask me, ask her, she put the idea forward." But by a few weeks into the term, many of the pupils totally disregarded his presence after his stimulating and often provocative input at the start of the lesson. A further subsidiary, generative question became Are there significant differences between whole-class and small-group discussions in terms of pupils' learning?

The life of a researcher is never plain sailing! At this moment the "whole-class discussion" teacher left the school in which he was working to head the department of a school with a contrasting view of how mathematics should be taught, namely, quietly, with individual learning materials. Rather than enter as a new broom sweeping all along with him, he determined to change the departmental teaching approach by his own gradually changing example. Initially the classes he taught would still use the same individualized materials, but students would work at them in pairs. Although we lost the opportunity to gather more data on whole-class discussion, this change gave us the opportunity to observe discussion in a quite different, structured environment. The nature of our methodology meant that this for us was nothing but an advantage. A different context for the discussion might enable us to spot important features of pupil-pupil discussion that were not evident to us previously, which did indeed prove to be the case.

An interesting variation of the category of "collaborative checking" came to light, as the following episode demonstrates. Jona and Bette were working on the same material, sometimes together and sometimes doing the tasks individually and then looking at each other's work to check what the other was doing. Presumably because talking was an encouraged but unfamiliar activity for these pupils in a mathematics classroom, they frequently talked aloud, but ostensibly to themselves, as they worked.

Jona: [They are expanding $(x-2)(x+3)$ and Bette has written $x^2 + 3x + 2x - 6$ and $x^2 + 5x - 6$] Tell me how you did that again. [She has obviously overheard Bette talking her way through her work.]

Bette: Right, so you times the x's, x squared, OK? Then x times 3 ...

Jona: ... plus $3x$ [writing $x^2 + 3x$].

Bette:	Then you do the minus 2. Times *x*.
Jona:	[Writing] minus 2*x*.
Bette:	… and the numbers make minus 6.
Jona:	[She has written $x^2 + 3x - 2x - 6$. Below she writes $x^2 + x - 6$.] Last time you said five. Five *x*, but it's 3 *subtract* [emphasis] 2. You put add there. That's where I didn't get it, what you'd done.

Here the notion of working individually while being encouraged to talk about their work had offered Bette an opportunity to correct a mistake in her working. We created a subcategory of "collaborative checking" and called it "revealing errors to themselves." In terms of our category groupings outlined previously, this episode was coded (c,h,q); they were reviewing their understanding of a task because Bette's original result did not fit with Jona's understanding—c, mathematical language was present—h, and the statements were operational—q.

When Can I Stop?

The third phase of data collection and analysis was conducted with the same methods as before but in the new, changed and focused environments. Each new set of data analyzed was used to confirm existing categories or suggest new ones. In the latter situation, all previous data were examined to see whether the new classification was an anomaly of the particular data set or a universally important grouping. This may sound very tedious and time consuming, but of course with each new analysis, the researcher becomes very familiar with the previous data. In addition, the process is not of itself unending. The aim is to attain theoretical saturation in each category. This is judged to have been achieved when new examples of the category add nothing to the development of its properties. When similar instances are encountered repeatedly, the researcher can be empirically confident that the category is saturated and can then cease to examine such data in the future. Data collection is then concentrated on filling gaps in other areas pointed up by emerging theories and questions based on existing data. When further data sets suggest no new categories, then the research can be considered theoretically stable.

SUMMARY

By offering a detailed account of the design of a specific research project, I have illustrated three key considerations that need to be addressed if we are to successfully adapt the research paradigms of other disciplines to appropriate use within mathematics education. The first of these concerns the research question. Tempting as it is to wish to demonstrate our independence from the enumerative methods of mathematics, the research question must always drive the choice of methodology. Too often we hear such statements as "I'd like to do an ethnographic study" before the focus of the study has been selected. Only when first the broad interest and then the refined questions have been teased out is it appropriate to turn to the selection of a methodology. This second key decision, the choice of methodology, should not be undertaken hastily. We must review imaginatively the range of possible approaches to answering our research questions. One approach may at first sight appear seductive, but it is in the details that the connections between questions and successful explorations lie. The final consideration is one concerning reporting. It is necessary for us to be very explicit, when writing about our research, about what exactly *are* our data, so others may, for themselves, judge the validity of the conclusions and recommendations that we make. Are we basing our analysis on the tape itself (whether video or audio), on transcripts of the tape, on field notes made at the time of the incident, on notes written up afterwards, or on some combination? Any of these and more can be appropriate data sources, but the kinds of analyses that we can make will differ (Pirie, 1996b). That said, we must also be explicit about *how* we performed the analysis of these data. If we are to hasten the day when it will be "possible to codify methods of qualitative analysis with ... clarity," then I suggest that we need to pay close attention to the three considerations outlined, but most especially to the last.

The purpose of this chapter was to demonstrate a qualitative approach to the research design for a specific project and to illustrate systematic theoretical sampling with constant comparison as a possible methodology for mathematics education research that intends to build rather than test theory. It would be cruelly tantalizing, however, to leave the reader with no insight into the theory emerging for the specific project described, and so I conclude with a postscript that traces the emergence of one particular category and present the inferences we drew from it. I then state very briefly some of the tentative answers that are emerging to our generative questions.

Postscript

I referred above to the emergence of new categories from the data we collected in the "thwarting individualized learning" environment. There were several such categories, the most striking of which we called "pupil as teacher." This category was characterized by one of the pupils clearly enacting the role of a teacher in the interaction. We took as evidence for this role play the pupil's adoption of the functions of teacher talk and language offered by Sinclair and Coulthard (1975). Having reanalyzed all previous episodes of discussion for the possibility of inclusion within this new category and, interestingly, having found very few examples in any other collections of data, we looked in detail at each included episode. Some of the more extreme episodes we separated into further new categories labeled "using pupil answer book" and "pupil as lecturer," and the main category was subdivided according to whether the pupil spontaneously adopted the role of teacher or was cast as teacher by another pupil. We also looked at how faithfully each pupil played the assigned role. This subcategorization is explained in detail in Newman and Pirie (1990). In the cases in which the pupils were working on the individualized materials, which by their very design had to have progression built in, the criterion we used for judging the effect on understanding in the short term was whether the pupils were able to successfully complete the task or move to the next activity.

It is important to remember that we are not in a position to make sweeping generalizations from our data. Instead, we wish to draw out common features that form significant factors in the creation of a theory describing pupil-pupil discussion. One such feature is that when pupils elected to spontaneously adopt the role of teacher, they tended to stay faithful to the role of *mathematics* teacher, using mathematical language and making abstractive statements (group r). Those cast as pupils, too, tended to play their role in an almost caricature, typical manner (listening carefully, trying to do what was asked of them, responding politely), and the outcome was successful in the short term at least. We could theorize that pupils who choose the teacher's role, who offer to help their peers, see the situation as one in which mathematical language must be used and the discussion cannot be at the operational level. As a consequence of the adoption of the role, they believe it necessary to continue the interaction until there is evidence that the "pupil" has gained in understanding. In contrast, when forced into the role of teacher, the majority of the "teacher" pupils do not use mathematical language, nor do the discussions contain abstract statements. In addition, there is no guarantee of a successful outcome, which might lead one to suggest that simply asking one pupil who "knows" to explain or discuss some piece of mathematics with another is not necessarily an activity of value. This latter statement is born out by evidence we have, in the category "confusing each other," of occasions where confusion, sometimes of both pupils, results from the event (Pirie, 1991a).

The category "pupil as lecturer" illustrates how discussion does seem to be of value. There were also other categories for which this was the case, such as "into algebra." Here pupils were seen to create their own *personal* "algebra," usually in an attempt to generalize or represent a problem symbolically. This frequently involved an extended discussion, which led to a much clearer understanding of the mathematical problem. This contrasts strongly with "using algebra," a category in which pupils discussed the use of standard algebraic techniques, often with disastrous results (Pirie 1991a)!

As previously indicated, much data still remain to be analyzed and reported. Indeed the richness of the data collected ensures that much still lies to be discovered by those who care to revisit the data. Perhaps the mark of a fruitful piece of research is that it fulfills some or all of its original intentions but uncovers the way to further avenues of exploration. To be of value, theory must remain a living comment, adapting to new environments as they arise.

Chapter 7

Studying the Classroom Negotiation of Meaning: Complementary Accounts Methodology

David J. Clarke

The research procedures that form the focus of this chapter were developed in an attempt to study learning in legitimate classroom settings while minimizing the need for researcher inference regarding participant thought processes and maximizing the richness of the research data base. The focus of the research stems from a perceived need to model empirically the process of learning in classrooms and, in particular, the so-called "negotiation of meaning." The use of the metaphor of negotiation grounds learning in social activity, but this research adopts the epistemological stance that the meaning that is constructed as a consequence of this social activity is experienced as personal meaning, and any theory of learning must accommodate this constructed self. Classrooms are complex social settings, and research that seeks to understand the learning that occurs in such settings must reflect and accommodate to that complexity. This accommodation can occur through a data-collection process that generates an appropriately rich data set. Such a complex data set can be adequately exploited only to the extent that the research design employs analytical techniques sensitive to the multifaceted and multiply connected nature of the data.

The focus of this chapter is a qualitative research approach I have called "complementary accounts methodology." Available technology is utilized to combine videotape data with participants' reconstructions of classroom events. This integrated data set then provides the basis for complementary accounts constructed by the research team. Complementary accounts methodology is distinguished from other approaches to classroom research by—

- the nature of the data collection procedures, leading to the construction of "integrated data sets" combining videotape and interview data;
- the inclusion of the reflective voice of participant students in the data set;
- an analytical approach that utilizes a research team with complementary but diverse areas of expertise to carry out a multifaceted analysis of a common body of classroom data.

I would like to express my gratitude to Sue Helme, whose insightful interpretative suggestions contributed greatly to the research reported in this chapter.

Within the scope of this monograph, it is possible to set out only certain key features of the research activity: the principal means of data collection, and an overview of the multiple forms of analysis that are demanded by the complexity of the setting and made possible by the complexity of the data. In the discussion that follows, specific research techniques of data collection and analysis are outlined, by which the nature of classroom learning might be put on a more empirical footing.

PURPOSE IN CLASSROOM RESEARCH

The particular aim of the research discussed here is to contribute to a constructivist model of learning that adequately accommodates the social activity typical of classroom settings with specific regard to negotiation and the construction of meanings by learners in mathematics classrooms.

Attempts to model the learning process in classroom settings have employed the metaphor of the "negotiation of meaning," and we need explicit, viable, and falsifiable models for the process represented by this phrase. Such models would then serve to direct our attention to those constructs and associated behaviors that we might study productively and, subsequently, to the methodological tools demanded by such research.

A research procedure is required that is designed to reveal the process by which meanings are negotiated and constructed by students in mathematics classrooms. At the heart of such research is the question of whose accounts of classroom activity are privileged for the purpose of understanding learning processes in such settings. The key to the approach described here is to ground student accounts of classroom activities (including thoughts, motivations, and construed meanings) in a videotape record of specific shared classroom events and to supplement each student's account with an associated data base of other students' accounts, researcher field notes, and transcribed videotape records. By this approach, the research techniques of classroom videotape analysis and student clinical interview are combined to best effect in a manner designed to be reciprocally validating and illuminating.

The theoretical constructs of meaning (Bakhtin, 1979), sources of conviction (Frid, 1992), and classroom consensus processes (Clarke, 1986) informed the interpretative framework for the study and, therefore, the method of data collection. *Sources of conviction* refer to how one determines facts, legitimacy, logicality, consistency, and accordance with accepted mathematical or scientific principles and standards (i.e., academic content meanings) and to the authorities cited by individuals to justify their statements, actions, or interpretations. *Consensus processes* are typified by group compromise, refinement, and accommodation—taken to be those interactions whereby conjectures and arguments arising in classroom discourse are compared and assessed (including the development of social-context meanings).

With regard to meaning: The presumptions of meaning are based on community, purpose, and situation. It is futile to discuss the meaning of a word or term

in isolation from the discourse community of which the speaker claims member-
ship, from the purpose of the speaker, or from the specific situation in which the
word was spoken. Indeed, it is not the word that has meaning, but the utterance.
The emphasis on utterance, derived from Bakhtin (1979), is evident later in this
chapter in a discussion and an illustrative analysis focusing on intersubjectivity.

The resultant framework based on the characterization of these terms served to
identify key data types (and the associated research techniques) essential to the
research design and also provided the theoretical framework for the interpretation of the resultant data. Data related to negotiative situations and associated
social activity were considered essential to any analysis of such consensus
processes. The structural analysis of classroom text is informed significantly by
the theoretical emphasis on utterance. It must be stressed that a theoretical framework used in such a way confers coherence on the research design and tells the
researcher where to look without predetermining what will be found.

The challenge for this type of classroom research was to portray the learning
process of an individual embedded in a highly complex social context. This
learning process was taken to be an integration of not just the obvious social
events that might be recorded on a videotape, but also the individual's construal
of those events, the memories invoked, and the constructions that arise as a consequence. The research procedure recounted here was designed explicitly to
achieve this integration.

Central to this research procedure was the use of videotaped classroom lessons
and video-stimulated recall techniques within an interview protocol that sought
to obtain the following:

1. Students' perceptions of their own constructed meanings in the course of a
lesson and the associated memories and existing meanings employed in the constructive process

2. Students' sources of conviction for the construction of their mathematical
meanings

3. The individuals, experiences, arguments, or actions in which students
believed mathematical (academic content) authority to reside

Since the concern was with the context of learning and descriptions of teachers' and learners' mathematical (and social) interpretations in classroom settings,
the research methods were qualitative in character.

THE PRACTICALITIES OF DATA COLLECTION

Procedure: In the Classroom

Two video cameras were used: One focused consistently on the teacher, and the
other, on a selected group of about four students. This approach did not assume
that the students would be working in collaborative groups, only that they were
seated sufficiently close to one another that the entire group could be simultane-

ously in view and a single microphone could be used to record the conversations of all four students. The teacher's conversation was recorded through a radio microphone. Once in place, the video camera focused on the students required no attention unless the students changed location within the classroom; however, a research assistant was required to keep the teacher in view on the other camera.

The dual video images of teacher and pupils were combined into a single image through a compact audiovisual mixing board situated at the rear of the classroom. This image was viewed on a small portable monitor. The composite image was structured so that the students occupied most of the viewing screen with the teacher included as a small insert in one corner of the screen. The same mixing device combined the audio input from both microphones. The relative volume of teacher and student conversations could be adjusted.

The combined image was recorded onto video-8 tape using a very compact video recorder. This video recorder was linked to a laptop computer. The researcher was seated at the rear of the classroom with easy access to the mixing board and the ability to view the image recorded on the video monitor. Using headphones, the researcher was able to listen simultaneously both to the students' conversations and to the teacher's utterances. Using the CVideo software (Roschelle, 1992), the researcher was able to record field notes onto a word processing document on the computer and also "time-tag" the notes to the corresponding events in the video record.

The following example illustrates a typical set of field notes (numbers refer to hours:minutes:seconds elapsed on the video tape):

00:15:04 to 00:18:35   Students doing number 2
K says something;   A: "I don't get it"
After some time A hesitantly puts her hand up and withdraws it.
A puts her hand up again without getting a response; USE THIS
00:18:36 to 00:22:19   Students still working on number 2
T demonstrates a particular method
Students call out "122" [K moves her mouth—thinking what? PURSUE THIS]
A hesitant but attentive. K staring at her pencil—discouraged?

Such field notes serve two purposes: first, as a record of the researcher's immediate impressions of significant social interactions and learning events; second, as reference markers for the subsequent interviewing of the student subjects.

Relating the Interview to the Video Record

In the video-stimulated interview, priority was given to those events to which the student attached significance. The research emphasis on negotiation, consensus, and conviction was used to attach significance to other events (not necessarily regarded as significant by the student) involving disagreement or uncertainty that then became the subject of student reconstruction. This process, as with all research techniques, has its limitations. It is possible that later analysis of the videotape might identify an event, whose significance was not recognized at the time by either the student or the researcher. As with any clinical interview, the researcher may miss one insight through the pursuit of another. Nonetheless, the videotape record was substantially enriched by the student's immediate reconstruction of those events perceived to be significant at the time. Subsequent analysis of interview and videotape transcripts can be used to reveal relationships of meaning that were not apparent at the time of the interview.

An important design consideration is that without the videotape as stimulus, the student's account is likely to be superficial and grounded not in actual classroom events but rather in the student's uncertain reconstruction of the lesson. Inconsistencies among student accounts of classroom lessons provide a fascinating study in themselves, but it is the learning stimulated by the student's participation in particular classroom events that is the focus of this research, specifically, the relationship between these events and the student's consequent knowings. Where the purpose of analysis is an understanding of the learning process, the researcher's interpretation of the videotape data is likely to be inadequate and possibly misguided without the student's account. The researcher would lack insight into the associations, memories, and meanings that each classroom event evoked for the student.

Procedure: The Interview

At the end of the lesson, using the video record as stimulus, the researcher interviewed the target students individually. This technique is in widespread use (see, e.g., Anthony, 1994). For the interview stage, the researcher used the video recorder, the video monitor, the laptop computer, and a compact audio recorder to record the interview on audiotape. The video record of the lesson was sampled as required in response to the identification of a particular episode by either the student or the researcher. The following example is typical of the commencement of such interviews.

I: What do you think that lesson was about?

S: Oh, linear functions and how you graph them.

I: Was that something that you understood before the lesson started?

S: Not really. I mean I knew about linear functions, and we had done a bit of stuff on graphing, but I couldn't say I really understood it.

I: Would you say that you understand it now, after the lesson?

S: Yes, I think so.

I: At what point in the lesson would you say that you came to "understand" about graphing linear functions?

S: I'm not sure. Probably after I had tried a few of the problems in the book, and they seemed to be coming out OK.

I: Was there something that happened in the lesson that really helped you to understand?

S: Maybe. I'm not sure.

I: It seemed to me that you spent a lot of time talking to Simone at one point, what was all that about?

S: Really. I don't remember. I suppose it was something to do with the problems. Yeah. She asked me about the first one, and then we started talking about how to do them.

I: Let's look at that bit now, and you can tell me what you were thinking.

The use of the CVideo software enabled the researcher to locate within the field notes reference to actions of the student that seemed to be of significance either to the researcher or to the student. Having found this point in the word document, the software was used to find the corresponding moment on the video record, which was then played back and discussed. The contrast between the superficiality of the student's recollections without the aid of the videotape and the comparative richness of the student's subsequent comments regarding a specific videotaped incident provide a recurrent endorsement of this technique.

The audio record of the interview was transcribed onto the relevant section of the word document and time-tagged to the corresponding video incident. Together, the video record and the word document incorporated the student and teacher actions and utterances throughout the lesson, the researcher's field notes, and the student's interpretations and explanations of significant events. This integrated data source was then available for analysis. One example of such an integrated word document is given below (**bold** = field notes; plain text = transcript from videotape; *italics* = transcript from interview). The following sample text includes two students' reconstructed accounts of the same event, after viewing the video record of the interaction transcribed below.

00:39:27 to 00:41:30 T(teacher) asks students K and L what they've done. K explains, T is dubious, then says I think you're right, L explains, says we're right.

T: Where'd you get 180 from?

K: Width. Equals point—

T: Why did you multiply them together?

K: To get the area. Forty-five thousand, therefore you'd need.

T: Forty-five thousand?

K: Forty-five thousand. That's what we got.

T: Forty-five thousand? Can you place that—can you place that—can you do that again? Two hundred and fifty times one hundred and eighty, oh, hang on, hang on, I think you're right. I think they're wrong.

K: Yup, they're wrong. We're right.

[L holds up calculator].

I (Interviewer with student L): Uh huh. So why were you so sure your answer was right? Or were you sure your answer was right?

L: Um, because when she asked us what it was, she thought it was right too.

I: I'd like you to tell me this last bit. So say that again for me.

L: She came and asked us to do the answer that we found and we had a different answer to the one that another group had given her and when she heard our answer it must have clicked that, um, it sounded more right than the other one did, so she went to tell them that they were wrong.

I: It must have clicked with her, so that's why she thought it was right. Why did you think it was right?

L: *'Cause if Mrs. Burton thinks it's right, it probably is.*

I (Interviewer with student K): *There she's going over to your group.*

[videotape continues] Yeah, so you seem pretty sure, you got the, you had answers for everything she said.

K: *Yeah, because, um don't say anything to her, but the girls said that she'd pick on me a bit because I'm new, so if I show her that I know what I'm talking about then she'll lay off.*

I: *Oh, well that makes sense.*

K: *Because I don't want to seem like I'm going, "Well, you're right."*

I: *But you did know, didn't you?*

K: *Yeah, but I just thought it, 'cause yeah.*

I: *Yeah.*

K: *So I just wanted to show her that I know what I was talking about, because otherwise she'd keep on at me.*

I: *Yeah.*

K: *Admit that actually sort of think that she made a little bit of a mistake. Yeah. I knew she'd lay off if I sort of had an answer for everything, so that's why I just said, straightaway she'd ask me a question, I'd have an answer, and she'd go, um, think about it for a while and then straightaway say, "You're right" or "You're wrong." Yeah, I just wanted to say everything quickly so she didn't have time to think of another question.*

In combination, the researcher's field notes, the transcribed classroom dialogue, and the student's explanations augment the video record to provide a rich data base for subsequent analysis. Other examples are given in the following discussion of data analysis.

ANALYSIS: FINDING STRUCTURE IN DIVERSITY

There are many comments that might be made about the preceding data. Comparisons might be made of the two students' interpretations of the exchange with the teacher. In a study whose major focus is classroom negotiation, student K's account of her motives and her perception of the interaction offer some insight into what it is that is actually being negotiated in an exchange whose surface content is mathematical. The example above strongly suggests that without the student's reconstruction, the researcher's account of the interaction would be unlikely to capture the student's motivations and construal of the particular social situation. Yet, lacking this detail, any inferences the researcher might make regarding the student's participation in the classroom and her associated learnings would be extremely restricted.

Inference is an obligation the researcher cannot escape; the minimization of the inferential gap remains a methodological imperative if our research is to claim either authority or application different from that of the novelist or the poet. To infer student thought processes and the significance of classroom events on the basis of only videotape data seemed an unnecessary and unjustified extrapolation. An important, possibly essential, perspective on the classroom was obtained from the students themselves in interview situations with the assisting prompt of the classroom video record. Students reconstructed, in full knowledge of the ultimate outcomes of those actions, the significance of the events and their associated motivations and meanings. Such accounts inform the researcher's interpretation of events, either by their similarity with the researcher's interpretation of the interaction or by their difference from that interpretation.

This chapter focuses on two fundamentally related research activities: the collection of a rich set of data and the use of analytic processes essential to the realization of the potential of these data. This section describes a set of different interpretative techniques that can be used to provide multiple and complementary interpretations to adequately portray the many facets of classroom learning contained in the integrated data sets. Examples from the videotape transcripts are used to illustrate analysis by exemplification and a structural analysis of text. A brief discussion is then presented of several other analytic methods.

Analysis by Exemplification

The key constructs from which our theories of classroom learning are constructed must be empirically well founded. The operationalization of these constructs occurs through the accumulation of research examples, in which the obligations of the researcher are to provide theoretical justification of the claimed exemplifications and to subject the proposed operationalized constructs to the scrutiny of the informed community of researchers and learning theorists.

The following discussion illustrates the use of "analysis by exemplification" to identify empirical examples of the key constructs of "negotiation" and "intersubjectivity." The sample analysis from the integrated data set that follows starts from evidence of students' intersubjectivity and documents alternative forms of uncertainty and the negotiative process whereby resolution is achieved—a process in which intersubjectivity has a central role. In this account of classroom learning, intersubjectivity enters as a mediating agency, essential to the negotiative process, whereby uncertainty is resolved and new knowings are constructed. Both negotiation and intersubjectivity, and the relationship between them, require definition to provide a theoretical framework for the analysis that follows.

Negotiation has been characterized in some detail elsewhere as a cyclic process of refraction (construal), reflection, and representation—the goal of which is consensus (Clarke, 1996). Lave and Wenger associate learning with participation in practice and assert that "participation is always based on situated negotiation and renegotiation of meaning in the world" (Lave & Wenger, 1991, p. 52). Cobb and Bauersfeld define the negotiation of meaning succinctly as "the interactive accomplishment of intersubjectivity" (Cobb & Bauersfeld, 1995, p. 295).

Negotiation depends on language (or at least on some form of communicative process), and language is constitutively intersubjective (Todarov, 1984, p. 30). Thus, a level of student-student and student-teacher intersubjectivity is prerequisite to the negotiative processes by which the resolution of uncertainty is attempted. A relationship between the constructs negotiation and intersubjectivity can be summarized in the argument that one pathway to knowing is by means of the resolution of uncertainty, that the process of resolution is fundamentally negotiative, that negotiation is mediated by language, that language presumes intersubjectivity, and that the matter of intersubjectivity is meaning (Clarke & Helme, 1997, p. 117).

The theoretical constructs of negotiation and intersubjectivity both require empirical substantiation. Similarly, general statements of principle, which define one construct in terms of another, require empirical demonstration of the postulated relationship. This is particularly obligatory when the proposed relationship is one of process and product. Since classrooms represent legitimate sites of situated mathematical practice, this perspective supports the need for the empirical documentation of negotiative processes in the classroom. For example, an understanding of the means by which the resolution of uncertainty might be achieved requires an understanding of intersubjectivity as a phenomenon of social interaction. To establish this point, consider the following videotape transcript. (All utterances are by students. K and L were subsequent interviewees, S19 and S20 were not.)

Episode 1

1. *S19:* It says how many sheets of graph paper would you need to show one million 1-millimeter squares.

2. *L:* To show one million, you know you don't divide it by 100, because there's more than a hundred 1-millimeter squares. I mean you're going to find the area of this.

3. *K:* What?

4. *L:* You've got to find the area of this, there's more than one hundred 1 millimeters.

5. *K:* That's right. I was doing length by—oh screw that.

6. *L:* One hundred 1-millimeter squares. Take length ...

7. *K:* Um, there's how many down here?

8. *L:* And along that side there is ...

9. *K:* 10, 20, 30, 40, 50. How many are there down there?

10. *L:* There's a hundred 1 millimeters there.

11. *L:* No, there wouldn't be.

12. *K:* There wouldn't be, that's not right.

13. *L:* There'd be 250.

14. *K:* Yeah.

15. L: Yeah, there'd be 250.

16. *K:* And we just totally screwed it all ...

17. *L:* Length of graph.

18. *K:* OK, so it would be length times width [inaudible]

19. *L:* And uh, 250 millimeters. Width ...

20. *K:* What's width?

21. *L:* That's ...

22. *K:* That's 10, 20, 30, 40, 50, et cetera.

23. *L:* 18, 180.
24. *K:* Times 180. OK here we go. 250 times 180 equals 45 thousand. OK, that's 45 thousand. We need a million. What's a million divided by 45 thousand and times it by that?
25. *L:* Hang on, hang on, hang on, hang on. Don't go too fast. OK. Therefore there are 45 thousand million millimeter squares.
26. *S20:* 45 thousand million?
27. *L:* Yeah.
28. *S20:* 45 thousand.
29. *K:* 22.2.
30. *L:* On one piece. Of graph paper.

The goal of analysis by exemplification, in this instance, is the operationalization of intersubjectivity through the accumulation of examples. In the preceding transcript are several indicators of intersubjectivity. First, much of the recorded dialogue is incoherent as written text: That is, sentences are ungrammatical or incomplete; pronouns are used without textual clues as to their referents; single-word utterances are frequent. Communication in this form is interpreted as being sustainable only because the participants share understandings of the referents of the pronouns or key words and of the processes, actions, or relationships suggested (but not stated) by the sentence fragments and the participants' gestures. Second, evidence of intersubjectivity can be interpreted from the manner in which one speaker completes the sentence of the previous speaker, as occurs in lines 8 and 9, and in 28 and 30 (I am using *line* as a shorthand for *utterance*). The overt text in the form of the literal transcription is here being distinguished from the implicit text being coconstructed by the participants. The existence of an implicit text is inferred on the basis that the interaction appears to have been both purposeful and successful.

The findings of this type of analysis reside in the claim that the preceding episode constitutes an example of intersubjectivity in a classroom setting. Evidence for the enactment of the construct of intersubjectivity should assist us in theoretically locating intersubjectivity within the learning process as agency or as outcome or as both.

Structural Analysis of Text

Another type of analysis of the integrated data sets used to achieve the research goals involves the classification of the text into three levels: the episode, the negotiative event, and the utterance. Episodes comprise the dialogue and activities that students engage in as they approach, work on, and complete a particular classroom activity, such as a problem-solving task. Thus, each episode is a coherent unit of activity unified by a single purpose. Each such episode may involve several negotiative events. A negotiative event is defined by an identifiable intermediate purpose—a purpose whose realization is an intermediate goal within the encompassing episode. Each negotiative event may be composed of several utterances, each with its own immediate purpose. The interpretation of the significance of a given episode requires an interpretation of each constituent level: the negotiative event and the utterance.

The following episode illustrates the partitioning of text according to the occurrence of "negotiative events" within an "episode." (K and L are student interviewees, S20 and S22 student noninterviewees, and T is the teacher.)

Episode 2

EVENT 1

1. *L:*   [Writing] 500 sheets. Height equals.
2. *K:*   OK, question 2 [Find the height of a stack of one million sheets of paper].
3. *L:*   Does everyone understand what we did with number one?
4. *K:*   No, but. Anyway. 500 sheets.
5. *L:*   And how many sheets do we need?
6. *K:*   500 sheets of what? 500 sheets.
7. *L:*   Their height equals five point eight.
8. *S20:*   We've done that.
9. *K:*   I know. But we've got to do it all together so.
10. *L:*   One point oh times ten to the power of six divided by five hundred.
11. *K:*   Oh yeah sure everyday what are you talking about? What are you talking about?
12. *L:*   Finding out how many five hundreds there are in a million.
13. *K:*   How many five hundreds there are in a million. That would make it one thousand. How many thousands are there in a million? That would make a thousand, two thousand. What? [to another S]. I have a lot to say.
14. *L:*   [Uses calculator] Two thousand. Well done!
15. *K:*   This is called skill. This is what you do. Five hundred into a hundred which is two. Then you do a hundred [correcting herself] which is a thousand.
16. *L:*   Times five point eight. Shush.
17. *K:*   Which is 2. Then you do a thousand into a million which is one thousand, so one thousand times two is two thousand.
18. *L:*   Eleven thousand six hundred.

EVENT 2

19. *T:*   With your working out folks I want you to tell me what you are mult—Matthew—what you are multiplying by, and you simply put a little arrow telling me what and why.
20. *K:*   What are we doing? Is it a million sheets of paper though?
21. *L:*   Yeah. One point ...
22. *K:*   We're doing a million sheets of paper.
23. *L:*   Yeah, you need ...
24. *K:*   Yes we do. We do, shut up.
25. *L:*   Therefore, I did that wrong.
26. *K:*   Two thousand times five point eight is eleven, six, zero, zero. [*i.e.,11,600*]
27. *L:*   [*Sounding out letters*] M-ms?
28. *K:*   Centimeters—which would make it eleven point six meters, right?

EVENT 3

29. *L:*   Or eleven—yeah. It'd be eleven point six meters, wouldn't it, 'cause you take off one to get the centimeters, and another one, yeah. [*pause*]

30. *K:*   [*Looking up*] That's quite high, isn't it?

31. *L:*   All right. And you've got to point out what the units [?] are, right?

32. *K:*   You've got to point out what the what is?

33. *L:*   We have to show what we're multiplying by.

     [*S22 says something to K, K laughs*]

34. S20:   That's not how you know, you look like you know what you're doing and you just do it.

35. *K:*   Exactly, you go into a state of total concentration, it lasts about 2 seconds, that's when you get the answer, and then you don't know what you're doing, so it doesn't matter. Five hundred sheets equals, height equals five point eight centimeters. I don't even understand what I wrote. [*pause as L, K write*]

EVENT 4

36. *K:*   But why do we divide a million by five hundred to get that answer?

37. *L:*   Because you know, if you know what the height is ...

38. *K:*   So what am I doing? Tell me what I'm doing here, tell me what I've done.

39. *L:*   All right. You know that five hundred sheets equals fifty-eight ...

40. *L and K:*   Five point eight centimeters.

41. *K:*   There is a point there, it's up there.

42. *L:*   Oh, I can't see it.

43. *K:*   Get some other glasses.

44. *L:*   Now, we need to know—we need to know the height of a million sheets of paper. Therefore you must divide a million by five hundred and times that number by five point eight.

45. *K:*   [*Writing*] Equals two thousand. Sheets of paper.

46. *L:*   OK.

47. *K:*   Two thousand times five point eight centimeters equals eleven thousand six hundred centimeters, equals eleven point six meters of paper. [*bell rings*]

The preceding transcription may be considered one episode in a lesson consisting of many episodes. Using structural analysis, I partitioned this episode into four events that can be characterized as follows:

- Event 1 combines the refinement of intersubjectivity within the group with L's first solution attempt (1 to 18).
- Event 3 involves the negotiation of appropriate units of measurement (29 to 35).
- Event 2 revisits the procedure employed in Event 1 (19 to 28).
- Event 4 reviews the procedure again and links it to the task (36 to 47).

These structural elements identified within the text may reflect parallel structures within the process of learning.

Analysis of Dialogue as Text

The use of indexing software packages for textual analysis of the dialogue in the integrated data sets can identify points at which the student's state of knowing demonstrably changes from uncertainty to comparative certainty or conviction. It may be that a student recounts, in an interview, a situation in which he or she came to "know" or to "understand" something related to the topic dealt with in the observed lesson. In particular, any student use of the verbs *know, understand,* or *learn* can be analyzed in detail with regard to the subject and object of each verb's use. That is, what sort of things can be known, understood, or learned; what sort of experiences, events, images, or people appear to be associated with learning, understanding, or coming to know; and who is it that knows, understands, or learns things?

In this form of analysis, such software packages as NUD•IST (Qualitative Solutions and Research, 1994) can be employed to undertake textual analyses of the frequency of association of terms, such as those mentioned above, in student classroom discourse and in student discussion of videorecorded classroom situations (Clarke & Kessel, 1995). Such software is in widespread use in studies in which text analysis is a key feature. The use of an indexing tool such as NUD•IST offers a form of replicability for textural searches not previously associated with conventional content analysis.

Complementary Accounts

Different perspectives, reflecting different objects of study within the encompasing goal of modeling classroom learning, can be used to analyze the integrated data sets. For example, Clarke and Helme (1997) used the data in Episode 2 to discuss the role of negotiation in the resolution of uncertainty in mathematics classrooms. Episode 2 is also amenable to analysis with respect to the several instances of student metacognition contained within the text (Lines 13, 20, 25, 35, 38) and the function of these self-evaluative reflections within the learning process.

These two accounts of Episode 2—one from the perspective of the resolution of uncertainty and one from the perspective of student use of metacognition—are not in competition; they represent complementary interpretations of the same integrated data set. Such complementary accounts have the potential to be mutually informing and to constitute in combination a richer portrayal of classroom learning than would be possible by the consideration of either account separately. The acknowledgement of the relativist character of any particular account of social activity commits us to defining explicitly the nature of our focus of inquiry, and those terms we employ in the analysis and comparison of the various accounts, since we are no longer able to presume any specific (absolute) meaning by implicit appeal to the authority of culture or the conventions of use.

A key design element in the complementary accounts methodology is the bringing together of a research team with sufficiently diverse expertise to adequately implement this approach. The research project from which the examples in this chapter were taken used an international team of more than a dozen university academics with expertise in mathematics education, developmental psychology, sociology, epistemology, values analysis, motivation, mathematics, science education, children's conceptual frameworks, metacognition, gender, and a range of qualitative and quantitative research methodologies. Rather than seek a consensus interpretation of an event, an episode, or an interaction, individual members of the research team were encouraged to interpret the documented interaction from their own distinct, carefully articulated theoretical perspective and use their particular selection for focus of study. The goal of such a process is complementarity rather than consensus, and each researcher's interpretation is accorded parity of status, subject to the same criteria of coherence, consistency with the videotape data, and plausibility.

CONCLUSION

In the research discussed in this chapter, an attempt was made to optimize the use of currently available technology through the synthesis of classroom videotape and interview data in an integrated video and text document. An important, possibly essential, perspective on the classroom was obtained from the students themselves in interview situations, in which the significance of classroom events and their associated thought processes were reconstructed by the students with the assisting prompt of the classroom video record. The analysis of the resultant data was enhanced by a framework for text analysis that distinguished episode, negotiative event, and utterance and the use of an indexing tool with the capability to undertake complex analyses of textual data.

Recent developments in educational research (and in learning theory) have led to the acceptance of the idiosyncratic and legitimate subjectivity of both the research subjects and the researcher and to the consideration of what can be learned from the comparison of the multiple stories compiled from the accounts of the various participants in the social setting and from the reconstructed accounts of a research team. Judgments regarding the relative merit of one account over another relate to the purpose for which the comparison is being made and do not call into question the value of either account with regard to any other purpose. I would like to suggest that it is through the accumulation of such complementary accounts in relation to a common integrated data set that our portrayal of classroom learning will approach the complexity of process we seek to model.

Chapter 8

The Centrality of the Researcher: Rigor in a Constructivist Inquiry into Mathematics Teaching

Barbara Jaworski

This chapter is about the research methods employed in a study that explored the nature of the teaching in a setting that might be called an "investigative approach" to the learning of mathematics (Jaworski, 1994). There were strong parallels between the teaching method and the investigative nature of the research itself. Both were embedded in a theoretical base of radical and, subsequently, social constructivism. The research methodology was broadly ethnographic, using data-collection techniques of participant observation and interviewing and verification techniques of triangulation and respondent validation. It was conducted from a researcher-as-instrument position; in other words, the main instrument in both data collection and analysis was the researcher. This was both inevitable and a source of serious issues, particularly where validation of interpretations and emergent theory were concerned. The meaning of research *rigor* in this context is central to the discussion that follows.

THE STUDY

I begin by briefly describing the theoretical background for the research. This description introduces needed terminology and raises some questions and issues that will be addressed in the subsequent discussion.

The Theoretical Background to the Research

The term *investigative approach* is one that gained some popularity with respect to mathematics learning and teaching in the United Kingdom during the 1970s and 1980s. It was not well defined, but was related to the use of mathematical investigations and inquiry methods in the classroom. The research study was undertaken to explore more precisely what such an approach involved, in terms of classroom practices and teachers' thinking, and what issues it raised for

I should like to thank Doug Grouws and Anne Watson for their very helpful comments on an earlier version of this chapter.

the mathematics teacher. A purpose of the research was to try to *characterize* an investigative approach.

It seemed obvious from the inception of the project that the subjects of the research would be teachers of mathematics and their pupils and that the research would take place in mathematics classrooms and their relevant surroundings. An early issue arose in choosing teachers to participate. Should their teaching be required to be investigative in order to study its characteristics? If so, what characteristics would one look for in selecting such teachers? The circularity here was a problem. This problem was resolved initially by choosing, for the first phase of the research, secondary mathematics teachers who were interested in exploring what an investigative approach might mean in their classrooms.

Working with these teachers led to a clarification of the theoretical basis of the research, which resulted in the embedding of the theory of an investigative approach into a *constructivist* view of mathematical knowledge and learning. Initially, this was a *radical* constructivist perspective (e.g., von Glasersfeld, 1987). During the later phases of the research, it developed into a *social* constructivist perspective (Jaworski, 1994). In the radical view, learners were conceived of as constructing their own knowledge, not as taking knowledge from outside of themselves. The process of construction was seen to be an adaptation of their existing knowledge (resulting from previous experience) to accommodate new experience. This constructivist position implied that a teacher could not *give* mathematical knowledge to students: teaching had to be seen as more than just a transfer of knowledge.

An investigative approach, based in this constructivist framework, was seen as providing experiences for students through which they could build a broad relational understanding of mathematics (Skemp, 1976). Implicit in references to mathematical understanding here is that students would be (a) encouraged to address mathematical concepts recognizably standard to most secondary school curricula and (b) encouraged to develop a conceptual understanding involving wide contextual embedding and linking of concepts.

The need to move, theoretically, from radical to social constructivism was apparent to the researcher as soon as the influence of classroom ethos and social interaction on the development of mathematical understandings was addressed. In the classrooms observed, social processes—including school and classroom norms and interactions between students and between teacher and students—formed a major part of the data and hence were significant to the analysis. In any classroom, shared norms and expectations instigate and guide the learning process. The relationship between social or common knowledge and individual knowledge construction was a source of issues for the teachers concerned as well as for the researcher. Two chief issues were involved:

1. The reconciling of knowledge constructed by students in exploratory situations in the classroom with knowledge as defined by the curriculum, that is, knowledge from the thinking and negotiation of mathematicians throughout

history, which has resulted in a socially derived body of knowledge: Although socially derived, this knowledge takes on perceived absolutist properties. Those interacting with it, teachers and students, may come to regard it as objective and external to human endeavor. Noddings (1990) addresses this issue from an epistemological viewpoint.

2. The interactive construction of knowledge in the classroom: It seemed that through discussion and negotiation between participants, knowledge grew in the social domain. However, the status of this knowledge is problematic from a constructivist perspective, particularly from a radical view. This phenomenon is important to a social constructivist perspective and needs to be taken into account (Ernest, 1991; Jaworski, 1994).

These two issues resulted from observations of teaching and learning in classroom events and rationalization with a constructivist theoretical perspective. They figured strongly in the analysis of data. Practical manifestations of the theoretical issues were significant in illuminating and challenging established theory.

Since the research process itself is designed to generate knowledge, it too can be regarded from a constructivist perspective. What is learned can be seen to derive from the constructive process of the researcher. In qualitative research of an interpretative nature, this knowledge depends heavily on a reconciling of interpretations, or *intersubjectivity*, between participants in the research. The research might therefore be considered *social* constructivist in nature. Such a rationale can lead to very dangerous ground where research rigor is concerned. For example, how is it possible to validate conclusions that are no more than a synthesis of interpretations? Hammersley (1993) has pointed out the potentially slippery slope leading from research into fiction or ideology. However, given the epistemological base outlined previously for the scrutiny of mathematics teaching, it seemed unavoidable that the research would be conducted from a constructivist perspective. It is perhaps unsurprising, therefore, that issues of validity dominated much of the analysis and, ultimately, the synthesis that led to conclusions.

The Practical Basis of the Research

In the second and third phases of the research, teachers were selected to fit the outlined theoretical framework. They were chosen because they seemed to be developing an investigative approach in their teaching. In some cases this was their declared aim, and in others it was a judgment of the researcher after initial observations.

The study of the practice of selected teachers led to the identification of practical manifestations of the outlined theory and subsequently to the theory's clarification, modification, and enhancement. As indicated, throughout the research there was a symbiotic relationship between theory and practice that is central to the methodological issues addressed in this paper.

In the research, I wished to characterize investigative teaching on the basis of its practical manifestations in classrooms. I therefore decided to look toward ethnography as a methodological approach. An ethnographic approach involved a classroom observer studying and trying to make sense of the whole activity of a classroom—perhaps beginning with a clean slate and writing on it some description of what was seen to occur that would then form the basis of future analysis. I learned that this was a somewhat simplistic view of ethnography, particularly with respect to the relationship between interpretations of observations and the theoretical perspectives of the research. No researcher goes into a classroom as a blank slate. There are always theories and preconceptions, often implicit, that guide observation and that need to be made explicit for the rigor of the research.

In my study, development of methodology and awareness of theoretical implications went hand in hand. I had to start from the simplistic view, previously expressed, and learn from the questions that arose as I proceeded. This necessity is supported by Ball (1990), who writes the following:

> The prime ethnographic skills cannot be communicated or learned in a seminar room or out of the textbook. Students can be prepared, forewarned, or educated in ethnography, but the only way to learn it is to do it. The only way to get better at it is to do more of it. My point is that ethnographic fieldwork relies primarily on *the engagement of the self* [italics added], and that engagement can only be learned enactively. (p. 157)

Ethnography seemed to allow the construction of knowledge regarding investigative teaching from observations of the practice of teaching. This led to the interrogation of my own previous knowledge and experience that formed broadly my theoretical base. The "engagement of self" was from the beginning a central feature of the research.

The field work took place over 4 years, in three phases. I studied six secondary school mathematics teachers, two in each of three schools, during a period of 6 to 9 months for each school. Typically, I visited a school for 1 day each week. Each teacher selected one class of students, in the 11 to 15 age range, for observation. The first phase acted as a pilot study in which research questions were refined and research methods evolved. I engaged in participant observation of lessons and informal interviewing of teachers and students as my chief methods of data collection. My levels of participation varied from being the teacher to being as unobtrusive as possible in observing the lesson of another teacher. Forms of interviewing varied, too. With students, I had to ask very specific questions. With teachers, interviews were often long monologues from the teacher with minimal interruption from me. Others involved unstructured conversations, with participants often seeking common understandings of issues that arose.

Significance

An important issue for the research was that of "significance." All observation is selective, if only because when one looks to the left, one misses something to the right. Neither my field notes nor audio or video recordings could capture the totality of the classroom. Whatever I recorded in field notes must have caught my attention and so had some level of significance. In the case of electronic recording, choices had to be made about where to point a camera or place an audio recorder. When I listened to a recording of a lesson or interview, some aspects stood out more than others; thus, they carried significance. A major part of my analysis was to recognize and account for items of significance.

The following text is structured to provide details of issues of significance through an example of an episode that was accorded significance. In the main text, I discuss the methodological concerns, whereas the indented text offers descriptions and analyses from the research.

A SIGNIFICANT EPISODE AND ITS ANALYSIS

In this episode, a teacher, Mike, in Phase 2 of the research, stopped himself in the middle of an instruction to his class. My description follows:

> He began with the words, "In groups, decide on different things to try, and ask ëwhat happens?' While you're doing it...." At this point he stopped and paused, then he said, "What am I going to ask you to do?" He started giving an instruction, seemed to think better of it, and instead asked the class what instruction he had been about to give. One response from the class was, "Keep quiet," which he acknowledged with a nod, but other hands were up and he took another response which was, "Ask questions." His reply was, "YES!" Other hands went down. It seemed to me that others had been about to offer this response too. (Jaworski, 1994, p. 113)

This episode struck me as being an important indicator of Mike's approach to teaching—thus it had significance for the research. This significance needed clarification and justification. First, it was important to be clear about what occurred in terms of classroom actions and spoken words. I can support my account with reference to my audio recording of the event. I also fed back to the teacher my writing about the event. His agreement when he read what I had written provided further justification—respondent validation. Second, I needed to explain the event's significance for the study. My analysis of this episode follows:

> The teacher's words seemed to say blatantly, "Guess what's in my mind," but it appeared that most of the class knew the answer to his question—"(You're going to ask us to) Ask questions!" As *I* hadn't known what he wanted them to do, I was very struck by this. A part of his classroom rubric was that the students should ask their own questions. He acknowledged in interview after the lesson that he was always asking them to ask questions, hence they knew that this is what he expected of them and knew what he wanted without his having to spell it out. When I subsequently offered him my text to read, for respondent validation, he further said, "I believe I did this deliberately to stress the 'you *can* get into my head, and *do*.' I had not had them long, remember." (Jaworski, 1994, p. 114)

In the preceding words, I have clarified the event's significance for me in terms of my own experience of it, and I have explained and justified my interpretation by pointing to sources of evidence. It was necessary then to fit the event into my theoretical perspective and explain its significance for my study. I shall say more of this shortly. Although I could be accused of indulging in subjectivity—perhaps of creating a fiction—if I were to offer my interpretation alone, it is the fitting of the event into its situational context as fully as possible that provides its credibility. Is the account as written valid in the eyes of the reader—initially the teacher, but eventually someone external to the research? A reader needs to know on what basis interpretations are made in order ultimately to judge the validity of what is presented.

Interpretation, Reflexivity, and Rigor

As I have indicated, an important part of my analysis was the attribution of meaning in classroom situations. In this context (of qualitative, interpretative, and possibly constructivist research), Burgess (1985) claims that the main research instrument is the researcher—the researcher is *central* to the research. The researcher's task is to seek out the meanings in a situation with reference to declared interests or goals. Cohen and Manion (1989) state, "One can only impute meaning to [experiences] retrospectively, by the process of turning back on oneself and looking at what had been going on" (p. 32). This reflection of significance back to the goals of the research is known as reflexivity. That is, reflexivity is a to and fro movement between the researcher and the research—a constant questioning and critiquing of observations and analyses relative to the total situation and context in which the research takes place. The personal theories of the researcher are one aspect of this totality.

I identified a reflexive cycle in analysis and synthesis throughout my research, whereby interpretations were central objects. Where possible, I sought to verify accounts by triangulating data—seeking the interpretations of the other participants in an event, for example, teacher and student, or of another observer. However, Cicourel (1973) points out limitations in this statement:

It is difficult for the observer "to verify his interpretation of the others' experiences by checking them against the others' own subjective interpretations."... The observer is likely to draw on his own past experiences as a common-sense actor *and* scientific researcher to decide the character of the observed action scene. (p. 36, citing Schütz, 1964)

Cicourel cites Schütz (1964), who goes further in recognizing the special position of the researcher:

The observer's scheme of interpretation cannot be identical, of course, with the interpretative scheme of either partner in the social relation observed. The modifications of attention which characterize the attitude of the observer cannot coincide with those of a participant in an ongoing social relation. For one thing, what he finds relevant is not identical with what they find relevant in the situation. Furthermore, the observer stands in a privileged position in one respect: he has the ongoing experiences of both partners under observation. On the other hand the observer cannot legitimately interpret the "in-order-to" motives of one participant as the "because" motives of the other, as do the partners themselves, unless the interlocking motives become explicitly manifested in the observable situation. (p. 36)

Cicourel further claimed that the researcher can "only objectify his observations by making explicit the properties of interpretative procedures and his reliance on them for carrying out his research activities" (p. 36).

Such interpretations, and the issues involved in making them, were the substance of this research. It was my task in presenting them to the reader to make their basis explicit. Cicourel's use of *objectify* was interesting to me because this seemed to mirror the sense in which I sought to avoid subjectivity. The word *objectivity* is redolent of positivist research, and in constructivist terms it is not definable because true objectivity in terms of knowledge external to an individual or social group can never be known (von Glasersfeld, 1987). The term *intersubjectiv*ity has been used by Ball (1982) and others to capture a sense of common knowledge arising from group negotiation in sharing and comparing interpretations. Shared meanings within a mathematics lesson might be regarded as *mathematical* intersubjectivity, central to an epistemology of the social construction of mathematical knowledge. In a research context, intersubjectivity involves the shared meanings that can be seen to develop through processes of interviewing, triangulation, and respondent validation. It derives from conversation and negotiation between participants in the research, which includes the researcher.

Such a reflexive accounting process in which intersubjectivity plays a part is the "rigor" that Ball (1990) speaks of when she talks of a research biography:

> The problems of conceptualizing qualitative research increase when data, and the analysis and interpretation of data, are separated from the social process which generated them. In one respect, the solution is a simple one. It is the requirement for methodological rigor that every ethnography be accompanied by a research biography, that is a reflexive account of the conduct of the research which, by drawing on fieldnotes and reflections, recounts the processes, problems, choices, and errors which describe the fieldwork upon which the substantive account is based. (p. 170)

So, in reporting my analysis of the episode of Mike, a research biography requires details of the incident itself, the classroom context in which it occurred, the environment in which this classroom was situated, the teacher's interpretation of the event, the teacher's comments on my analysis of the event, the reasons for this event's significance in terms of my theoretical base, and the relation of my analysis to my own experience as a practitioner and researcher.

I found this complexity of detail challenging and fascinating, but a major disadvantage was its lengthy nature both in the time required for analysis and in the space taken to present an account. This latter consequence meant that very few episodes could be reported in detail, and many that could have contributed valuably to conclusions were left out. For example, from two school terms of observation of lessons of a teacher and class, only three or four of those lessons were discussed in any detail in the report of the research. This made critical demands in ensuring that those episodes selected were sufficiently generic to represent the validity of the theory they supported.

Generalizibility and Theory Generation

In addition to fieldnotes, transcripts from audio- and videotapes, and one set of questionnaire data of student's views of mathematics lessons, I had as data my own reflective notes written throughout the study. These consisted of day-to-day jottings regarding incidents I had experienced and my own ideas and perceptions. Sometimes they were elaborations of anecdotes that had significance. Sometimes they involved incipient theorizing—expressing patterns I observed or attempting explanations. Eisenhart (1988) refers to this type of data collection as researcher introspection in which "the ethnographer tries to account for sources of emergent interpretations, insights, feeling, and the reactive effects that occur as the work proceeds" (p. 106).

The incipient theorizing attempted to express levels of generality within the research. A criticism of qualitative research methods is that it is very difficult to make and justify generalizations that apply to other settings. In-depth research necessarily results in small samples from which it can be hard to extrapolate. Delamont and Hamilton (1986) address this issue by recognizing the difficulty, yet claiming that some degree of generalization makes sense:

> Despite their diversity, individual classrooms share many characteristics. Through the detailed study of one particular context, it is still possible to clarify relationships, pinpoint critical processes, and identify common phenomena. Later abstracted summaries and general concepts can be formulated, which may, upon further investigation be found to be germane to a wider variety of settings. (p. 36)

In my own study, it was important to consider how far the classroom characteristics I found significant were indicative of investigative approaches more generally or were of relevance to other teachers wishing to interpret a constructivist philosophy in mathematics teaching. Furlong and Edwards (1986) make this comment:

> Although the ethnographer is committed to having as open a mind as possible during his period of observation, it is inevitable that he will begin his work with some preconceptions and some foreshadowed problems which will lead him to pay attention to certain incidents and ignore others. If he presents his observations as "objective description," he is probably naively unaware of his own selectivity. On the other hand, if he follows a theory too closely, he will be accused of selecting observations to support his own point of view. (p. 54)

There seems to be some skill required in weaving a path between the two polarizations expressed here, and I was very much aware of the implications of this for my own work. I recognized potential for what Glaser and Strauss (1967) refer to as "an opportunistic use of theory," which they call "exampling":

> A researcher can easily find examples for dreamed-up, speculative, or logically deduced theory after the idea has occurred. But since the idea has not been derived from the example, seldom can the example correct or even change it (even if the author is willing), since the example was selectively chosen for its confirming power. Therefore one receives the image of a proof where there is none, and the theory obtains a richness of detail that it did not earn. (p. 5)

For example, in the early stages of my research I was exhilarated by the way that radical constructivism (then, a theory that I had only just encountered) seemed to underpin my perceptions of an investigative approach to mathematics teaching. It was possible to look at examples of students' mathematical thinking as they arose in the lessons I observed and cast these in radical constructivist terms. However, it then became necessary to look critically at the relationships involved to see how a theory such as radical constructivism would fit the complexity of my research as a whole.

Consider again the episode of Mike's requiring his class to ask questions. This episode emerged, in my analysis, as significant from the lesson of which it was part; therefore, some selection had taken place from the data at this stage. I needed to account for this significance theoretically. The theoretical significance had two levels: (a) it fit with my own constructivist perspective of knowledge growth and hence learning, and (b) it contributed to emergent theory of the practical implications (for a mathematics teacher, for example) of a constructivist view of knowledge and learning.

I thus had to justify my analysis at these levels. This justification is summarized in the indented text that follows:

The process of asking their own questions encourages students to become immersed in the ideas that the teacher wants to be the focus of the lesson. From asking questions and the resulting investigation, students gain ownership of the mathematics they generate, which provides an experiential grounding for synthesis of particular mathematical ideas. The teacher's approach fosters questioning and investigating and, moreover, an independence of thinking and decision making that can lead to students taking more responsibility for their own learning.

This analysis rests on the constructivist view that (a) students' own constructions are central to their developing mathematical concepts and (b) the practical teaching acts (such as requiring students to ask questions) put emphasis on students' own constructions to make these more evident in students' knowledge growth.

Clearly, some statements here need further explanation and justification (e.g., the importance of experiential grounding and its practical manifestations). It was central to my research to provide this kind of critique, that is, the requisite explanations and justification. There were various levels of complexity. One of these involved the characterization of an investigative approach in terms of "asking questions," "ownership of ideas," and "taking responsibility for own learning." Were these constructs emergent from the data, or did they accord with the researcher's preconceptions? Was the researcher engaged in the production of grounded theory or in a process of exampling? Another level of complexity involved reconciling observations with theory such as radical constructivism—for example, in seeing the teacher's emphasis on students' asking their own questions and making their own decisions as contributing to students' construction of mathematical concepts.

Addressing these questions and issues required a very detailed study of the research data. A disadvantage of trying to provide a flavor of the research process through a particular episode is that, by its very nature, the episode cannot carry a sense of the interweaving of observations, perceived attributes, and analytical categories. It cannot show, for example, how "asking questions" related to "pattern spotting" and "making conjectures" in other lessons and other classrooms. It cannot show how this teacher's approach in this lesson compared or contrasted with approaches in his other lessons or in other teachers' lessons.

One episode cannot show that one teacher works according to an investigative approach, let alone have consequences for describing an investigative style of teaching more generally. The overall research synthesis demands a rational weaving of such research outcomes and a clarity of presentation that allows other researchers to judge its validity. Where an episode is concerned, I can say little beyond what this teacher aimed to achieve and what seemed to occur in his classroom. However, by taking many such episodes from different lessons of different teachers it is often possible to see a pattern of interactions in which students question and investigate mathematical situations and in which the groundwork for synthesis of mathematical concepts is prepared. Subsequently, it is possible to take these practical manifestations of aspects of theory and flesh out the theory. This is the symbiotic process that I described earlier.

In summary, initial theory gives starting points for observation and selection. Episodes selected are rich in details that the theory is too narrow to predict. From this richness, patterns emerge that not only substantiate the theory, but make clearer what such theory means for the practice of teaching and learning. This enhanced theory can then be reapplied to further practical situations for substantiation and enrichment.

THE THEORY-PRACTICE INTERFACE

In my research, an example of theory arising from data was a theoretical construct I called the *Teaching Triad* (Jaworski, 1992). This construct arose from a close scrutiny of all the data from one teacher, which involved categorizing attributes and classifying emerging patterns. It was possible to characterize her teaching under three headings: management of learning, sensitivity to students, and mathematical challenge. These categories had distinct as well as interrelated properties. This was theory generation. The teaching triad emerged directly from the data. I conjectured that this teacher's teaching could be characterized through the teaching triad. I tested the triad on further lessons that had not been part of the original analysis to see whether these also fit with the triad or whether the triad could offer a characterization. Considerable evidence supported the triad's potential to characterize this teaching. It was then important to test the triad against other teaching to see whether it had potential beyond one teacher. Again, evidence suggested it had. The next stage was to rationalize the teaching triad, an emergent construct, with the theoretical basis of the research, a constructivist view of knowledge and learning. Details of this rationalization can be found in Jaworski (1994).

Here, I am concerned with the methodological processes involved and shall explicate these further by showing how an analysis of a classroom episode (quoted from Jaworski, 1994) provided support for the teaching triad as a construct to characterize the teaching observed.

The Case of Packaging

The class was beginning a project on packaging. In the first lesson of the project, the teacher, Clare, and the students had brought into the classroom packages and bottles of various kinds from domestic products. Clare had organized a brainstorming session with the class, seeking questions that might be explored with regard to packaging of various kinds. A set of twenty questions had resulted, and Clare had photocopied a sheet of these for each member of the class. Students were encouraged to start by exploring a question of their own choice.

The videotaped episode consists of about 5 minutes of class time from the second lesson of the project. A number of girls sitting together at a table had chosen to work on the questions "Which shapes are scaled down versions of other shapes? How can you tell? How can you check?" They had identified three variables, volume, surface area, and shape, that they were trying to relate to one another. They had decided that they needed to fix one of these variables in order to explore the other two. The one they decided to fix was shape, and they decided to make it a cuboid. A transcription of the episode appears in Figure 8.1. An analysis of the episode follows.

It's a Cuboid

This involves a group of girls, including Rebecca and Diana, who were working on questions relating to volume and surface area using a large collection of packets from commercially produced products. The teacher, Clare, listened to their conversation for some moments, and then interjected:

(1) Cl   We're saying, volume, surface area and shape, three, sort of variables, variables. And *you're* saying, you've fixed the shape—it's a cuboid. And I'm going to say to you [pause] hm

[She pauses and looks around.]

      Cl   I'll be back in a minute

[but she continues talking.]

      Cl   *That* is a cuboid.

[She picks up a tea packet.]

      Cl   *That* is a cuboid.

[She picks up an electric light bulb packet.]

(5) Cl   and ...

[She goes away—then returns with a meter rule.]

(table continues)

Cl   *This* is a cuboid.

[She looks around at their faces. Some are grinning.]

Cl   And you're telling me that those are all the same shape? [Everyone grins.]

(8) Reb   Well, no-o. They've all got six separate sides though.

Cl   They've all got six sides. But I wouldn't say that that is the same shape as that.

(10) Reb   No-o

Cl   Why not?

Di   Yes you would …

[There is an inaudible exchange between the girls D and R.]

Cl   What's different?

[There are some very hard to hear responses here. They include the words *size* and *longer*.]

Cl   Different in *size*, yes.

[Clare reached out for yet another box, a large cereal packet, which she holds alongside the small cereal packet.]

(15) Cl   Would you say that those two are different shapes?

Reb   They're similar.

Cl   What does similar mean?

Reb   Same shape, different sizes. [They all laugh.]

[During the last four exchanges there was hesitancy, a lot of eye contact, giggles, each person looking at others in the group, the teacher seeming to monitor the energy in the group.]

Cl   Same shape but different sizes. That's going round in circles isn't it? [R nods exaggeratedly. Others laugh. Teacher laughs.] We still don't know what you mean by shape. What d'you mean by shape?

[She gathers three objects, the two cereal packets and the metre rule. She places the rule alongside the small cereal packet.]

(20) Cl   This and this are different shapes, but they're both cuboids.

[She now puts the cereal packets side-by-side.]

Cl   This and this are the same shape and different sizes. What makes them the same shape?

[One girl refers to a scaled-down version. Another to measuring the sides—to see if they're in the same ratio. Clare picks up their words and emphasises them.]

(22) Cl   Right. So it's about *ratio* and about *scale*.

Figure 8.1. Cuboid transcript (Jaworski, 1994).

The episode seems to split into three parts, which I characterize as follows: statements 1–7, the teachers' initial challenge; statements 8–14, students' engagement; and statements 15–22, further challenge. In terms of the teaching triad, parts 1 and 3 show strong elements of mathematical challenge, part 2 provides evidence of sensitivity to students, and the ethos within which the episode occurs is indicative of the teacher's management of the learning environment.

At the beginning of the episode, the teacher has listened to the students' discussion and made a decision to intervene. From her point of view, the problem seemed to be that a cuboid was not mathematically appropriate to their needs and she wanted somehow to draw their attention to this. She set up a dramatic little scene in which she asked them to compare three different cuboids. Her departure to get the meter rule added to the drama because there was a pause between her pointing to the two boxes and then returning with the rule. Her tone was provocative. The girls' attention was captured. There were half-smiles, almost as if they were asking, "What is she up to?" When she produced the rule they grinned. It seemed obvious that the rule was not the same shape as either of the boxes.

I saw this situation to be similar to Inhelder and Piaget's (1958) rods experiment, which was designed to get students to consider relationships between variables. In their experiment, researchers asked only neutral questions, not trying to teach but to elicit evidence of students' thinking and understanding. However, here there is a teaching act to be considered, and this might be seen rather in terms of Vygotsky's (1978) Zone of Proximal Development (ZPD)—judging students' potential for making progress and providing the necessary scaffolding. The teacher, it seemed, believed that students would not make the required progress without some intervention from her. Thus, she influenced their development, allowing them to progress in a way that might not otherwise have been possible. Of course we can never know what would have been possible without the intervention, which is one of the difficulties of using the ZPD construct in a practical arena.

One interpretation is that the teacher was aggressive. She was denying students the opportunity to formulate for themselves that this notion of "shape" is too imprecise a variable. She was forcing onto them her perspective, forcing the pace of their thinking, directing them mathematically. Asking more neutral questions, corresponding to the Piagetian position, would have left the girls to move forward only as their own thinking allowed.

An alternative interpretation is that the teacher saw the girls' thinking as fuzzy and not seeming to make much progress toward relating the variables. She could see an opportunity to focus their thinking in a way that would lead into some useful mathematics. She had to decide whether to push them in this direction. Having made the decision (for whatever reason), rather than offer an explanation of why cuboids would be too imprecise, she set up a provocative situation and challenged them with an apparent contradiction, capturing their interest and attention. This might be seen as promoting conflict discussion (Bell & Bassford, 1989), or, in radical constructivist terms, as creating constraints to challenge the viability of the girls' current knowledge (von Glasersfeld, 1987). In social constructivist terms, the situation could be seen as stimulating intersubjectivity through which meanings could develop; in Vygotskian terms, as providing scaffolding to enable progress (Bruner, 1985). There was a relaxed and friendly atmosphere, but at the same time, there was a build up of tension as the contradiction became apparent.

Clear evidence of a high degree of mathematical challenge can be seen in the first part of the episode. There was also considerable risk involved on the teacher's part. The girls might not take up the challenge. It might be inappropriate. They might not be able to cope with it. They might lose their own, perhaps precarious, thinking and possibly their confidence. The teacher, in having somehow to salvage the situation, might increase students' dependency on her. These were some of the dilemmas facing Clare as she chose her course of action with the students.

For Clare, mathematical challenge seemed always to be allied to sensitivity to students. She knew her students well, for which I had much evidence. The three girls had previously demonstrated their ability to think well mathematically. She believed that they had high mathematical potential. She also had a very good relationship with them. The risks she took were allied to this knowledge. These factors are all facets of the cultural ethos of the classroom and the teacher's role in encouraging students' mathematical constructions. Situations were created in which mathematics could be discussed—in this case, the packaging questions. Discussion and negotiation were actively encouraged, with the teacher providing stimulation or provocation where she believed it was needed. Such knowledge of students, creation of tasks, and acts of encouragement and stimulation were part of the teacher's management of the learning environment. The classroom ethos was a product of this management of learning.

The next part of the episode, in statements 8–14, shows a lessening of the tension as the girls began to think through what had been offered. It was almost as if they were thinking aloud, rather than participating in discussion. The shapes all have six sides. However, the meter rule and the bulb box are not the same shape. How are they different? Well, they are the same in some respects. In this section the teacher was less intrusive, perhaps providing space for students' constructive thinking to internalize the problem, but her remarks were still focusing. "What is different?"

Success in a situation like this depends very greatly on the teacher's sensitivity to students' perceptions, both mathematical and social. In analyzing why I believed that this episode was successful with regard to the teacher's objectives and the students' gain, I attributed it to the decision making by the teacher at various strategic points. Clearly the teacher had to make the initial decision to intervene and to do so as provocatively as she did. However, there was another crucial decision hovering in the middle stage of the episode. Were the students able to take up the challenge? Could they make progress? What else should she offer? It was in making an appropriate decision here that sensitivity to the students was most crucial. The success, or otherwise, of such episodes is very rarely due to just chance, but usually involves a high degree of vital decision making based on teaching knowledge and experience (Calderhead, 1987; Cooney, 1988).

Finally, in statements 15–22, the teacher seemed to decide that she should push further. She chose two cereal packets of different sizes but the same shape and asked if they were the same. She was rewarded instantly as one girl offered the crucial word, *similar*. So she pushed harder: "What does similar mean?" The reply was not helpful. They were going round in circles. She diffused the tension by acknowledging this and laughing, and they all laughed with her. However, she persevered, and in the interchange that followed, she was given further appropriate language by the students—*ratio* and *scale.*

She could, of course, have gone on to ask, "What does ratio mean?" However, she chose to leave it there. Her emphasis on ratio and scale, picking up the girls' own words, was probably sufficient to provide a new starting point for their thinking and progress. It seemed that the girls had entered into her thinking, as she had initially entered into theirs. She seemed to be convinced that the girls were involved sufficiently to be able to make progress.

There was evidence, subsequently, that the students' thinking became more focused as a result of the exchange with the teacher. They moved from vague articulations of shape to much more precise ones involving similarity, ratio, and scale. With a correspondingly more precise conceptual foundation, they could be more likely to make progress in relating their original variables. Ultimately some assessment could be made of the episode in terms of what the girls did next and where their thinking eventually led. However, judging only this episode, there seemed to be an effective balance between challenge and sensitivity. The teaching situation seemed to be effective in terms of what the girls gained from it and what the teacher might have hoped to achieve.

Decision making in the episode was well founded on knowledge and preparation by the teacher. She had created a situation in which students could engage in meaningful and potentially productive work. Students had a set of questions on which to start. They had been instrumental in devising these questions, so the questions were meaningful to them. They could choose whichever questions interested them most, which increased motivation. They were encouraged to work in groups—to articulate and share ideas, to develop intersubjectivity, and to challenge and support individual conceptions. Thus, what the students were engaged in here owed much to the teacher's overall management of the learning environment. I suggest that the three elements (management of learning, mathematical challenge, and sensitivity to students) can be seen in evident interaction in this episode, characterizing its nature in contributing to students' mathematical learning.

CONCLUSIONS

The preceding example illustrates my analysis of one episode from classroom practice against a theoretical construct that arose from earlier analysis. As a result, it is likely that the theoretical construct—the teaching triad—became clearer through its practical manifestations. It now becomes available to other researchers or practitioners to test against other theory or research. The detail of such manifestations and the bases of interpretations and judgments are crucial to this availability.

The relation between ethnography and theory raises thorny issues for ethnographic research. Hammersley (1990, p. 102) argues that too little theory results from such research, perhaps as "an over-reaction to positivism." He claims that ethnographic research in schools puts much emphasis on qualitative descriptions of behavior, supported by extracts from field notes or transcripts, but little on explanations for patterns discovered. He suggests that for the development and testing of theory to be pursued effectively, the research focus has to be narrower than is often the case in ethnographic research.

There is a serious tension here for the researcher. In my case I wished to study the nature of an investigative approach in mathematics teaching. It was necessary to be sufficiently aware of what this term meant in theory in order to select subjects for research. This was a narrowing; I did not go out to observe just *any* mathematics teaching. One possibility for following up my initial selection would have been to devise a coding schedule whereby I could identify, in classrooms, aspects of an investigative approach that my theory predicted. This would have been a further narrowing of focus and could have resulted in my finding little more to characterize an investigative approach in practice than was predicted by my theory. Thus, it seemed important to study the classrooms in as open a manner as possible, allowing for the diversity and richness, but also for the researcher being overwhelmed by too much complexity. It was the recognition of significance within this complexity that allowed further narrowing to occur and subsequently led to theory generation and enrichment.

Despite talk of narrowing, it is important to recognize, when talking of validity, that there is no way in which any of the interpretations or conclusions in this research could be regarded as right or true. Validity, here, does not have the objective meaning it takes from positivistic research. One might argue that such meaning often derives from unrealistic narrowing and definition. Research rigor in this study lay in embedding results in their fully situated nature and context, and in making the details of this embedding overt. The centrality of the researcher and the resulting implications must be judged through the validity of what is offered in this and other writings, since validity resides ultimately in the degree to which an informed reader is convinced by what is written.

Chapter 9

Using a Computer in Synthesis of Qualitative Data

Judith Mousley, Peter Sullivan, and Andrew Waywood

Forms of educational inquiry are shaped not only by the traditions of scientific and naturalistic research but also by researchers' epistemological assumptions—that is, by their beliefs about the nature and scope of knowledge itself. If it is believed that knowing is a matter of saying what is objectively real, then researchers will aim to describe and measure observable entities, to explain these, and then to suggest ways in which the resulting understandings might best be used. Such a belief about knowledge leads to the selection of relatively objective research methods and data, with researchers attempting to remove themselves from the subject matter of the study. However, if it is believed that knowing is a matter of having a stance within a world, then researchers will aim for new ways of participating in that world through the construction of tentative theories and through demonstrating an openness to changing understandings and alternative viewpoints. Such a belief about knowledge is likely to lead to research methods and data that are more varied and more qualitative in nature.

Contrasting beliefs about what it is to know are linked with different understandings of terms like *understanding*. Such serious words are difficult to define in that they come to have meaning only as they are situated (uttered) in particular discourses, such as in the alternative discourses currently vying for researchers' allegiances. What was initially a contrast of style between research in the physical sciences and that in the human sciences has become a methodological divide, and the notion of what it is *to understand* has become a measure of the very depth of this divide. In the physical sciences, the term clusters with words like *explain, cause, grasp,* and *discover.* However, in the human sciences, it clusters with *interpret, reason, express,* and *experience.* This contrast relates closely to discourses about knowledge in that the gaining of understandings in the physical sciences is about researchers grasping reality (e.g., by measuring or predicting an event), whereas in the human sciences it is about researchers being grasped by reality (e.g., by experiencing and interpreting an event). Although the former act necessitates a stance outside the event, the latter creates changes in the lifeworlds of researchers—altering lived experience in fundamental ways.

On the assumption of a dialectical relationship between understanding and interpretation, what it is *to interpret* is to be similarly defined within these contrasting discourses. Gadamer (1975) explains this relationship when he claims the following:

> Interpretation is not an occasional additional act subsequent to understanding, but rather understanding is always an interpretation, and hence interpretation is the explicit form of understanding. In accordance with this insight, interpretive language and concepts are also an inner structural element of understanding. (p. 274)

Gadamer's position moves the whole problem of language "from its peripheral and incidental position into the center of philosophy" (p. 274) and leads him further to question whether a researcher can escape the constraints of linguistic use. He questions whether language might perform thought and claims that this raises

> fundamental doubts about the possibility of our escaping from the sphere of influence of our education which is linguistic, of our civilization which is linguistic and of our thought which is transmitted through language, as well as the doubt about our capacity for openness to reality which does not correspond to our opinions, our fabrications, our previous expectations. (p. 491)

It might be assumed that using technology in qualitative data analysis in the human sciences would encourage movement of researchers away from the subjects of their studies as well as add an element of objectivity to processes of analysis and synthesis in that it would control the effects of human experience and operate outside human theoretical, methodological, and political frameworks. However, this can never be the case. The act of programming a computer, as well as such research processes as deciding on what will be considered useful data, resides within those frameworks. The beliefs that a program designer holds about *knowledge, understanding,* and *interpretation,* aside from those about effective research processes, shape the software produced and, consequently, shape the products (including data, interpretations, and explanations) of the projects for which it is employed.

Some developers of computer programs for data analysis recognize that value-laden and subjective choices are made at every instance of a research project and so have created environments that facilitate the recording of these choices as well as the keeping of notes as new understandings develop (or new theories are built). These records can make the role of the researcher more open to examination and, hence, render the role of human agency more recognizable. One such computer package, an application designed to be used as a tool in the analysis and examination of qualitative data, is NUD•IST. (Richards & Richards, 1990).

OUR USE OF NUD•IST

NUD•IST stands for Non-numerical Unstructured Data Index Searching and Theorizing. The version used was the most recent available at the time (version 2.3). Later versions have improved graphic displays, menu bars, and dialog boxes to make the whole process more user friendly.

This chapter focuses on how using NUD•IST made us more aware of the theories and expectations that we brought to the analysis task. Our working as a team to use this software for handling responses to a survey raised our consciousness of roles that researchers, and tools they employ, play in shaping the products of educational inquiry. In this chapter, our focus on a growth of understanding and on processes of interpretation signifies our attempt to stay close to the text of subjects, and to participate in its meaning, rather than to have our discourse produce an object that is distanced from ourselves. We recognize that the product of our research project is not one of the "things" of the physical sciences—it is an expression of a viewpoint and is open to critique as well as reworking by others as well as to further development by ourselves.

It is appropriate to describe briefly the processes in using this particular package. We stress that this description is not meant as an instruction guide and that we are not arguing that the program is better than other computer-based qualitative analysis tools.

Basically, NUD•IST is software that allows the management and organization of data through indexing. It can handle any digitized text—from one word-processed sentence to a whole book scanned into the computer's memory. Although off-line data (e.g., videotaped or audiotaped data) cannot be handled, they can be linked (using other software) to digitized data and thus be manipulated by text.

The first key decision is about the way the data are categorized. Ultimately the data will be entered into a treelike hierarchy, with the data points called nodes and subnodes. The nodes at the top of the tree may be determined by the research design or can be derived from the data themselves. In both cases, the subnodes will usually be determined by inspecting the data. One node, and its subnodes, can be reserved for factual information, such as gender, data source, and so forth, so that cross-categorization can draw on this at a later date. Note that all of this can be changed as the analysis unfolds, so researchers are not bound by initial categorizations.

The data are typed into text files in a particular style. One key decision is whether data are to be managed in words, phrases, lines, or paragraphs. The text units are separated by a <return>. The files are then imported into the program. It can be useful to get a printout at this stage, since the text units have associated line numbers.

The categorization structure is then applied to the data. Each text unit is assigned to one or more of the subnodes through a system of numerical codes. This can be done by researchers, or NUD•IST has the capability to conduct searches for key words or phrases and responds to Boolean commands. This facilitates the examination of current or potential subcategories.

NUD•IST offers options to support analyses from this stage onward. These include recoding and recategorizing entries and subnodes, adding and deleting subnodes, analyzing data by background categories, adding new material into the project, and recording notes at each stage of the analysis process.

The next section of this chapter elaborates our use of NUD•IST. It uses one application of the tool in a study by the first two authors. It outlines the stages of the research and the steps in the use of NUD•IST. Concurrently, some issues arising from the use of such tools are discussed as are some of the additional options available in the program.

THE EVOLUTION OF THE PROJECT

In the example of the application of NUD•IST reported in this chapter, we describe the evolution of the project, the instrument used, and the development of a conceptual framework. We attempt to develop a useful framework from the raw data and acknowledge the difficulty of accomplishing this goal.

In 1990, Clements and Mousley reported the results of their research into student teachers' perceptions of the teaching observed during practicum sessions (Mousley & Clements, 1990). Student teachers had reported, on questionnaires, that much of what they were observing in classrooms was the antithesis of both current theory and the behaviors espoused in their preservice teacher-education course. It seemed that despite its considerable cost to universities as well as the considerable energy expended by teachers and trainee teachers, the work experience was not enabling student teachers to observe the regular use of calculators and other technology, cooperative group work, mathematical discussions among students, problem-based teaching of mathematics, the asking of open-ended questions, and other nontraditional techniques. Further research by Sullivan involving teacher-education students from other institutions produced similar results (Mousley, Sullivan, & Clements, 1991).

It seemed likely either that (a) desirable practices were not being implemented in schools, and thus the observations made by the teacher-education students were an accurate portrayal of current teaching, or that (b) these teacher-education students may have witnessed some high-quality teaching but may not have identified the features of such teaching because of the subtle, sophisticated, and complex nature of classroom interaction. Probably, both hypotheses were correct, with the weighting of factors varying among different teachers, student teachers, and individual schools.

This raised the question of how teacher educators could prepare student teachers better for close observation of exemplary practices. The key seemed to be better preparation for school-experience rounds with the honing of observation skills by using a resource base that included examples of exemplary teaching.

This decision, in turn, led to discussion of *which* features experienced teachers and mathematics educators believe are desirable components of quality practice. It was realized that there would not be complete agreement about one set of features of quality teaching. The effectiveness of pedagogical decisions and actions depends on factors like their appropriateness for the subject matter at hand, the current incident, and the particular pupils' needs at any given moment. However, it was thought that it would be useful to gather data on some generally agreed-on features of high-quality teaching as identified by experienced teachers and mathematics educators and then to use these in creating a resource base that included videotaped lessons.

The "Quality Teaching" Questionnaire

The first step in this process was the development of a survey of mathematics educators to seek consensus on some characteristics of quality teaching of mathematics. Such a questionnaire was prepared and administered. Our research drew on both "quantitative" and "qualitative" paradigms to allow different but complementary sets of survey items to provide broader data with epistemological touchstones. The diverse methods of data collection were intended to make provision for later assimilation of evidence and for close examination of patterns and interesting inconsistencies.

The first section of the survey consisted of one open-response item:

> We want you to imagine a mathematics lesson, at any year level, where the students are learning, for example, to estimate the mass of various objects, or to add fractions, or to record given information as a graph.... Please write down the most important characteristics which a *quality* mathematics lesson on any of these concepts/skills would usually have.

Participants were asked to complete this item first, before they read any categories presented in the latter part of the questionnaire, in order to capture respondents' own initial reactions to the request.

The second, more structured, part of the instrument used fixed format items. Seventy-eight pairs of descriptors were compiled from research summaries (e.g., Bell, Costello, & Kuchemann, 1983), from teaching frameworks (e.g., Good, Grouws, & Ebmeier, 1983), from recent recommendations (e.g., Australian Education Council, 1990), and from the earlier questionnaire used with the student teachers (Mousley & Clements, 1990). The descriptors were clustered under the headings teaching environment, lesson aims, lesson content, presentation, class activities, questions, aids, assessment, and closure. Descriptors were presented as bipolars. For instance, one set of descriptors listed in the lesson aims cluster read as follows:

there was no clear purpose	⟷	there was a clear purpose
pupils were aware of the aims	⟷	pupils were not aware of the aims
the goals were not achieved	⟷	the goals were achieved
the aims were negotiated	⟷	the aims were imposed

Respondents were asked to (a) write in any important characteristics they thought were missing, (b) delete any pairs that seemed not necessary for quality mathematics lessons, then (c) mark on the continua whether quality teaching would be closer to one of the pair of features or the other, and (d) rank the features in order of importance. The analysis of the second structured component of the survey is not discussed here other than to note that the data can be linked to responses to the open-response items by using NUD•IST.

The survey was first piloted with twelve teachers and teacher educators. To test the layout, length, and complexity of the form; to determine participants' thinking during the completion process; and to discuss with them possible solutions for any difficulties experienced in completing the form, these respondents were observed and interviewed as they completed the questionnaire.

After revision in accordance with the feedback gained from the pilot study, the questionnaire was mailed to three groups of people involved in mathematics education. These were mainly colleagues and fellow members of two professional associations. Forty survey responses came from experienced teachers who were graduate students in mathematics education (100% return), 56 from Victorian teacher educators (80% return), and 29 from American teacher educators (40% return). These groups were selected because they represented an informed view of current issues in teaching and learning yet would present opportunities for comparisons to be made between sets of data from different groups of respondents.

DATA ANALYSIS

All 125 responses to the open-response item were word processed. The NUD•IST program produced a printout that identified the respondent's occupation, country, and so forth, and the raw data (a list of descriptors, a sentence, or a paragraph). For example, the printout reproduced as Figure 9.1 was the response from Number 70, a mathematics education colleague from Victoria, Australia.

```
*2
70    MESH                                                          2
* QUESTION 1                                                        3
- well-prepared, i.e., lesson structured appropriately             4
- if relevant, a related concrete/investigative project/activity  5
- guided interactive discussion leading to conceptual underpinnings 6
- should be related, where possible, to previous learning and related to  7
  children's conceptual experiences                               8
```

Figure 9.1. The format of the text.

The first step in the analysis process was to separate the phrases into units that seemed to convey a particular thought. The phrases were categorized by hand with a numerical classification system involving a taxonomy of classroom practices—a taxonomy not developed in advance of the categorization process, but resulting from discussions as each phrase was examined.

Initially, some key ideas were identified by inspection of the data. These formed the top-level nodes. One node was used for background data, such as the country of the respondent, years of experience, and so forth. Other top-level nodes included pupil activity and communication. Ideas that emerged within communication, such as clear explanation, became subnodes.

At times, further levels of division were created. New categories also needed to be formed for text that did not fit into existing categories. Similarly, if we found that data we had been splitting between two categories were so similar that the divide was somewhat artificial and arbitrary, the overlapping subcategories were merged. This process of placing data according to emerging ideas and categories continued until each phrase in the responses had been coded.

Key words and common phrases were useful in deciding on how to classify phrases. For instance, the phrases "sharing ideas," "time for sharing perceptions," "sharing alternative solutions," and "listening to alternative solution strategies" seemed to be linked by common words as well as conceptually, so all were classified as "sharing strategies."

Figure 9.2 shows a schematic representative of one section of the framework tree during one stage in this process. Pupil's activity represents a top-level node. There are subnodes of this node, which in this case are content and activities and interaction, and these in turn have their own subnodes.

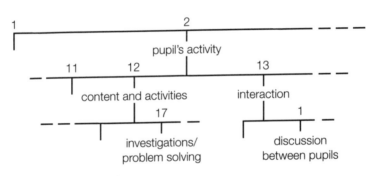

Figure 9.2. Schematic representation of one section of the framework tree.

Although we sketched out such possible ways of organizing the data on butcher paper, NUD•IST allows users to merge, cut and paste, compare, reorganize, and rename sets of data onscreen—with a log of such theory-building strategies being maintained by the program.

Our aim was to create a structure that could allow categorization and organization of the data rather than to devise a picture of some ultimate reality. Successful development of the taxonomy at this stage depended not on its correct interpretation (for many equally viable presentations could have resulted from the original data) but on its usefulness in building plausible understandings and richer insights about elements of quality teaching. The taxonomy could then be put to the mathematics education community for discussion and development of increased understanding in this area.

Putting the data into categories and subcategories was time-consuming but enlightening. The responses, and the need to decide where they fit, stimulated probing discussions about teaching and learning. There were some lively debates about possible interpretations of responses and the meanings of jargon, such as *nonthreatening*. Many problematic aspects of interpretation arose. Are there essential differences in what respondents call *problem solving* and *problem posing*, and if so, what might they be? Is the word *curriculum* being used to describe what is intended to be learned, what is learned, or the learning process? If *pedagogy* expresses a dialectical relationship, does it belong more with the *teacher's realm* or *student's actions*? Many such points raised our awareness of the difficulties that researchers face when dealing with the lack of specificity both of our professional language and of emerging categories.

We also discussed whether the structure arising from the data-reduction process was largely predetermined—either by our own pedagogical notions or by the wording of the original question. Although we never suffered from the delusion that categories for analysis emerge from data untouched by human hand (Glaser & Strauss, 1967), we became more and more aware of the impact that our experiences as teachers (including our teacher training), as teacher educators, and as readers of current mathematics education literature were having on the shaping of these categories. Our discussions led to a growing awareness that our theorizing shaped reality, rather than vice versa, and that our varied (but similar) prior experiences and preunderstandings limited possible subjective and intersubjective meaning as well as the ways in which we communicated about the data.

We were aware that as soon as researchers read or hear subjects' interpretation of particular phenomena, credence is given to those data. The new knowledge then influences the ways in which further data are interpreted. Thus developing understandings change researchers' stances (perhaps only by reaffirmation) so that they can never see raw data relating to the same phenomena in the same way. Thus data change researchers—they change the way they see as well as what can be seen. But, as Ödman (1988) points out, the synthesizing of qualitative data is not merely a process of attempting to mirror other people's understandings; interpretation and understanding interact closely, since making something explicit is likely to imply a change in the understanding of it:

> Interpretation, understanding, and pre-understanding are dialectically coupled with our existence as human beings. People's self-definitions and definitions of life are a result of their understanding, and their understanding develops through their experiences. The understanding of their lives is the ultimate hermeneutical circle. (p. 64)

As the data analysis progressed, there was also concern about practical issues, such as the effect of including a phrase in two different classifications or whether a particular term and an example of what was meant should be included as one or two entries. We decided that some of the responses fit neatly into two categories, and because we were less interested in the number of phrases in each category than in what was actually said (and what we could use in planning exemplary lessons), we allowed the methodology to respond to our needs as researchers rather than to be constrained by traditions of any research approaches.

It was to our benefit that we were working as a team at this stage; otherwise, individual understandings would not have been challenged so frequently. We found that the NUD•IST program is, as its manual claims (Richards & Richards, 1990), more than a "code-and-retrieve" system:

> The indexing data base can be of any level of complexity—from the flat lists of codes necessary for most code-and-retrieve programs to highly organized and complex tree-structured indexes of categories and sub-categories. This structuring allows indexing concepts to be organized and managed as theoretical systems, not just as labels. (p. 7)

Being forced to consider alternative interpretations, structures, and ways of working was an educative process in itself. We started to discuss the notion that the act of classification promotes theory building, and being able to use NUD•IST quickly and efficiently (to call up sets of phrases for comparison, combination, and redistribution) assisted this process. It is important to note that theory was developing as shared understandings within the group—not by the computer. As Richards and Richards (1990) note,

> what the user does with the retrievals, using such software, is essentially offline: all the theory-building, the shaping of understanding and the reshaping of the data in accordance with the changing understanding, is done outside the computer. (p. 6)

Emerging Categories

At this stage, number codes were assigned to each of the text units and entered into the computer. For the background data—for example, country of origin—the whole of the survey was coded at the particular subnode. This was done because NUD•IST checks aspects of one category against those of another rather than match information within any node. For example, a researcher may later wish to ask such questions as, "What did males say about problem solving and how does this compare with what females said?" or "How did comments about use of manipulatives vary between Australian and USA teachers?" Searches of this nature require the personal information to be stored in one node and the specific topics, such as "problem solving" or "manipulatives," to be in different nodes (or subnodes) so that sorting and matching processes can take place.

Initially, the major categories into which all data were placed were teacher action (1) and pupil action (2). Figure 9.3 shows a set of example phrases used by a respondent. The first number 2 given in the triple to the right of each phrase relates to the classification pupil action. The middle numbers indicate minor categories from the next level of the classification tree: content and activities (12) and interaction (13). The right-hand number in the triple designates a further subclassification—discussion between pupils (1) and investigations/problem-solving (17). It would have been possible to create many levels of classification, but we stopped at the point at which phrases about classroom action were grouped in relation to commonly used terms about teaching and learning strategies.

Physical involvement	(2	12	3)	4
Cooperative learning	(2	12	3)	5
Discussion	(2	13	1)	6
Problem solving	(2	12	17)	7
Risk taking	(2	12	8)	8

Figure 9.3. Examples of coding a response.

The numbers in the right-hand column of Figure 9.3 are not classifications—they are "addresses" for the original data. This program feature is important because it enables the machine, on request, to undertake searches for particular strings (words, phrases, and so forth) or to reorganize data while retaining links with particular respondents or identified groups of respondents. More important, it enables researchers to skip quickly to the original paragraphs—the context of the subject and his or her utterances—to check, for instance, that a phrase has been categorized with consistency of meaning despite shuffling of the data during the process of building and rebuilding categories. If we aim to stay close to the text of subjects and to participate in its meaning, such facilities for recall and review are vital.

In the process of refining categories, the collections placed into particular nodes and subnodes were printed and examined to determine whether they formed a coherent set. Any phrases not congruent with the others in the set were moved. To determine names for the categories that had been created, groups of descriptors were printed and academics were asked to suggest appropriate nomenclature. We found that most of the suggestions matched the names we had already been using in discussing the nodes.

It was realized afterward that it would have been useful to use a coding process to enable later ready identification of phrases that raised interesting points for further discussion—such as two obviously conflicting beliefs or a particularly thought-provoking comment. However, such data were not lost, for one of the benefits of using a computer for qualitative data analysis is that original words, phrases, sentences, or whole paragraphs (and indeed whole chapters, papers, or journals in other studies) can be called up later for further review. Data remain, relational and interactive, and can be traced back to their origins if necessary. The retention of original data also means that analyses can be replicated, for purposes of adding robustness, for checking the logic of the current categories, for testing the consistency and coherence of the conclusions, or for examining the impact of a different team of researchers.

Three facilities of the program enabled the keeping of an "audit trail" (Lincoln & Guba, 1985, p. 319) throughout the analysis stage. The first is the ability to save (as documents) and recall data from any stage of the analysis process. The second is that NUD•IST keeps a log of changes automatically. A history of what was done therefore forms the basis for keeping a record of, and retracing if desired, the research process. The third useful facility is the capacity for the researcher to notate any entry from within the program. These facilities allow researchers to enter questions arising, points of interest, links to published theory (including appropriate quotations), comments about the research process, and other notes. They therefore facilitate (a) the process of developing understandings, (b) the recording of conceptual developments that have taken place, and (c) the writing up at a later stage. They also open up the research process to examination by others.

The Categories Arising

The printout of respondent phrases categorized into two different subnodes is shown in Figure 9.4.

THINKING (2 12 18)

Aims to develop understanding opportunity for student thinking
Lesson requires thinking rather than repetition and mimicking
Promotes thinking
Lots of thinking by students about task
Speculating on how best to solve them and solving
Thought about the problem

CHALLENGING (2 12 9)

Challenging
Challenging task within reach
Challenging activities
Challenge
Should have ability for extension
Challenging but caters for individual differences

Figure 9.4. Responses categorized within two particular subnodes.

These groups of phrases are ready to be inspected for coherence, sense, and relevance. Phrases that do not fit can be easily moved elsewhere. From such data, we can infer that some teacher educators see student thinking and provoking challenge as characteristics of quality teaching, and so these constructs formed part of the model that we developed.

Data gathered under the headings used in the survey (teacher actions, content, activities, and so forth) had now been organized, through the process of allocation to emerging categories as described above, into six quite-new categories: building understanding, communication, engagement, problem solving, task orientation, and teacher concern.

Efforts to place particular phrases and the examination of the content of each node led to the realization that building understanding relied largely on factors and activities listed in other nodes, and it seemed that each of the other nodes could be considered a vehicle for building mathematical understanding. For instance, the phrases listed in such nodes as task orientation and communication, and in such subnodes as use of materials, although significant in themselves, seemed directed at teacher and student actions that in turn would lead to building understanding. In other words, the main categories and the subcategories arose from the process of grouping like comments together and establishing coherence and sense from the groups. The placement of the building understanding node at a higher level that the others was a decision of the researchers.

Figure 9.5 shows both the nodes and subnodes that illustrate the components of quality teaching that emerged from the analysis and also a taxonomy or hierarchy that we imposed on that data.

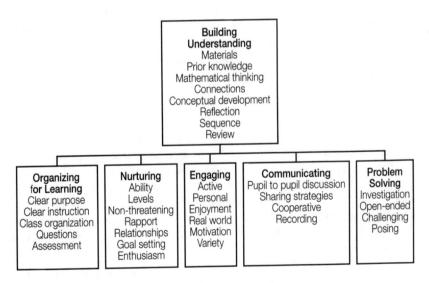

Figure 9.5. Hierarchy of categories of quality mathematics teaching arising from the data.

Other Possibilities for Analysis

Having the data formatted appropriately in the NUD•IST program would enable the comparison of comments by experienced teachers (e.g., 5+ years) with those of less-experienced teachers or with teacher educators. Similarly, words and phrases used by teacher educators from different countries, or of different gender or from different age groups, could be compared. Although such lists were not called up, it would only be a matter of a minute's work to request and print any lists of interest.

Further cross-referencing, cross-indexing, and reindexing became possible as the data were refined, and the potential for using NUD•IST for manipulating data to answer new research questions became clearer. For instance, the results from other sections of the questionnaire could be fitted with the new categories and the reasons for inconsistencies explored with the synthesis of disparate information serving as clues for more complex and richer readings. Similarly, the addition of new data—perhaps from repeating the study with other samples from the mathematics-education community—would allow interfaces and contrasts between different sets of data to be examined. To carry out such comparisons by hand, and at several levels of the inquiry tree, would be a huge and daunting task. It is at this stage that NUD•IST makes such analyses practicable.

Although we were not interested in using the qualitative data for statistical analysis at this stage, it is now in a form where this would not be difficult. For instance, it is easy to examine the data to find out that the node building understanding was outstanding in terms of the number of times respondents referred to its features (112 times out of the 125 responses), so this proportion could be compared with responses to such features in the structured section of the survey. An analysis such as this would have the potential to be informative but would be in danger of removing from the reporting process much of what is useful for our specific purposes.

COMPUTER ANALYSIS AND QUALITATIVE DATA

It is important to note that although reduction to general categories has involved some loss of depth of meaning as well as a coalescence of discrete ideas, the conclusions remain open to verification. All the richness of the original data is retained and can be recalled at any stage of the project—or even in further processes of inquiry. The original and sorted data can all be used and reported meaningfully. Handling data in this way is one solution to the common qualitative data-analysis problem that Sowden and Keeves (1988) identified when they claimed that

> while an increasing amount of empirical research using qualitative data is being carried out, … it is being reported in such a way that the conclusions cannot be verified …. This gives rise to the anomalous situation that while in research the evidence is rich and detailed, the very richness and detail of the data collected prevent presentation in a coherent form that would lead to acceptance of the findings as a contribution to scholarly inquiry. (p. 525)

In comparison with manual indexing and matrixing systems, it is clear that using a program like NUD•IST enables the efficient handling of large quantities of textual materials and offers several advantages for educational inquiry. Readers of research reports generally rely on accurate classification of raw data by authors and usually have no way of checking the interpretations made or the appropriateness of orienting constructs. However, when data are stored as electronic documents and readily accessible, looking anew at material gathered or the replication of the analysis processes by other researchers does not require the repetition of a lengthy processes. Whereas the reduction of data to generalities frequently closes off options for cross-indexing and reindexing, or at least requires the use of a tedious index-card system, NUD•IST enables—and in fact encourages—such processes. Similarly, numerical data (such as frequencies for sets and subsets of data) can easily be reworked in the light of new research questions or developing understandings. In addition to their use for indexing, programs such as NUD•IST become tools for the building of theory by emphasizing the emerging nature of understandings while maintaining links between original utterances and their discursive contexts.

Notwithstanding the contribution that computer-based tools can make to qualitative analyses, there are limitations. Using a computer for categorizing qualitative data does not overcome some of the problems inherent in the research design. It does assist with the focusing of data, enabling it to be reduced to a state where it can be analyzed in terms of quantity, discussed under broad headings, or compared with other data. Data can then be displayed in a compressed, organized form that is accessible to teachers, teacher educators, and other researchers. Conclusions can be drawn. As theory about mathematics pedagogy is developed further, irregularities, patterns, and plausible explanations together with the notions of robustness, sturdiness, and validity can be explored (Miles and Huberman, 1990, p. 349).

Although the original data are still accessible, the act of classification involves a reorientation, rebuilding, and modification of the original data as well as removal of individual words and phrases both from their original contextual paragraphs and from their speakers. Whereas the aim of the researcher might be to keep as close as possible to the intention of the contributor of a given phrase, two factors impinge on this process. First, the act of categorization is by its very nature subjective. Selection of orienting categories depends on researchers' personal constructs of the task at hand. These, in turn, are shaped by perceived possibilities within the fields of research and educational theory and then by developing notions of the overall "findings." Second, phrases and terms used to describe the teaching and learning of mathematics are themselves attempts to capture nebulous qualities and diverse ways of behaving. These are used in various ways according to participants' prior experiences and understandings as well as their perceptions of audience. To place phrases within categories is to assume a meaning and a set of associative properties and perhaps to "bend" the data to fit with an emerging structure. As with most analysis of most qualitative data, factors (such as inflection and body language) that would have assisted the accuracy of placement or summation are lost in the transcription process.

It can be noted that these problems are related to the subjective nature of decision making and the interpretation of human beliefs and actions and are not in any way specific to the use of NUD•IST. As Giddens (1984) notes, knowledge is framed as individuals view the real world in terms of their personal understandings, and these interpretations can be made only in the light of their current understandings of the theories, ideas, and concepts. Further interpretation takes place as the ideas are published and take new form in the praxis of everyday social use. Although "moments" of decision making are not so apparent in empirical research, they are still present, and attempts to control such factors bring their own set of limitations to research projects.

It must be recognized that using a computer does not change the fact that interpretive research is based on the gathering of qualitative data and that such research aims to understand rather than to explain. The intention is to capture and interpret rather than to generalize or predict. The complexities and uniqueness of an event (such as the beliefs of professionals at a particular time) are recognized as objects worth studying and using. These objects can bring about change in the stance of individual researchers but should not be considered the replicable phenomena of empirical research.

ISSUES FOR CONSIDERATION

Using a computer for handling qualitative data has certainly facilitated our exploration of social actions and understandings and assisted in the construction of tentative understandings about these. One group of questions raised in our discussions about the use of tools such as NUD•IST related to how we, as educational researchers, make judgments regarding what information to seek, how to seek it, how to analyze it, and how to use it. We discussed how the resolution of these questions is influenced by, and also limited by, our own sociocultural history as well as by our individual professional histories, personal understandings, and current needs.

Another group of issues raised in our discussions was about the sharing of findings and what is considered by a researcher to be worth sharing. What is withheld from the reader? How do we share our findings with particular audiences, and is this done selectively? How accessible are the ideas presented to the consumers and producers of educational theory in use, that is, teachers in classrooms?

There was also discussion about how we raise the issues of the problematic nature of judgements that have been made during the research process. At each stage of the process, decisions were being made about how to handle the data in its current form, but in most research reports, the nature of this decision making is not presented as problematic. The collaborative nature of the coding, and the verification process using other researchers, provided checks and balances and was an integral part of the research method. We also sought to address such issues explicitly in reports.

The experience of thinking about the research processes undertaken has sensitized us to the workings of interpretation within educational research. Starting points and further developments, analyses and theory, conceiving and reconceiving, part and whole, what-is-seen and what-is-to-be-seen—the interplays among these are ongoing throughout the research. All reflect a process of gaining understanding. The researcher is involved not only in processes of representation and the creation of boundaries but also in processes of expanding horizons of understanding. However, readers of published articles rarely see them as artistic creations—pictures of the educational researchers' experiences, intentions, and growing conceptions. And the act of reading a research report in many ways parallels the creative acts of the researchers themselves in that the theoretical stances of the readers inform their interpretations of, as well as their abilities to use, the work at hand.

The data-analysis process using NUD•IST taught us as much about our own (as well as each others') concepts of quality lessons and the act of writing a questionnaire item as it did about the beliefs our colleagues hold about quality mathematics teaching. We also learned a lot about the way different phrases are used in describing teaching and were reminded continually of the vagueness of most of the terms used. It is now hoped that we can use our collected data to engage people in further discussion about the appropriateness of the categories formed and about the possibilities of developing a more common language for describing teaching. It might be noted that the development of a common language is one of the characteristics of a discipline of study, and one that educational research generally could well pursue more actively.

Chapter 10

Using Research as a Stimulus for Learning

Beatriz S. D'Ambrosio

Teacher research provides a tool for developing, encouraging, and sustaining teachers' reflective practice. The process of carrying out such research leads teachers to analyze their classrooms, their practice, and their students' learning to depths that are difficult to reach with other types of professional activities. Furthermore, the results of such research provide the larger mathematics-education community with greater insight into aspects of successful teaching. Qualitative methods furnish essential tools for teachers to use in this endeavor, as they study the reality of their classrooms and their students' learning.

In this chapter, I describe a preservice and an in-service experience in which teacher research was used to engage teachers in exploring how students learn mathematics. First, I discuss the importance of teacher research in bridging the gap between research and practice. Then I examine the parallels between the act of learning and the act of researching and the use of practitioner research in developing K–12 mathematics instruction that is more constructivist in nature. The chapter focus on qualitative research methods is then presented through an example of a teacher-research experience developed for, and implemented with, preservice secondary mathematics teachers, followed by the description of an in-service experience centered on the use of teacher research as the primary teaching methodology.

ISSUES IN TEACHER RESEARCH

The question of how to bridge the gap between research and practice is a concern of the international academic research community in mathematics education. Several participants at the Eighth International Congress on Mathematics Education, held in Seville, Spain, in July 1996 addressed this issue in a working group that explored the theme "connections between research and practice in mathematics education." Among the many dimensions that exacerbate the gap are the lack of communication between academic researchers and practitioners, the silenced voices of practitioners in much academic research, the demeaning approach to practitioner knowledge in much academic literature, and the view of practitioners as users of knowledge about teaching and learning rather than as active participants in the generation of that knowledge.

It has been useful to me to invite teachers to engage in research activity and to learn from this experience what constitutes some of the issues that result in the lack of communication between researchers and practitioners. Two issues, in my mind, need resolution if we hope to involve teachers in the dialogue about teaching and learning: the acceptance of teacher research as scholarship and the acceptance of teacher research as part of the process of generating the knowledge base about teaching and learning.

In recent encounters with colleagues, I have been asked why I insist on using the phrase *teacher research* in my work with teachers. My colleagues have suggested that I instead use the phrase *practical wisdom* to describe what we might learn from teachers' research activity. I am very concerned that using the phrase *practical wisdom* instead of the word *research* undermines the legitimacy and authority of the knowledge base of teachers—a knowledge base that is grounded in the articulation of theoretical frameworks, personal histories, and practice. Teachers' research on teaching and learning provides an insider's perspective on the complexities of the lives of teachers and students as they interact to construct understanding and meaning about the world around them.

The acceptance of teacher research as scholarship requires that the academic community look to that body of work as a new genre of research with its own criteria of rigor, unique methodology, form, and style. It also requires a reconsideration of the purposes of research. Teacher researchers do not look to academic research for the accumulated "knowledge base" about teaching and learning. Instead, academic research serves as a source for them of intriguing interpretations, conflicting information, multiple conceptual frameworks, confirming or discrepant evidence from other settings, and new questions and problems. As teachers problematize their teaching and seek to understand their classrooms, their students, and their practices, they build theoretical frameworks, raise new questions, and contribute to the knowledge base on teaching, learning, and research. As a community, we face the challenge of including teachers' ways of knowing and understanding in our dialogue about teaching, learning, and research.

Also, to more fully embrace the research of practitioners, our traditional views of theory must be redefined. This new genre of research, still in its early stages of development, requires an understanding of theory as a combination of perspectives, that is, as a set of interrelated conceptual frameworks grounded in practice (Cochran-Smith & Lytle, 1993).

LEARNING THROUGH TEACHER RESEARCH

Current reform initiatives in the teaching of mathematics have placed new demands on teachers. In particular, the curricular perspectives adopted by the National Council of Teachers of Mathematics require teachers to take on roles in the classroom that differ from those that have typically engaged teachers. These new roles include guiding and encouraging children's investigations of mathematics, basing instruction on children's prior knowledge, tying mathematics to the world of applications, and being a learner and researcher themselves. For preservice teachers and practicing teachers, these new expectations often differ greatly from their beliefs about the activities of a teacher.

An effective source of change of teachers' conceptions of teaching and learning is that of the teacher as researcher (e.g., Darling-Hammond, 1996; Hubbard & Power, 1994; Meyer, 1995; Nias & Groundwater-Smith, 1988; Short & Burke, 1996; Wells, 1994). This approach is believed to develop an investigative disposition in teachers, helping them to become reflective, questioning, and flexible.

The area of language arts has the longest history of teacher as researcher (Goswami & Stillman, 1987; Phinney & Ketterling, 1997; Sega, 1997; Short, Harste, & Burke, 1996). The work done by teachers in this field, as they study their students' learning of reading and writing, reveals how practitioner research can serve as an agent of change. The impact on teachers of conducting classroom-based research includes the following: (a) teachers come to better understand their classrooms, (b) they are in a better position to make decisions about their classroom practice and the classroom environment, (c) they take ownership of change initiatives, (d) they come to better understand their students by listening to them in ways they have never listened before, (e) they model and foster an inquisitive disposition in their classrooms by redefining learning as research, and (f) they engage in classroom-based research that renews their enthusiasm for learning. Finally, classroom-based research will bring the voice of the teacher to the research community and the voice of the researcher to the classroom, thus bridging the everlasting gap between research and practice (Altrichter, Posch, & Somekh, 1993; Boero, Dapueto, & Parenti, 1996; Bullock, 1987; Cochran-Smith & Lytle, 1993; Crawford & Adler, 1996; Goswami & Stillman, 1987).

The parallels between the act of learning and the act of researching are remarkable when learning is understood as a constructive process as is advocated in many current reform initiatives. In fact, one might venture to claim that learning is a research process. Teachers' pursuit of research studies in their classrooms provides opportunities for teachers to learn more about student understanding of mathematics, mathematics itself, and themselves as teachers. These insights enable teachers to tackle the new roles envisioned by reform initiatives.

Creating an environment that encourages students to construct mathematical ideas requires teachers to understand what students bring to the learning experience. Effective classroom activities capitalize on students' prior understandings of mathematics, which allows students to construct new meanings to solve problems. Teachers not only must assess student understanding of mathematical ideas prior to planning experiences, but they must also devise means of assessing student growth in knowledge during the activities.

Teachers are encouraged to assess much more than students' knowledge of mathematics. The *Curriculum and Evaluation Standards for School Mathematics* (National Council of Teachers of Mathematics, 1989) recommends that teachers assess students' willingness to pursue an investigation, perseverance, flexibility of use of heuristics, decision-making processes, and other process skills that enhance their participation in the community of learners of mathematics—in this case, the mathematics classroom. Creating a research disposition in teachers is essential if they are to successfully assess the many dimensions of student thinking.

To successfully plan investigative activities for students, teachers must understand mathematics as an inquiry-based discipline (Borasi, 1992; Siegel & Borasi, 1994). This requires teachers to actively investigate mathematics themselves. For many teachers, this is a totally new perception of the nature of mathematics that requires them to reconstruct their understanding of the act of learning mathematics. Many teachers perceive mathematical research as an activity restricted to research mathematicians. It is crucial, if changes in the nature of classroom activities are to occur, that teachers believe that they too can investigate mathematics and pursue research in that field of inquiry. The disposition toward mathematical inquiry fostered in their students must be one that they themselves practice.

Professional-development experiences can be used to create an investigative disposition in teachers. Research activities in mathematics can be used that are similar to the research activities that teachers would engage in with their students as they participate together in the community of mathematics learners. Activities designed to encourage teachers to reflect on their practice would stimulate teachers to reconsider their perception of what constitutes successful teaching. In addition, teachers should be encouraged to systematically plan innovations and analyze the successes and difficulties encountered during the implementation of these innovations.

In conclusion, classroom-based research, carried out by teachers, provokes teachers to analyze their classrooms, their practice, and their students' learning to depths that are difficult to reach with other types of professional-development activities. Furthermore, such research provides the larger mathematics-education community with greater insight on aspects of successful teaching. In the following pages, I describe two programs that have been designed to engage teachers and future teachers in research activities. A goal of these programs was to engage participants in reflective practice. I give examples of the ways in which participants were able to reflect on their students' learning, on mathematics itself, or on their teaching practice through their research studies.

A PRESERVICE EXPERIENCE

A teacher-education seminar held at the Catholic University of S„o Paulo in Brazil is an example of how a teacher-research experience was designed for preservice secondary mathematics teachers. The goal of the seminar was to initiate the participants in research experiences that would shape their beliefs about the teaching and learning of mathematics and about the nature of mathematics. Together, the seminar participants (future teachers, university faculty, and guests) constituted a research team. The charge to the research team was to identify a research question, propose a study, collect data, analyze the data, and write up the findings in the form of a report (Research report, no date).

The group decided to work on studying children's understanding of fractions. They proposed to design a diagnostic test, apply the test to a large number of students, and analyze the data. Unlike most research seminars, the group was purposely not taught any research methodology. The philosophy adopted by the faculty was that knowledge is constructed by the learner; thus the approach taken to learning about research should be constructivist as well. Hence, students would experience research activities and construct their own understanding of what constitutes research on the basis of reflections on the experiences themselves.

This research group was not "hindered" by criteria and standards of what the mathematics education research community would consider "good" research. Instead, the driving force for their research study was the pressing questions that had emerged during their field experiences in preparing to become teachers.

The research group met twice a week until data collection began. During data collection, meetings occurred once a week. During data analysis, meetings occurred twice a week. The role of the faculty members during the meetings was to serve as participant observers. They took field notes of the discussions and asked questions that focused the groups' attention on the research activity. For example, as items were produced for the diagnostic tests, the faculty would often ask the group for a rationale for including specific test items. Also, the students often turned to the faculty to identify readings that were related to the questions they were asking.

The group's initial research design reflected their beliefs about research—beliefs gained from much of the reading they had done on educational research in general and on mathematics education research in particular. They were convinced that they would not be able to say much about children's understanding of fractions unless they tested a very large number of students. Thus, the first step taken by the group was to test 182 students between fifth and eighth grades. This was followed by an analysis of the test results. This analysis was, in a first instance, focused on the frequency of correct and incorrect answers. The research team was amazed at the results and distressed about how little they could say about the results. Only vague comments could be made, such as "88% of the children solved question 15 incorrectly" (Research report, p. 6). As the research team was pressed by the faculty to say more about the findings, they began to look beyond the numerical results. The research team began to raise many conjectures as indicated by the following comments: "It seems that the 7th and 8th graders were so worried about using the correct rules for operating with fractions that they were unable to finish the test.... We could not understand how 8th graders had to find a common denominator in order to solve $1/2 + 1/4 + 1/4$. It seems they couldn't transfer their informal learning of part/whole to the formalization of the ideas" (Research report, p. 6).

Many more questions were raised from this first step than were answered. The students refined the study by restructuring the diagnostic instrument. They revised the instrument so that it no longer focused on both procedural and conceptual knowledge of fractions, but instead focused on items that might reveal students' conceptual understanding of fractions. The second test was administered exclusively to 10- to 12-year-old children and was given to only 76 children. As the students searched for meaning and for explanations of how children were making sense of fractions, tests were analyzed much more qualitatively.

Although this second test was a lot more revealing than the first, it was clear that another form of data collection was needed before the questions raised could be adequately addressed. It is worth mentioning that there was evidence of growth in these preservice teachers' thinking about children's understanding of fractions even as they developed the second instrument. Every question had a rationale behind it, and many children's answers were anticipated. For every potential children's answer, the students had a conjecture for a possible explanation.

It was during the analysis of the results of the second test that the students became aware that the interview process might be a more effective form of data collection for the types of questions they wished to address. Discussions of the various readings on research about the learning of fractions and the ineffectiveness of the initial data in giving insight into children's understanding of fractions pointed the group to the use of interviews.

Reflections on the Preservice Experience

It is not the purpose of this chapter to report on the findings about children's learning of fractions. As stated earlier, my goal is to report on the study of preservice teachers' growth in understanding of the research process and how an investigative disposition becomes an important part of the teaching process.

The decision to use interviews with the children was an important breakthrough in the students' thinking about research. It was also interesting to see how creative they were in thinking of ways to elicit children's thinking. The decisions they made about the interview process were the following: (a) they would interview some children individually and others in pairs, with the hope that the children in the pairs would communicate with each other and that their thinking would be verbalized; (b) they would have two members of the research team conducting an interview (one interviewing, the other taking notes); (c) they would audiotape the interviews; and (d) they would pilot the interviews before finalizing the interview structure to improve the questions posed and to learn how to conduct interviews.

Decisions were also made about how to pick the children to be interviewed. Children were classified into three groups on the basis of the results of the second test: children who got everything correct, those who made consistent errors, and those whose errors were inconsistent. The pairs were chosen in various ways: (a) one child who made no errors was paired with one who made errors, (b) one child who made consistent errors was paired with one who made inconsistent errors, and (c) one child who made errors was paired with a child who made a very different type of errors. At this point it was clear that this research group was struggling with a very important question that faces researchers using interview procedures. The most effective means of conducting interviews with children is not clearly established in the research community. This research group was exploring an open-ended question about pairing students for interviewing purposes in an effort to elicit as much information as possible about their understanding of fractions.

Some of the indicators of growth in reflective thinking among the students were the following: (a) the research group's ability to anticipate children's responses to the questions posed, (b) the rationale given for each question posed, (c) the emerging need for the use of different research methods to further investigate a question, (d) the emerging new questions arising with the analysis of each new data set, (e) the emerging feelings of anxiety about teaching as they analyzed the consequences of traditional learning experiences, and (f) a realization by the students of how children construct knowledge and make sense of their experiences. There was also evidence that teaching experience alone would not generate the level of reflection necessary to analyze the data about children's work with fractions that was gathered in this project. A group of practicing teachers was asked to use in their classes the second diagnostic test produced by the research group and to analyze the results. The teachers had very little ownership in the diagnostic test, they had little sense of why the questions were composed as they were, and they themselves had not raised the research questions driving the analysis of the test results. This resulted in a much less sophisticated analysis of the test results as evidenced by the teachers' informal papers prepared for an in-service course they were attending at the time.

The following comments from three student members of the research group may help the reader sense how reflective the students were toward the end of the group research project, and especially how open they were to continuous learning and self-assessment.

> I feel that I am still not secure about what to do, but I realize that I have changed tremendously in what I believe about teaching and about evaluation.... I feel anxious every time I correct a test, and I know I am expected to quantify the results rather than describe the students' understanding. (Maria, interview, March 1989)

> I am now concerned with the directions taken in education, with my students.... We have taken the first step, to detect and worry about the problems in learning (even if we are still unable to resolve them fully).... This is my expectation, to continue my quest for changes in my practice. (Ana, interview, March 1989)

> ... reflect about students' perspectives. This is important in all of pedagogical practice, in the objectives, lesson plans, content analysis, and methodology ... the classroom has become one big laboratory, which in fact motivates one's work. (Roberto, interview, March 1989)

AN IN-SERVICE EXPERIENCE

The setting for the in-service experience described next was a graduate class called Teachers as Researchers, held at the University of Delaware. The class was a requirement for the master's degree in education and usually had an enrollment of about 30 students. The intent of this class was to engage practicing teachers in classroom-based research activities. Most of the students in the class were practicing teachers, and their research studies were carried out in their own classrooms.

The main goal of the class was to encourage teachers to identify a research question related to their classroom practice and to conduct a study addressing the question they had identified to gain insight into their teaching practice and how it relates to their beliefs about teaching and learning. Questions, ranging from a focus on a single child to a focus on school policies and procedures, varied greatly among teachers.

Built into the process was a support network for the teachers as they pursued their studies. The class met formally on a weekly basis for 3 hours. Part of the class meeting consisted of teachers working in small groups to share their progress, their struggles and difficulties, and their insights. During this time, the instructor circulated throughout the class and noted the similarities and differences in the issues addressed by the various groups. These issues became the focus of the large-group discussion during the final hour of the class meeting.

Inquiry began as the teachers were asked to keep personal journals from which a research question would emerge. The journals were described to the teachers as a personal record of their day. Teachers were asked to write in the journal regularly, daily if feasible, and reflect on the accumulated journal entries weekly. Their goal throughout the first month of the experience was to use the journal as a tool to help them reflect on their practice. They were to find something that intrigued them about their practice or about their students or, more generally, about their lives as teachers. These journals took on many different roles for the different teachers. Whereas some kept a journal that resembled a log or diary of classroom activities, others used the journal to raise issues about teaching and learning and to reflect on the issues. The importance of the teacher's journal in identifying a research question is reflected in Strieb's (1993) comment:

> I'd found my ideal mode of data collection. In the introduction of the published version of my journal, I wrote, "the more I wrote, the more I observed in my classroom, and the more I wanted to write." As I re-read my journal I got more ideas for teaching. (p. 122)

Initially the readings used for the course included primarily work done by teachers (see examples in Bissex & Bullock, 1987; Goswami & Stillman, 1987; Rowland, 1984). Many teachers entered the course with great skepticism about research and the research process. Even those who viewed research as an activity limited to members of the university community were interested in, and intrigued by, the pieces written by teachers themselves. According to Kincheloe (1991), "Traditional researchers had weeded out the self, denied their intuitions and inner voices, in the process producing restricted and object-like interpretations of socio-educational events. Using the traditional definitions, these object-like interpretations were certain and scientific" (p. 30). Whereas university-based authors typically strive for "objectivity," purposefully stripping their writing of any emotion or passion, practicing teachers write with all the emotion and passion that characterize their lives. The experiences of teachers in this class were clearly resonating with the experiences described by the writings of teacher researchers, that is, classroom teachers who had systematically studied a question of concern to them in their professional practice.

As questions began to emerge for each of the teachers, I noticed certain patterns in teachers' choices of research questions. Several teachers chose to look at how to better manage their classrooms. Their focus was on discipline and behavior. Their rationale was typically that the class as a whole would benefit if it were more effectively managed. Others chose to study a student or a small group of students and their learning difficulties. All of these latter studies clearly focused on children.

Several teachers used the research literature and the findings in that literature as the springboard for their inquiries. One teacher came to question the assumptions within the misconceptions in literature in science education. Another teacher used her learnings about problem solving to analyze what implications it had for her and her teaching. Several teachers studied emergent literacy in their students. One teacher piloted the use of a curricular program, *Mathematics Their Way* (Barrata-Lorton, 1976), in her first-grade classroom.

Two teachers focused on policy issues that affected classroom practices. One teacher realized from reflecting on her journal entries how often she was interrupted throughout her teaching and chose to study how interruptions affected her teaching and her students' learning. Her systematic inquiry provided evidence to argue that school policies concerning classroom interruptions from the office and administration be revised. Yet another teacher set out to prove how resistant teachers would be toward including research as a part of their daily activities. She was convinced that this was an impossible task to include in their daily lives and set out to convince the class what a crazy idea this was. Interestingly, in spite of all her "evidence," she could not argue the case strongly, and in fact, her colleagues' experiences seemed to disprove her conjectures rather than support them.

To enable teachers to develop a study that could be managed within a semester, my role in the initial phase of the study was to help them focus their questions. Similar to the process in the typical masters' study or doctoral study, much effort was put into clearly defining the research question and focusing on that question. Once each question was defined, my task became one of advising the teacher on the research methodology that was most reasonable for addressing the question and most feasible to fit as unobtrusively as possible within the teacher's classroom practice.

The methodology used by the teacher researchers varied according to the types of questions they addressed and included primarily qualitative sources of data. Throughout the experience, many teachers were reluctant to accept qualitative data sources as legitimate research tools. However, as they addressed the feasibility of using quantitative experimental designs in the classroom and the nature of the types of questions they were asking, it soon became clear that the most informative sources of data would be mostly qualitative. The methodology used turned out to be quite dynamic, and new sources of data and forms of data collection were tried throughout different stages of many of the studies.

The analysis of the data was done throughout the study. Every week the teachers presented their findings to their small working group. The group discussion often led to insights and suggestions. My role at this stage was to point out some of the research literature that could offer insight into what the teachers were observing and finding in their own studies. I realized that the process of analyzing and interpreting the data provided intrinsic motivation for reading the existing, related research literature, a level of motivation that I had little success in generating with other forms of in-service experiences.

Susan's Inquiry and Her Growth as a Teacher

The following example is used to illustrate the reflectiveness of one of the participating teachers, Susan, as she conducted her study. This teacher used her journal entries and her reflections about children's success in problem solving as a springboard for her thinking about her practice.

In her early journal entries, Susan begins her reflections by describing her teaching style and philosophy of education as expressed below:

> My style and philosophy of teaching has been very much centered around the mastery of the basics and teaching the methods that allow one to arrive at the answers. My instruction has often started with manipulatives and hands-on practice to define how a basic operation, such as multiplication or division, worked. However, from there I would revert to the text and practice as many problems as possible with the students, developing a step-by-step plan to arrive at a correct answer. I have found that I am very effective at teaching this way, and I have seen students master the four basic operations through this method of teaching.

Susan was a teacher in her second year of teaching. The teacher as researcher class was the very first class in her master's program. She had felt rewarded in her teaching experience with fourth graders by getting children to master the basic facts in mathematics. It was the journal entries related to this research project that led Susan to realize that the students were not performing as well on problem-solving tasks as they were on the mastery of the basic facts.

> The start of this research began with my own realization that, in the real world, my students would rarely come across problems such as 27×15. They would rarely find key words to hint at a solution. Real math problems come in the form of words and numbers without a sign telling you what to do. Real math problems require critical thinking and planning before a solution can be reached.

In analyzing her thinking about problem solving and her approach to teaching problem solving, she began to notice some patterns of behavior.

> I did not dwell on the problems for more than one or two class periods. I wanted to get them completed, and I did not concentrate on the "how do you know what to do"

aspect of the problem.... I found myself encouraging strategies taught in the earlier grades, such as locating key words, that were now ineffective because the mathematical operations were more advanced.

The focus of her study turned to the children's strategies for solving word problems. She interviewed children, she observed their work in small groups, and she reflected on her actions and their consequences for the students' learning of problem solving.

> I was horrified when I realized the pattern in some of these problem-solving methods and the ways in which I had been helping students to solve these problems.... I knew as I began to see these methods applied that I had indeed said in one of the earlier subtraction lessons that to spend money you must subtract since money is being taken away.... I also knew that when we started the year with addition and subtraction I had displayed a chart of key words typically found in word problems requiring students to add and subtract. I found that such an ordered, nonanalytical method of teaching would come to haunt me only several months later.

In the midst of her study, I noticed a shift from Susan's thinking about what she was doing in her classes to concentrating on what she could learn from the children. The focus of her inquiry changed dramatically toward the children's thinking strategies. From observing and interviewing the successful students and comparing their thinking strategies with those of the less successful students, Susan tried to extrapolate the thinking strategies that she could encourage all students to use.

> The more successful problem solvers were the students who could analyze the size of the solution, attribute meaning to the words, and generate a diagram or picture relating to the problem.

Susan's efforts to understand students' thinking about problem solving helped shape her own views about problem solving. Although she had clearly studied what problem solving was about in her preservice teacher-education program, what it really meant to teach children to solve problems had not been incorporated into her practice. It is likely that Susan had not internalized the meaning of a problem-solving approach to teaching mathematics from her teacher-preparation experiences. During the research experience, Susan found and reread the articles about problem solving that she had already been exposed to during her preservice training. At this point, she was able to draw conclusions about the implications of that literature for her practice much more effectively than she had been able to do prior to this experience. She was able to tie her findings to the literature on students' problem-solving strategies and to plan for changes in her teaching of problem solving.

> Since uncovering the different types of problem-solving strategies (both effective and ineffective), I have tried to change my teaching methods as well as my attitude about teaching problem solving.

Stimulated by this experience, Susan came to question her values for mathematics instruction. She had been pleased with her results, yet the reflections on her practice and the group interactions with her peers led her to question her assumptions and beliefs about teaching problem solving. The questioning and raising problems from within through self-analysis took on a very different dimension than it might have if an outsider were trying to point to "faults" in her teaching. This is but one of the many examples whereby the teachers who engaged in teacher research found themselves questioning their practice and wondering and planning what they might do differently.

CONCLUSION

This chapter was intended to point to some of the dimensions of teacher research that can serve to foster a disposition toward inquiry in teaching. In both the preservice and in-service experiences described here, teacher research was used as a tool for developing, encouraging, and sustaining teachers' reflective practice. In these experiences, qualitative methods were the main tool used by teachers to study the reality of their classrooms and the learning of their students. The preservice experience in particular points out how traditional quantitative methods are unsatisfying; it is not feasible to use these methods to address the questions that teachers raise regarding the teaching and learning occurring in their classrooms.

The chapter also points out how the teachers' voices are an important component of our understanding of the effectiveness of teacher research experiences. Their voices also constitute an important component of our understanding of the reality of the classroom and of children's thinking and learning. As teachers participate in contributing to the knowledge base about teaching and learning, they become empowered, autonomous decision makers. At the same time, the academic research community gains insights about teaching and learning through the teachers' perspectives as they interpret, analyze, and describe the complexities of their lives as teachers and their students' lives as learners.

Chapter 11

Where Do We Go from Here?

Susan Pirie

"Education literature has usually treated the alternatives to traditional positivistic research as a single approach—often called the 'qualitative' approach" (Jacob, 1987, p. 1).

Even a brief study of this book would be sufficient to dispel this notion of a singularity of definition for qualitative research within the field of mathematics education. Indeed, had the editor managed to assemble all the authors of the preceding chapters in one room, it is my contention that a very lively debate would have ensued and that no one approach to qualitative research on the learning and teaching of mathematics would have emerged as triumphant and representative. It is not even clear to me that the authors would have been in unanimous agreement on their placing of the variety of methods in relation to the boundaries of legitimate mathematics research mentioned in Chapter 2. What we, as researchers, have done is taken the traditions of other, older disciplines and made them our own to apply them to specific questions arising within mathematics education. We have, in addition, attempted to make overt the variations and precautions that we have been obliged to employ to remain faithful to our own notions of genuine "research."

The range of approaches, methods, attitudes, foci, concerns, and situations encompassed is dramatic. In Chapter 3, Ernest attempts to construct a definition of what he calls "the qualitative research paradigm," but he is quick to draw attention to the fact that this term can be misleading because it can enshroud a confusion between methods and methodology; a qualitative methodology may well utilize quantitative methods (Jacob, 1987). It is this confusion that sometimes gives rise to inappropriate criticisms of the validity of certain research, and I will return to this topic later in this chapter.

Teppo opens the book with a focus on the diverse ways of knowing, and subsequent authors capture some of the myriad ways of coming to know that are available to us. They have not provided recipes for success but illustrations of the reality of qualitative research—its problems and its strengths. Recurrent themes run through the chapters that address some of the fundamental questions facing qualitative research in mathematics education. It is appropriate, therefore, to close this book, but not the debate, by teasing out some of these themes and acknowledging the tasks that lie ahead.

THE ROLE OF THEORY

Possibly the most crucial consideration, if not always the most dominant in the presentations, is that of the role of theory in qualitative research. There are in fact two issues here: first, the intention of the research itself in regard to its contribution to the development of general theory within mathematics education and second, the theoretical standpoint of the researcher and the theoretical basis for the methods and instruments used. A subsidiary of the second issue is the ability to shift theoretical positions relative to methods and instruments within the research process. In other words, theoretically, where is the research going, where does it have it roots, and how flexible should those roots be?

Teppo touches on the first issue in her introduction when she considers the different goals the authors have with respect to the outcomes of their research. Each chapter thereafter seeks to characterize, or account for, or classify aspects of, the teaching and learning of mathematics. There is an intention to work toward a greater understanding of the whole area of mathematics education, whether the current particular focus be on overarching classroom phenomena such as discussion (Pirie), or on more detailed specificities, such as school beginners' conceptions of number (Neuman). The encompassing notion is that theory will (eventually) be generated that will explain in legitimate and precise ways the events and occurrences of classrooms, although in some cases, before this can happen we need simply to better understand the nature of the phenomenon.

For Clarke, the starting point is a little different. He intends not to build new theory but to challenge an existing theoretical assertion. He does not set out, however, to scientifically disprove the current model of "negotiation of meaning" within the classroom. Rather, employing a qualitative, deeply investigative method based on case study, he attempts to elaborate the model by providing a better characterization of the ways in which meanings are constructed within the classroom. Only then will he be in a position to refute the value of current metaphorical ways of seeing the meaning-making process. Attempts to quantify or rigorously test the inappropriateness of the current position would themselves be inappropriate. In this respect, one of the firm characteristics of qualitative research—that of the focus on concrete practices and particulars—is being enacted.

The second issue concerning the theoretical aspects of the roots of the reported research is more contentious. Because of its broad and diverse nature and the span of historical backgrounds from which qualitative research springs, it is essential for the community to have some understanding of where in this spectrum particular researchers are situating themselves (see Chapters 1 and 2). Since we do not have a unified methodology built over time and universally accepted by the mathematics education community, we need to make explicit where we, as individuals, stand theoretically in relation to our work (Silver & Kilpatrick, 1994). Pirie is an excellent case in point. She does not approach the research with a preconceived attitude about the appropriate theoretical stand but begins with her research question and seeks out an appropriate theoretical starting place

(Denzin & Lincoln, 1994; Shulman, 1981). Goldin, indeed, states explicitly, in the words of Davis (1984, p. 22), "without an appropriate theory, one cannot even state what the 'facts' are," although some of the authors might disagree about what constituted an appropriate theory.

Related to the second issue is the interactive nature of the relationship between the theoretical underpinnings and the understandings that develop during the research process. It is clear that there is a need to make overt our own theoretical underpinnings in the way that Jaworski makes very explicit in her initial radical constructivist approach. What is of especial interest here is that we then see one of the inner strengths of qualitative research at work—namely, the ability of the researcher to make design decisions throughout the research process and to draw on multiple perspectives to understand the phenomenon in question (Denzin & Lincoln, 1994; Janesick, 1994). As her gathering of data and initial analysis dictate the making of certain pragmatic decisions, she acknowledges the transformation of this theoretical position to that of social constructivism. I use the word *strengths* here because it is the paradigmatic denial of an absolutist epistemology that allows for the human element, allied to the specific goals of the research, to be influential. Indeed, for D'Ambrosio, the shifting of theoretical positions within the thinking of the teachers she was studying was one of the major facets in the achievement of her goals.

The ability of preliminary research findings to influence underlying methodological choices is also illustrated by Pirie (see Chapter 6) and by Mousley, Sullivan, and Waywood (see Chapter 9). Their requirements for multiple, overlapping classifications of certain sets of data in no way contradict the theoretical backgrounds of their methods. In contrast to the scientific tradition, there is need here not for a dichotomy between right and wrong categorizations, but for a systematic, controlled searching for informative classifications that will lead to greater understanding of the teaching and learning processes.

The various ways that theory is treated by the authors, both as a framework for research and as the end result of the inquiry process, illustrate the situated role that theory plays in qualitative research. Selection of an appropriate framework should be relative to the contextual needs of each research question. Additionally, theory that is elaborated on, or generated by, the research should be understood within the context of that research (Cobb, 1994; Janesick, 1994). This recognition of contextual relevance makes it crucial that researchers carefully position and describe their use of theory within the contexts of their work. To form judgments related to research, we must know from where the researcher is coming.

VALIDITY AND RELIABILITY

Not anything goes, of course. Research is not simply looking to see what happens. "Traditions are important, even when one takes an open stance, because they provide a set of orienting assumptions" (Jacob, 1987, p. 40). To undertake even theory-building research, we must have specific, justifiable aims that are based to some degree within a theoretical reasoning. One approach that has a substantial following among researchers is to seek to define and justify qualitative research from the perspective of its emergence as a new paradigm. Many of the authors do this, giving legitimate, powerful, theoretical foundations for their approaches. An indication of the length of the road ahead, however, is given by the set of theoretical questions posed by Goldin, to which he (modestly) claims to give only preliminary and partial answers. He faces squarely an awareness of the need to answer those who challenge the value of qualitative research *on their own terms.* This is evident from the struggle he reveals (and it is this detailed revelation that is of such value to the emergence of a coherent research paradigm) as he attempts to align his research with the criteria for acceptability imposed by the traditional methodologies.

If our findings are to be considered of value by readers external to, or unfamiliar with, qualitative approaches, we must at the very least offer evidence that the traditional notions of "validity" and "reliability," if not directly applicable, have their counterparts within the new research paradigm (Eisenhart & Howe, 1992). We cannot say with impunity that these notions are of no consequence to us; we must seek to put in their place equally cogent arguments and tests for the value of what we report.

The question that must also be explicitly addressed is, "Of what are we trying to establish the validity?" Is it the description we are offering of the phenomenon? The inferences drawn from that description? The theory based on these inferences? At every stage we must remain credible, yet also realize that "validity is relative to [the] purposes and circumstances" of the research (Maxwell, 1992, p. 283).

It is clear that as yet, no neat textbook tests or arguments exist by which qualitative research can be judged. Indeed it is unlikely, by the very nature and intent of the research, that such tests will ever exist (Silver & Kilpatrick, 1994). At the most, only very general guidelines for credibility can be applied across all research. One such standard that was touched on in the preceding section refers to that of the coherence or goodness of fit of research design—the fit among the theoretical framework, research questions, data-collection procedures, and interpretative techniques (Eisenhart & Howe, 1992). Pirie's hypothetical framing of her intended research within different qualitative methodologies illustrates how the requirements of coherence would have created a range of different studies within the given context of student classroom discourse—these differences reflecting the need to fit all elements of the research design into a methodologically coherent whole.

It is more appropriate to consider design-specific standards that relate judgments of quality to particular methodological perspectives. Thus, Jaworski concerns herself with "rigor" within her interpretative, ethnographic stance; Goldin, with reproducibility, comparability, and generalizability in his use of scientific inquiry; and Neuman, with the phenomenographic criteria of interpretative awareness. Making these criteria explicit helps us differentiate the perspectives needed to judge individual research. In addition, the nature of the knowledge sought by each author is heightened by understanding the relevant criteria whereby the different research is evaluated.

A crucial element that researchers must address is that of openness, both in carefully reporting the research design and in making explicit the subjective nature of the researcher's role in collecting and analyzing qualitative data. Jaworski's use of a research biography illustrates how detailed descriptions of context, researcher reflections, and respondent validations illuminate and make credible her interpretations of "significant" events relative to the goals of her research.

For many of the authors, it is the explicitness of the reporting (Ernst; Goldin; Jaworski; Mousley et al.) and the awareness of the need to remain "open to discussion and challenge" (Goldin) that give strength to the value of the research. As Merton remarked in 1968, when we have a considerable body of qualitative research *in which the researchers have exposed their actions and thinking in the kind of detail necessary for external scrutiny,* we can attain the security of footing accorded to quantitative research. A quarter of a century later, that need has yet to be met.

WHAT ARE THE DATA?

A common method of data collection is through audio and video recording. The rationale for this method is usually that these recordings offer the best available way of preserving as much of the phenomena under scrutiny as possible. Leaving aside the decisions along the lines of whether to use one static camera, or to use a camera for each group of pupils with a fixed microphone, or to use a radio microphone attached to the teacher, the researcher is still faced with the decision about what to do with the tapes. This is not a trivial decision, and pragmatic influences must be acknowledged (Pirie, 1996b). There are those who remain faithful to the original intention of recording everything, and for them *the data are the tapes* and all analysis is done purely from watching or listening to the tapes. This leads to a very cumbersome working environment, although modern software such as C-video is beginning to make the process of scanning, and selecting data on which to focus, a more manageable task. There are others who realize that something will be lost by the process, but for whom, nevertheless, transcribing is still considered a more appropriate way to work. For them *the data are the transcripts.*

Field notes form another common source of data in qualitative work. Within the scientific paradigm, these will be in the form of codings on some preselected grid; once they have left the classroom, they can be operated on, as symbols, exactly as they stand. The field notes of the qualitative researcher, however, may consist of sheets of notes, diagrams, prose, and personal comments. Are these to be the data as they stand? Does the researcher reduce them to coherent summaries and work with those? Or indeed do they serve as aide-mémoire to the writing of a fuller account of events witnessed? What exactly is used for the analysis? The interaction here is not to set up one method as preferable to another, but in the interests of credibility when reporting, we must, once again, return to the notion of being as explicit as possible in the details we make available to those who would judge our research.

LANGUAGE

In their opening paragraphs, Mousley, Sullivan, and Waywood raise one of the fundamental considerations within qualitative research that is not given sufficient prominence by other authors. This is the issue of language. By its very nature, qualitative research demands that we move "the whole problem of language from its peripheral and incidental position into the center." This means more than acknowledging and defending loss of detail when we reduce aural and visual data to written verbal data. We trade in words—the words of the teachers, the words of the students, the words of our own reporting. We need to concern ourselves with the reality that we can only define and describe categories and emergent theories through language. We observe and personally interpret classroom contexts, and, leaving aside the question of whether we need language for thought, we certainly need language to attempt to convey these thoughts to an audience.

"Texts are not simple mirrors of reality" (Nielson, 1995, p. 8). When we give voice to our interpretations, our meaning is mediated through words, both by ourselves and by our audience. The category labels we assign and the constructs we define are frequently attempts to capture initially nebulous qualities and behaviors. We can, as Goldin does in his scripted interviews, take great care with our own language, but the responses are not given with such care! Students respond to tasks spontaneously and without attention to the possibility of misinterpretation. In the very structured setting in which he works, Goldin is able to endeavor to confirm his interpretations by encouraging "the child to construct a concrete, external representation." In more open classroom settings, such confirmatory evidence is rarely available. We construct our own personal meanings of the discourse that we hear—and indeed we can do no other—but there is a need to be alive to the notion that the meanings are ours and, further, that others will, in turn, impose meanings on *our* words that are dependent on *their* histories and culture. Mousley et al. make overt their awareness of the eventuality that as ideas are published they inevitably take on new form in the everyday praxis of social use. Language is not merely one of "a new set of research emphases" (Ernest) but at the very core of all we do in a qualitative approach to the study of mathematical education.

REPORTING THE RESEARCH

Whatever form of data is selected for analysis and however careful we attempt to be in the linguistic interpretations of these data, one further problem remains when it comes to reporting qualitative data. As Jaworski says, "a major disadvantage" of qualitative data are their "lengthy nature … in the space taken to present an account." Whether they take the form of shelves of videotapes or reams of transcripts and field notes, it simply is not feasible to offer the reader all the data on which conclusions have been based. We are obliged to offer our summaries, interpretations, and selections of what we deem important for the reader know. We may claim that a single reported case can indicate a general conceptual category or property, that it is sufficiently generic to be taken as indicative of the theory we are suggesting. Necessarily, however, it is ultimately "the degree to which an informed reader is convinced" (Jaworski) that proves to be the test by which the research and resultant theoretical implications are judged. We are forced to return again to the problem and necessity of validating our work, *for others.*

As Mousley et al. suggest, developing technology may be coming to our aid. Software such as NUD•IST makes handling the vast quantities of data somewhat easier, but more than that, such products allow others to access the data and see the analytical decisions that were made by the researchers. The actual paths of theory building become accessible; the actual data become available for replicating the analysis or, indeed, for carrying out alternative analyses for the same or different purposes. This latter suggested use of the data raises new questions concerning the ethics implied by the transference of ownership of data. This and other ethical issues are discussed in the next section. Until technological advances become even more accessible to the general reader, however, we are dependent on the extent to which we are seen to be trustworthy in our reporting—until perhaps the definition of reader takes on another meaning, and research is communicated through alternative technologies as yet undreamed.

ETHICAL ISSUES

One final concern, conspicuous by its absence within this collection of writings, needs raising: a consideration of some of the fundamental ethical issues that qualitative research raises. These, I contend, are more acute than in quantitative approaches. There is the danger that we are less able to accord anonymity to the people involved. Caught by the need to give sufficient detail to enable readers to exercise their powers of judgment about the validity of the research findings, we may find that merely changing the names of the participants may not disguise their identity. The specifics of the detail may be enough to identify the school, class, or subject. Of even greater concern is the widespread use of video data. At oral presentations of research, such as at conferences and seminars, the temptation to illustrate, enhance, or at least enliven the delivery with video clips from the data is very strong. Anonymity here is impossible. Traditionally, subjects have been assured of the confidentiality of their contribution to the advancement of knowledge, but nowadays an additional factor is at play. With the ease of widespread, international dissemination of research, there is the desirability, even necessity, to specifically illustrate or define the cultural and educational background against which it takes place, thus making the masking of identities more difficult.

How far can, or should, a confidentiality agreement hold? Locally? Nationally? Internationally? For the main participants? For the bystanders? For those whose voices can be heard off camera? Do, and should, ethical considerations prevent us from gathering certain classroom data? Can we never reveal our original data to others? At what loss to the growth of understanding of the mathematical education process? Do our answers to the previous questions conflict with the intent to make data more widely available through modern technology as suggested by Mousley et al.? Where does the balance lie between personal and societal concerns? There is a tension here between the need to report in detail and the protection of those involved—a dilemma of nontrivial proportions that needs to be grappled with, since the publication of research is no longer confined to the pages of traditional journals.

CLARIFYING THE RESEARCH PROCESS

It should be evident from the foregoing chapters that we are not out of the woods in regard to the general acceptance of qualitative approaches as legitimate research paradigms for exploring the understanding of mathematics education. It is also evident that the approaches offered by the authors in this book have power and merit and, in many cases, offer the only way that today's quest for understanding can be furthered. As researchers, we must be critical participants in the debate that will eventually lead to the clarification of what is acceptable research in the emerging discipline of mathematics education. There is "an intimate relationship between the research process and the findings it produces," and by studying these processes, we gain insights not only into them but also into the problems of qualitative, interpretative research (Altheide & Johnson, 1994, p. 486). As participants, we need to address the challenge issued by Jacob (1987, p. 41) that it is a "better understanding of the various qualitative traditions (that) offers the hope of a richer and fuller understanding of education."

References

Ahlberg, A. (1992). *Att möta matematiska problem: En belysning av barns lärande.* [Meeting mathematical problems: An elucidation of children's learning]. Göteborg: Acta Universitatis Gothoburgensis.

Altheide, D. L., & Johnson, J. M. (1994). Criteria for assessing interpretative validity in qualitative research. In N. K. Denzin & Y. S. Lincoln (Eds.), *Handbook of qualitative research* (pp. 485–499). Thousand Oaks: Sage Publications.

Altrichter, H., Posch, P., & Somekh, B. (1993). *Teachers investigate their work: An introduction to the methods of action research.* New York: Routledge.

Anthony, G. (1994). Learning strategies in the mathematics classroom: What can we learn from stimulated recall interviews? *New Zealand Journal of Educational Studies, 29*(2), 127–140.

Ascher, M. (1991). *Ethnomathematics.* Pacific Grove, CA: Brooks/Cole.

Aspray, W., & Kitcher, P. (Eds.). (1988). *History and philosophy of modern mathematics* (Minnesota Studies in the Philosophy of Science, Vol. XI). Minneapolis: University of Minnesota Press.

Austin, J. L. (1962). *Sense and sensibilia.* (G. J. Warnock, Ed.). Oxford: Oxford University Press.

Australian Education Council. (1990). *A national statement on mathematics for Australian schools.* Canberra: Australian Education Council.

Bakhtin, M. (1979). *The aesthetics of verbal creation.* Moscow: Bocharov. Cited in Todorov (1984).

Ball, S. J. (1982). The verification and application of participant observation case study. In case study methods 5. *Perspectives on case study: Ethnography* (pp. 141–164). Deakin, Australia: University of Deakin Press.

Ball, S. J. (1990). Self doubt and soft data: Social and technical trajectories in ethnographic fieldwork. *Qualitative Studies in Education, 3*(2), 157–171.

Barnes, D. (1982). *From communication to curriculum.* London: Penguin.

Barnes, D., Britton, J., & Rosen, H. (1971). *Language, the learner and the school* (revised). Harmondsworth: Penguin.

Barnes, D., Britton, J., & Torbe, M. (1986). *Language, the learner and the school* (3rd edition). Harmondsworth: Penguin.

Barnes, D., & Todd, M. (1977). *Communication and learning in small groups.* London: Routledge & Keegan Paul.

Barrata-Lorton, M. (1976). *Mathematics their way.* Menlo Park, CA: Addison-Wesley.

Bartolini-Bussi, M. G. (1994). Theoretical and empirical approaches to classroom interaction. In R. Biehler, R. W. Scholz, R. Straesser, & B. Winkelmann (Eds.), *The didactics of mathematics as a scientific discipline* (pp. 121–132). Dordrecht: Kluwer.

Bassey, M. (1990–1991). On the nature of research in education (Parts 1–3). *Research Intelligence, 36,* 35–38; *37,* 39–44; *38,* 16–18.

Bauersfeld, H. (1992). Classroom cultures from a social constructivist's perspective. *Educational Studies in Mathematics, 23,* 467–481.

Bauersfeld, H. (1994). Theoretical perspectives on interaction in the mathematics classroom. In R. Biehler, R. W. Scholz, R. Straesser, & B. Winkelmann (Eds.), *The didactics of mathematics as a scientific discipline* (pp. 133–146). Dordrecht: Kluwer.

Bell A. W., & Bassford, D. (1989). A conflict and investigation teaching method and an individualised learning scheme—a comparative experiment on the teaching of fractions. *Proceedings of the 13th International Conference for the Psychology of Mathematical Education,* (pp. 125–132). Paris.

Bell, A. W., Costello, J., & Kuchemann, D. (1983). *Research on teaching and learning.* Windsor: NFER-Nelson.

Berger, P., & Luckmann, T. (1966). *The social construction of reality.* Reprinted. London: Penguin Books, 1967.

Bishop, A. J. (1985). The social construction of meaning: A significant development for mathematics education? *For the Learning of Mathematics, 5*(1), 24–28.

Bishop, A. J. (1988). *Mathematical enculturation.* Dordrecht: Kluwer.

Bishop, A. J. (1992). International perspectives on research in mathematics education. In D. A. Grouws (Ed.), *Handbook of research on mathematics teaching and learning* (pp. 710–723). New York: Macmillan.

Bissex, G., & Bullock, R. H. (Eds.). (1987). *Seeing for ourselves: Case-study research by teachers of writing.* Portsmouth, NH: Heinemann.

Blaikie, N. (1993). *Approaches to social inquiry.* Cambridge: Polity Press.

Bloor, D. (1976). *Knowledge and social imagery.* London: Routledge & Kegan Paul.

Bodner, B. L., & Goldin, G. A. (1991a). Drawing a diagram: Observing a partially developed heuristic process in college students. In F. Furinghetti (Ed.), *Proceedings of the Fifteenth International Conference for the Psychology of Mathematics Education (PME)* (Vol. 1) (pp. 160–167). Genoa, Italy: Dipartimento di Matematica dell'Universià di Genova.

Bodner, B. L., & Goldin, G. A. (1991b). Cognitive obstacles of developmental-level college students in drawing diagrams. In R. G. Underhill (Ed.), *Proceedings of the Thirteenth Annual Meeting of the North American Chapter of the International Group for the Psychology of Mathematics Education* (Vol. I) (pp. 8–14). Blacksburg, VA: Virginia Polytechnic Institute and State University Division of Curriculum & Instruction.

Boero, P., Dapueto, C., & Parenti, L. (1996). Didactics of mathematics and the professional knowledge of teachers. In A. J. Bishop, K. Clements, C. Keitel, J. Kilpatrick, & C. Laborde (Eds.), *International handbook of mathematics education* (pp. 1097–1121). Dordrecht: Kluwer.

Borasi, R. (1992). *Learning mathematics through inquiry.* Portsmouth, NH: Heinemann.

Bredo, E. (1994). Reconstructing educational psychology: Situated cognition and Deweyian pragmatism. *Educational Psychologist, 29*(1), 23–35.

Breiter, C. (1997). *Mathematical knowledgeability.* Paper presented at the meeting of the American Educational Research Association, Chicago, IL.

Brissiaud, R. (1992). A tool for number construction: Finger symbol sets. In J. Bideaud, C. Meljac, & J. P. Fischer (Eds.), *Pathways to number* (pp. 41–65). Hillsdale, NJ: Lawrence Erlbaum Associates.

Brown, D. (1997). Teachers as researchers: Some historical issues. In V. Zack, J. Mousley, & C. Breen (Eds.), *Developing practice: Teachers' inquiry and educational change* (pp. 193–202). Geelong, Australia: Centre for Studies in Mathematics, Science and Environmental Education.

Bruner, J. (1985). Vygotsky: A historical and conceptual perspective. In J. V. Wertsch (Ed.), *Culture, communication and cognition.* Cambridge: Harvard University Press.

Bruner, J. S. (1990). *Acts of meaning.* Harvard, MA: Cambridge Press.

Bullock, R. H. (Ed.). (1987). Teachers talk about their research: A round-table discussion. In G. Bissex & R. H. Bullock (Eds.), *Seeing for ourselves: Case-study research by teachers of writing* (pp. 145–163). Portsmouth, NH: Heinemann.

Burbules, N. C., & Rice, S. (1991). Dialogue and differences: Continuing the conversation. *Harvard Educational Review, 61*(4), 393–416.

Burgess, R. G. (1982). *Field research: A source book and field manual.* London: Allan & Unwin.

Burgess, R. G. (1984). *In the field.* London: Unwin Hyman.

Burgess, R. G. (1985). *Strategies of educational research.* London: Falmer Press.

Calderhead, J. (1987). *Teachers' classroom decision making.* London: Holt Rinehart & Winston.

Carpenter, T. P., & Moser, J. M. (1984). The development of addition and subtraction concepts in grades one to three. *Journal for Research in Mathematics Education, 15*(3), 179–202.

Carr, W., & Kemmis, S. (1986). *Becoming critical.* London: Falmer.

Carter, K. (1993). The place of story in the study of teaching and teacher education. *Educational Researcher, 22*(1), pp 5–12, 18.

Charles, R. I., & Lester, F. K. (1984). An evaluation of a process-oriented instructional program in mathematical problem solving in grades 5 and 7. *Journal for Research in Mathematics Education, 15*(1), 15–34.

Cicourel A. V. (1973). *Cognitive sociology.* London: Penguin.

Cizek, G. J. (1995). Crunchy granola and the hegemony of the narrative. *Educational Researcher, 24*(3), 26–28.

Clarke, D. J. (1986). Conceptions of mathematical competence. *Research in Mathematics Education in Australia,* (No. 2), 17–23 (Australia).

Clarke, D. J. (1996). Refraction and reflection: Modelling the classroom negotiation of meaning. *RefLecT, 2*(1), 46–51.

Clarke, D. J., & Helme, S. (1997). The resolution of uncertainty in mathematics classrooms. In F. Biddulph & K. Carr (Eds.), *People in mathematics education: Proceedings of the Twentieth Annual Conference of the Mathematics Education Research Group of Australasia* (pp. 116–123). Waikato, New Zealand: MERGA.

Clarke, D. J., & Kessel, C. (1995). To know and to be right: Studying the classroom negotiation of meaning. In B. Atweh & S. Flavel (Eds.), *Galtha: MERGA 18: Proceedings of the 18th Annual Conference of the Mathematics Education Research Group of Australasia* (pp. 170–177). Darwin, NT: University of the Northern Territory.

Cobb, P. (1986). Clinical interviewing in the context of research programs. In G. Lappan & R. Even (Eds.), *Proceedings of the Eighth Annual Meeting of the North American Chapter of the International Group for the Psychology of Mathematics Education: Plenary speeches and symposium* (pp. 90–110). E. Lansing, MI: University of Michigan Department of Mathematics and Department of Teacher Education.

Cobb, P. (1989). Experiential, cognitive, and anthropological perspectives in mathematics education. *For the Learning of Mathematics, 9*(2), 32–42.

Cobb, P. (1994). Where is the mind? Constructivist and sociocultural perspectives on mathematical development. *Educational Researcher, 23*(7), 13–20.

Cobb, P. (1995). Continuing the conversation: A response to Smith. *Educational Researcher, 24*(6), 25–27.

Cobb, P., & Bauersfeld, H. (Eds.). (1995). *The emergence of mathematical meaning: Interaction in classroom cultures.* Hillsdale, NJ: Lawrence Erlbaum Associates.

Cobb, P., Jaworski, B., & Presmeg, N. (1996). Emergent and sociolcultural views of mathematical activity. In L. P. Steffe, P. Nesher, P. Cobb, G. Goldin, & B. Greer (Eds.), *Theories of Mathematical Learning* (pp. 3–19). Mahwah, NJ: Lawrence Erlbaum Associates.

Cobb, P., & Yackel, E. (1996). Constructivist, emergent, and sociocultural perspectives in the context of developmental research. *Educational Psychologist, 31*(3/4), 175–190.

Cochran-Smith, M., & Lytle, S. (1993). *Inside/Outside: Teacher research and knowledge.* New York: Teachers College Press.

Cockcroft, W. H. (1982). Mathematics counts: Report of the committee of inquiry into the teaching of mathematics in schools. London: Her Majesty's Stationery Office.

Cohen L., & Manion, L. (1989). *Research methods in education* (3rd ed.). London: Routledge.

Confrey, J. (1995a). How compatible are radical constructivism, sociocultural approaches, and social constructivism? In L. P. Steffe & J. Gale (Eds.), *Constructivism in education* (pp. 185–225). Hillsdale, NJ: Lawrence Erlbaum Associates.

Confrey, J. (1995b). Student voice in examining "splitting" as an approach to ratio, proportions and fractions. In L. Meira & D. Carrher (Eds.), *Proceedings of the 19th International Conference for the Psychology of Mathematics Education* (Vol. 1) (pp. 3–29). Recife, Brazil: Universidade Federal de Pernambuco.

Cooney, T. J. (1988). Teachers' decision making. In D. Pimm (Ed.), *Mathematics teachers and children.* London: Hodder and Stoughton.

Cooney, T. J., & Henderson, K. B. (1972). Ways mathematics teachers help students organize knowledge. *Journal for Research in Mathematics Education, 3,* 21–31.

Crawford, K. (1996). Cultural processes and learning: Expectations, actions, and outcomes. In L. P. Steffe, P. Nesher, P. Cobb, G. Goldin, & B. Greer (Eds.), *Theories of mathematical learning* (pp.131–147). Mahwah, NJ: Lawrence Erlbaum Associates.

Crawford, K., & Adler, J. (1996). Teachers as researchers in mathematics education. In A. J. Bishop, K. Clements, C. Keitel, J. Kilpatrick, & C. Laborde (Eds.), *International handbook of mathematics education* (pp. 1187–1205). Dordrecht: Kluwer.

D'Ambrosio, U. (1985). Ethnomathematics and its place in the history and pedagogy of mathematics. *For the Learning of Mathematics, 5*(1), 44–48.

Darling-Hammond, L. (1996). The right to learn and the advancement of teaching: Research, policy, and practice for democratic education. *Educational Researcher, 25*(6), 5–17.

Davis, P. J. (1993). Applied mathematics as social contract. In S. Restivo, J. P. van Bebdegem, & R. Fisher (Eds.), *Math worlds: Philosophical and social studies of mathematics and mathematics education* (pp. 182–194), Albany: State University of New York Press.

Davis, P. J., & Hersh, R. (1980). *The mathematical experience.* Boston: Birkhauser.

Davis, P. J., & Hersh, R. (1988). *Descartes' dream.* London: Penguin Books.

Davis, R. B. (1984). *Learning mathematics: The cognitive science approach to mathematics education.* Norwood, NJ: Ablex Publishing.

Davis, R. B. (1992). Reflections on where mathematics education now stands and on where it may be going. In D. A. Grouws (Ed.), *Handbook of research on mathematics teaching and learning* (pp. 724–734). New York: Macmillan.

Davis, R. B. (1994). What mathematics should students learn? *Journal of Mathematical Behavior, 13*, 3–33.

Davis, R. B., Maher, C. A., & Noddings, N. (Eds.). (1990). *Journal for Research in Mathematics Education, Monograph No. 4, Constructivist views on the teaching and learning of mathematics.* Reston, VA: National Council of Teachers of Mathematics.

DeBellis, V. A. (1996). *Interactions between affect and cognition during mathematical problem solving: A two-year case study of four elementary school children.* Unpublished doctoral dissertation, Rutgers University Graduate School of Education, (University Microfilms No. 96-30716).

DeBellis, V. A., & Goldin, G. A. (1991). Interactions between cognition and affect in eight high school students' individual problem solving. In R. G. Underhill (Ed.), *Proceedings of the Thirteenth Annual Meeting of the North American Chapter of the International Group for the Psychology of Mathematics Education* (Vol. I) (pp. 29–35). Blacksburg, VA: Virginia Polytechnic Institute and State University, Division of Curriculum & Instruction.

DeBellis, V. A., & Goldin, G. A. (1993). Analysis of interactions between affect and cognition in elementary school children during problem solving. In J. R. Becker & B. Pence (Eds.), *Proceedings of the Fifteenth Annual Meeting of the North American Chapter of the International Group for the Psychology of Mathematics Education* (Vol. II) (pp. 56–62). Pacific Grove, CA: San Jose State University Center for Mathematics and Computer Science Education.

DeBellis, V. A., & Goldin, G. A. (1997). The affective domain in mathematical problem-solving. In E. Pehkonen (Ed.), *Proceedings of the Twenty-first Conference of the International Group for the Psychology of Mathematics Education (PME)* (Vol. II) (pp. 209–216). Helsinki, Finland: University of Helsinki Department of Teacher Education.

Delamont, S., & Hamilton, D. (1986). Revisiting classroom research: A cautionary tale. In M. Hammersley (Ed.), *Controversies in classroom research* (pp. 25–43). Milton Keynes: Open University Press.

Denzin, N. K., & Lincoln, Y. S. (1994). Introduction: Entering the field of qualitative research. In N. K. Denzin & Y. S. Lincoln (Eds.), *The handbook of qualitative research* (pp. 1–17). Thousand Oaks, CA: Sage Publications.

Descartes, R. (1955). *A discourse on method.* Translation in R. Descartes, *Philosophical works,* Vol. 1. New York: Dover Press. (Original work published 1637)

Devlin, K. (1997). *Mathematics: The science of patterns.* New York: Scientific American Library.

Donmoyer, R. (1996). Educational research in an era of paradigm proliferation: What's a journal editor to do? *Educational Researcher, 25*(2), 19–25.

Dossey, J. A. (1992). The nature of mathematics: Its role and its influence. In D. A. Grouws (Ed.), *Handbook of research on mathematics teaching and learning* (pp. 39–48). New York: Macmillan.

Dryfus, T. (1991). Advanced mathematical thinking processes. In D. Tall (Ed.), *Advanced mathematical thinking.* Dordrecht: Kluwer.

Dunne, M., & Johnston, J. (1992). An awareness of epistemological assumptions: The case of gender studies. *International Journal of Science Education, 14*(5), 515–526.

Eco, U. (1984). *Semiotics and the philosophy of language.* Bloomington, IN: Indiana University Press.

Edwards, A. D., & Furlong, V. J. (1978). *The language of teaching.* London: Heinemann.

Edwards, D., & Mercer, N. (1987). *Common knowledge—the development of understanding in the classroom.* London: Methuen.

Eisenhart, M. A. (1988). The ethnographic research tradition and mathematics education research. *Journal for Research in Mathematics Education, 19*(2), 99–114.

Eisenhart, M. A., & Howe, K. R. (1992). Validity in educational research. In M. D. LeCompte, W. L. Millroy, & J. Preissle (Eds.), *The handbook of qualitative research in education* (pp. 643–680). San Diego: Academic Press.

Eisner, E. W. (1993). Forms of understanding and the future of educational research. *Educational Researcher, 22*(7), 5–11.

Erlwanger, S. H. (1973). Benny's conception of rules and answers in IPI mathematics. *Journal of Children's Mathematical Behaviour, 1*(2), 7–26.

Ernest, P. (1991). *The philosophy of mathematics education.* London: Falmer Press.

Ernest, P. (1994a). *Mathematics, education and philosophy: An international perspective.* London: Falmer Press.

Ernest, P. (Ed.). (1994b). *Constructing mathematical knowledge: Epistemology and mathematics education.* London: Falmer Press.

Ernest, P. (1994c). *An introduction to educational research methodology and paradigms.* Exeter: University of Exeter.

Ernest, P. (1994d). A perspective on research in mathematics education. In J. Kilpatrick, J. Fey, & A. Sierpinska (Eds.), *What is research in mathematics education and what are its results?* (ICMI Study Pre-Conference Proceedings). College Park, MD: University of Maryland.

Ernest, P. (1997). *Social constructivism as a philosophy of mathematics.* Albany, NY: State University of New York Press.

Fenstermacher, G. D., & Richardson, V. (1994). *Promoting confusion in educational psychology: How is it done? Educational Psychology, 29*(1), 49–55.

Feyerabend, P. (1975). *Against method.* London: New Left Books.

Fischer, J. P. (1992). Subitizing: The discontinuity after three. In J. Bideaud, C. Meljac, & J. P. Fischer (Eds.), *Pathways to number: Children's developing numerical abilities* (pp. 119-131). Hillsdale, NJ: Lawrence Erlbaum Associates.

Flanders, N. A. (1970). *Analyzing teacher behaviour.* Reading, MA: Addison-Wesley.

Foucault, M. (1972). *The archaeology of knowledge.* London: Tavistock.

Freeman, K. (Ed.). (1956). *Ancilla to the pre-socratic philosophers.* Oxford: Basil Blackwell.

Freire, P. (1972). *Pedagogy of the oppressed.* London: Penguin Books.

Freudenthal, H. (1991). *Revisiting mathematics education: China lectures.* Dordrecht: Kluwer.

Frid, S. (1992). *Undergraduate calculus students' language use and sources of conviction.* Unpublished doctoral dissertation, Department of Secondary Education, University of Alberta.

Fuller, S. (1988). *Social epistemology.* Bloomington, IN: Indiana University Press.

Furlong, V. J., & Edwards, A. D. (1986). Language in classroom interaction: Theory and data. In M. Hammersley (Ed.), *Controversies in classroom research* (pp 51–61). Milton Keynes: Open University Press.

Fuson, K. (1992). Relationships between counting and cardinality from age 2 to age 8. In J. Bideaud, C. Meljac, & J. P. Fischer (Eds.), *Pathways to number* (pp 127–149). Hillsdale, NJ: Lawrence Erlbaum Associates.

Gadamer, H. G. (1975). *Truth and method.* New York: Seabury.

Gage, N. L. (1989). The paradigm wars and their aftermath: A "historical" sketch of research on teaching since 1989. *Educational Researcher, 18*(7), 4–10.

Galbraith, P. (1991). *Paradigms, problems and assessment: Some ideological implications.* Paper presented at Mathematics Education Research Group of Australasia Conference, Perth, Australia.

Galton, M., Simon, B., & Croll, P. (1980). *Inside the primary classroom* (the ORACLE project). London: Routledge.

Gardner, H. (1983). *Frames of mind.* New York: Basic Books.

Gardner, H. (1987). *The mind's new science* (rev. ed.). New York: Basic Books.

Garfinkel, H. (1967). *Studies in ethnomethodology.* Hemel Hempstead: Prentice Hall.

Geertz, C. (1973). Thick description: Towards an interpretive theory of culture. In C. Geertz (Ed.), *The interpretation of cultures* (pp. 3–32). New York: Basic Books.

Gelman, R., & Gallistel, C. R. (1978). *The child's understanding of number.* London: Harvard University Press.

Gerdes, P. (1985). Conditions and strategies for emancipatory mathematics education in underdeveloped countries. *For the Learning of Mathematics, 5*(1), 15–20.

Gerdes, P. (1996). Ethnomathematics and mathematics education. In A. Bishop (Ed.), *International handbook of research in mathematics education* (pp. 909–943). Dordrecht: Kluwer.

Gergen, K. (1985). The social constructionist movement in modern psychology. *American Psychologist, 40,* 266–275.

Giddens, A. (1984). *The constitution of society.* Oxford: Polity Press.

Gillies, D. A. (Ed.). (1992). *Revolutions in mathematics.* Oxford: Clarendon Press.

Ginsburg, H. (1981). The clinical interview in psychological research on mathematical thinking: Aims, rationales, techniques. *For the Learning of Mathematics, 3,* 4–11.

Ginsburg, H. (1983). *The development of mathematical thinking.* New York: Academy Press.

Giorgi, A. (1986). A phenomenological analysis of descriptions of concepts of learning obtained from a phenomenographic perspective. Göteborg: *Publikationer från institutionen för pedagogik, Göteborgs Universitet, 18.*

Gitlin, A. D. (1990). Educative research, voice, and school change. *Harvard Educational Review, 60*(4), 443–466.

Glaser, B. G., & Strauss, A. L. (1967). *The discovery of grounded theory: Strategies for qualitative research.* London: Weidenfeld & Nicholson.

Goffman, E. (1971). *The presentation of self in everyday life.* London: Penguin Books.

Goldin, G. A. (1982). The measure of problem-solving outcomes. In F. K. Lester, Jr. & J. Garofalo (Eds.), *Mathematical problem solving: Issues in research* (pp. 87–101). Philadelphia, PA: Franklin Institute Press (acquired by Lawrence Erlbaum Associates, Hillsdale, NJ).

Goldin, G. A. (1985). Studying children's use of heuristic processes for mathematical problem solving through structured clinical interviews. In S. Damarin & M. Shelton (Eds.), *Proceedings of the Seventh Annual Meeting of the North American Chapter of the International Group for the Psychology of Mathematics Education* (pp. 94–99). Columbus, OH: Ohio State University Department of Educational Theory and Practice.

Goldin, G. A. (1986). Comments on structured individual interview methods for the study of problem solving. In G. Lappan & R. Even (Eds.), *Proceedings of the Eighth Annual Meeting of the North American Chapter of the International Group for the Psychology of Mathematics Education: Plenary speeches and symposium* (pp. 111–119). E. Lansing, MI: University of Michigan Department of Mathematics and Department of Teacher Education.

Goldin, G. A. (1987). Cognitive representational systems for mathematical problem solving. In C. Janvier (Ed.), *Problems of representation in the teaching and learning of mathematics* (pp. 125–145). Hillsdale, NJ: Lawrence Erlbaum Associates.

Goldin, G. A. (1992a). Toward an assessment framework for school mathematics. In R. Lesh & S. J. Lamon (Eds.), *Assessment of authentic performance in school mathematics* (pp. 63–88). Washington, DC: American Association for the Advancement of Science.

Goldin, G. A. (1992b). On developing a unified model for the psychology of mathematical learning and problem solving. In W. Geeslin & K. Graham (Eds.), *Proceedings of the Sixteenth International Conference for the Psychology of Mathematics Education (PME)* (Vol. III) (pp. 235–261). Durham, NH: University of New Hampshire Department of Mathematics.

Goldin, G. A. (1993). Observing mathematical problem solving: Perspectives on structured, task-based interviews. In B. Atweh, C. Kanes, M. Carss, & G. Booker (Eds.), *Contexts in mathematics education: Proceedings of the Sixteenth Annual Conference of the Mathematics Education Research Group of Australasia (MERGA-16)* (pp. 303–310). Queensland, Australia: Queensland University of Technology—Kelvin Grove Campus (MERGA).

Goldin, G. A., DeBellis, V. A., DeWindt-King, A. M., Passantino, C. B., & Zang, R. (1993). Task-based interviews for a longitudinal study of children's mathematical development. In I. Hirabayashi, N. Nihda, K. Shigematsu, & F-L. Lin (Eds.), *Proceedings of the Seventeenth International Conference for the Psychology of Mathematics Education (PME)* (Vol. I) (pp. 197–203). Tsukuba, Japan: PME Program Committee.

Goldin, G. A., & Landis, J. H. (1985). A problem-solving interview with "Stan" (age 11). In S. Damarin & M. Shelton (Eds.), *Proceedings of the Seventh Annual Meeting the North American Chapter of the International Group for the Psychology of Mathematics Education* (pp. 100–105). Columbus, OH: Ohio State University Department of Educational Theory and Practice.

Goldin, G. A., & Landis, J. H. (1986). A study of children's mathematical problem-solving heuristics. In L. Burton & C. Hoyles (Eds.), *Proceedings of the Tenth International Conference for the Psychology of Mathematics Education (PME)* (Vol. I) (pp. 427–432). London: University of London Institute of Education.

Goldin, G. A., & McClintock, C. E. (Eds.). (1980). *Task variables in mathematical problem solving.* Columbus, OH: ERIC Clearinghouse for Science, Mathematics and Environmental Education. Reissued by Franklin Institute Press, Philadelphia (1984) (acquired by Lawrence Erlbaum Associates, Hillsdale, NJ).

Goldin, G. A., & Passantino, C. B. (1996). A longitudinal study of children's fraction representations and problem-solving behavior. In L. Puig & A. GutiÈrrez (Eds.), *Proceedings of the Twentieth International Conference for the Psychology of Mathematics Education (PME)* (Vol. III) (pp. 3–10). Valencia, Spain: Universidad de València Dept. de Didàctica de la Matemàtica.

Good, T. L., Grouws, D. A., & Ebmeier, H. (1983). *Active mathematics teaching.* New York: Longman.

Goswami, D., & Stillman, P. (1987). *Reclaiming the classroom: Teacher research as an agency for change.* Upper Montclair, NJ: Boynton/Cook.

Gray, E. M., & Tall, D. O. (1994). Duality, ambiguity and flexibility: A proceptual view of simple arithmetic. *Journal for Research in Mathematics Education, 25*(2), 115–141.

Greer, B. (1996). Theories of mathematics education: The role of cognitive analysis. In L. P. Steffe, P. Nesher, P. Cobb, G. Goldin, & B. Greer (Eds.), *Theories of mathematical learning* (pp. 179–196). Hillsdale, NJ: Lawrence Erlbaum Associates.

Guba, E. G., & Lincoln, Y. S. (1989). *Fourth generation evaluation.* London: Sage.

Habermas, J. (1971). *Knowledge and human interests.* London: Heinemann.

Habermas, J. (1981). *The theory of communicative action* (2 vols.) (T. McCarthy, Trans.). Cambridge: Polity Press.

Hammersley, M. (1990). *Classroom ethnography.* Milton Keynes: Open University Press.

Hammersley, M. (1993). On constructivism and educational research methodology. *PME News* (May). Oxford: Oxford University Department of Educational Studies.

Hammersley, M., & Atkinson, P. (1990). *Ethnography principles in practice.* London: Routledge.

Harding, S. (Ed.). (1987). *Feminism and methodology: Social science issues.* Milton Keynes: Open University Press.

Harding, S. (1991). *Whose science? Whose knowledge?* Milton Keynes: Open University Press.

Harré, R. (1979). *Social being.* Oxford: Basil Blackwell.

Harré, R., & Gillett, G. (1994). *The discursive mind.* London: Sage Publications.

Hart, K. (Ed.). (1981). *Children's understanding of mathematics: 11–16.* London: John Murray.

Hart, L. (1986). Small group problem solving as a data source for the individual. In G. Lappan & R. Even (Eds.), *Proceedings of the Eighth Annual Meeting of the North American Chapter of the International Group for the Psychology of Mathematics Education: Plenary speeches and symposium* (pp. 120–127). E. Lansing, MI: University of Michigan Department of Mathematics and Department of Teacher Education.

Hatano, G. (1982). Learning to add and subtract: A Japanese perspective. In T. P. Carpenter, M. M. Moser, & T. A. Romberg (Eds.), *Addition and subtraction: A cognitive perspective.* Hillsdale, NJ: Lawrence Erlbaum Associates.

Henriques, J. H, Urwin, W., Venn, C., & Walkerdine, V. (1984). *Changing the subject: Psychology, social regulation and subjectivity.* London: Methuen.

Hitchcock, G., & Hughes, D. (1992). *Research and the teacher.* London: Routledge.

Hobbes, T. (1651). *Leviathan.* (Reprinted in Fontana Library.) Glasgow: William Collins, 1962.

Hoyles, C., Healey, L., & Sutherland, R. (1990). The role of peer group discussion in mathematical environments: Report to the Leverhulme Trust. London: University of London.

Hubbard, R., & Power, B. M. (1994). *The art of classroom inquiry: A handbook for teacher researchers.* Portsmouth, NH: Heinemann Press.

Ihde, D. (1997). *Experimental phenomenography.* New York: Longman.

Inhelder, B., & Piaget, J. (1958). *The growth of logical thinking from childhood to adolescence.* London: Routledge & Kegan Paul.

Jacob, E. (1987). Qualitative research traditions: A review. Review of Educational Research, 57(1), 1–50.

Janesick, V. J. (1994). The dance of qualitative research design: Metaphor, methodolatry, and meaning. In N. K. Denzin & Y. S. Lincoln (Eds.), *The handbook of qualitative research* (pp. 209–219). Thousand Oaks, CA: Sage Publications.

Jaworski, B. (1992). Mathematics teaching, what is it? *For the Learning of Mathematics,* 12(1), 8–14.

Jaworski, B. (1994). *Investigating mathematics teaching: A constructivist enquiry.* London: Falmer Press.

Joseph, G. G. (1991). *The crest of the peacock.* London: I. B. Tauris.

Kennedy, M. M. (1997). The connection between research and practice. *Educational Researcher,* 26(7), 4–12.

Kieran, C. (1994). Doing and seeing things differently: A 25-year retrospective of mathematics education research on learning. *Journal for Research in Mathematics Education,* 25(6), 583–607.

Kieren, T. E., & Pirie, S. E. B. (1991). Recursion and the mathematical experience. In L. P. Steffe (Ed.), *Epistemological foundations of mathematical experience* (pp. 78–101). New York: Springer-Verlag.

Kilborn, W. (1979). *PUMP-project—backgrund och erfarenheter* (The PUMP-project, background and experiences). FoU nr. 17. Stockholm: Liber.

Kilpatrick, J. (1987). What constructivism might be in mathematics education. In J. C. Bergeron, N. Herscovics, & C. Kieran (Eds.), *Proceedings of PME 11 Conference,* (Vol. 1, pp. 3–27). Montreal: University of Montreal.

Kincheloe, J. (1991). *Teachers as researchers: Qualitative inquiry as a path to empowerment.* New York: Falmer Press.

Kitcher, P. (1984). *The nature of mathematical knowledge.* Oxford: Oxford University Press.

Kitcher, P., & Aspray, W. (1988). An opinionated introduction. In W. Aspray & P. Kitcher (Eds), *History and philosophy of modern mathematics* (Minnesota Studies in the Philosophy of Science, Vol. XI, pp. 3–57). Minneapolis: University of Minnesota Press.

Kline, M. (1980). *Mathematics: The loss of certainty.* Oxford: Oxford University Press.

Kuhn, T. S. (1970). *The structure of scientific revolutions* (2nd ed.). Chicago: University of Chicago Press.

Kvale, S. (1989). To validate is to question. In S. Kvale (Ed.), *Issues of validity in qualitative research* (pp. 73–91). Lund: Studentlitteratur.

Kvale, S. (1994). Ten standard objections to qualitative research interviews. *Journal of Phenomenological Psychology, 25,* 147–173.

Lakatos, I. (1976). *Proofs and refutations.* Cambridge: Cambridge University Press.

Lakatos, I., & Musgrave, A. (Eds.). (1970). *Criticism and the growth of knowledge.* Cambridge: Cambridge University Press.

Larson, S. (1993). Om kvalitet I kvalitativa studier. (On quality in qualitative studies). *Nordisk Pedagogik,* 4(93), 194–211.

Lave, J., & Wenger, E. (1991). *Situated learning: Legitimate peripheral participation.* Cambridge: Cambridge University Press.

LeCompte, M. D., Millroy, W. L., & Preissle, J. (Eds.). (1992). *The handbook of qualitative research in education.* San Diego: Academic Press.

Lerman, S. (1996). Intersubjectivity in mathematics learning: A challenge to the radical constructivist paradigm? *Journal for Research in Mathematics Education, 27*(2), 133–150.

Lesh, R., & Lamon, S. J. (Eds.). (1992). *Assessment of authentic performance in school mathematics.* Washington, DC: American Association for the Advancement of Science.

Lester, F. K., Jr., Kehle, P. E., & Birgisson, G. (1996). *In pursuit of practical wisdom in mathematics education research.* Paper presented at the Research Presession of the Annual Meeting of the National Council of Teachers of Mathematics, San Diego, CA.

Lincoln, Y. S., & Guba, E. (1985). *Naturalistic inquiry.* Beverly Hills, CA: Sage.

Livingston, E. (1986). *The ethnomethodological foundations of mathematics.* London: Routledge & Kegan Paul.

Lybeck, L. (1981). *Arkimedes i klassen: En ämnespedagogisk berättelse.* (Archimedes in the classroom: A subject pedagogical story) Göteborg: Acta Universitatis Gothoburgensis.

Lyotard, J. F. (1984). *The postmodern condition: A report on knowledge.* Manchester: Manchester University Press.

Maher, C. A., & Martino, A. M. (1996). Young children invent methods of proof: The gang of four. In L. P. Steffe, P. Nesher, P. Cobb, G. Goldin, & B. Greer (Eds.), *Theories of mathematical learning* (pp. 431–447). Hillsdale, NJ: Lawrence Erlbaum Associates.

Marton, F. (1981). Phenomenography: Describing conceptions of the world around us. *Instructional Science, 10,* 177–200.

Marton, F., Beaty, E., & Dal'Alba, G. (1993). Conceptions of learning. *International Journal of Educational Research, 19,* 277–300.

Marton, F., & Booth, S. (1997). *Learning and awareness.* Hillsdale, NJ: Lawrence Erlbaum Associates.

Marton, F., & Neuman, D. (1996). Phenomenography and children's experience of division. In L. P. Steffe, P. Nesher, P. Cobb, G. A. Goldin, & B. Greer (Eds.), *Theories of mathematical learning* (pp. 315–334). Mahwah, NJ: Lawrence Erlbaum Associates.

Maxwell, J. A. (1992). Understanding and validity in qualitative research. *Harvard Educational Review, 62*(3), 279–300.

McLeod, D. B., & Adams, V. M. (Eds.). (1989). *Affect and mathematical problem solving: A new perspective.* New York: Springer-Verlag.

McLeod, D. B., Carpenter, T. P., McCornack, R. L., & Skvarcius, R. (1978). Cognitive style and mathematics learning: The interaction of field independence and instructional treatment in numeration systems. *Journal for Research in Mathematics Education, 9,* 163–174.

Mead, G. H. (1934). *Mind, self and society.* Chicago: University of Chicago Press.

Mehan, H. (1979). *Learning lessons: Social organization in the classroom.* Cambridge: Harvard University Press.

Mehan, M. (1985). Structure of classroom discourse. In T.A. Van Dijk (Ed.), *Handbook of discourse analysis* (Vol. 3) (pp. 119–131). London: Academic Press.

Mellin-Olsen, S. (1987). *The politics of mathematics education.* Dordrecht: Reidel.

Merton, R. K. (1968). *Social theory and social structure.* New York: The Free Press.

Meyer, R. (1995). Servicing-in: An approach to teacher and staff development. *Teacher Research, 2* (1), 1–16.

Miles, M. B., & Huberman, A. M. (1990). Animadversions and reflections on the uses of qualitative inquiry. In E.G. Eisner & A. Peshkin (Eds.), *Qualitative inquiry in education* (pp. 339–357). New York: Teachers College Press.

Minsky, M. (1986). *The society of mind.* New York: Simon & Schuster.

Mousley, J., & Clements, M. A. (1990). The culture of mathematics classrooms. In M. A. Clements (Ed.), *Whither mathematics?* (pp. 397–406). Melbourne: Mathematical Association of Victoria.

Mousley, J., Sullivan, P., & Clements, M. A. (1991, July). *The perceptions which student teachers have of teaching practices in classroom observed during field experience.* Paper presented at the annual conference of the Mathematics Education Lecturer's Association, Perth.

National Council of Teachers of Mathematics. (1989). *Curriculum and evaluation standards for school mathematics.* Reston, VA: National Council of Teachers of Mathematics.

Neuman, D. (1987). *The origin of arithmetic skills: A phenomenographic approach.* Göteborg: Acta Universitatis Gothoburgensis.

Neuman, D. (1993). Exploring numbers through subtraction in primary mathematics. In T. Breitig, I. Huntley, & G. Kaiser-Messmer (Eds.), *Teaching and learning mathematics in context* (pp. 37–50). New York: Ellis Horwood.

Neuman, D. (1994). Five fingers on one hand and ten on the other: A case study in learning through interaction. In J. P. da Ponte & J. F. Matos (Eds.), *Proceedings of the Eighteenth International Conference for the Psychology of Mathematics Education,* (Vol. 2, pp. 352–359). Lisbon: Departamento de Educaçio, Faculdade de Ciências da Universidadi de Lisboa.

Neuman, D. (1997). Immediate and sequential experiences of numbers. In E. Pehkonen (Ed.), *Proceedings of the Twenty-first International Conference for the Psychology of Mathematics Education,* (Vol. 3, pp. 288–295). Lahti: University of Helsinki.

Newman, C. F., & Pirie, S. E. B. (1990). *Watching the growth of understanding.* Midlands Mathematics Education Seminar, University of Birmingham.

Nias, J., & Groundwater-Smith, S. (1988). *The enquiring teacher: Supporting and sustaining teacher research.* New York: Falmer Press.

Nielson, H. B. (1995). Seductive texts with serious intention. *Educational Researcher, 24*(1), 4–12.

Noddings, N. (1990). Constructivism in mathematics education. In R. B. Davis, C. A. Maher, & N. Noddings (Eds.), *Constructivist views on the teaching and learning of mathematics* (pp. 7–18). Reston, VA: National Council of Teachers of Mathematics.

Noddings, N. (1994). William Brownell and the search for meaning. *Journal for Research in Mathematics Education, 25*(5), 524–525.

Nunes, T. (1992). Ethnomathematics and everyday cognition. In D. A. Grouws, (Ed.), *Handbook of research on mathematics teaching and learning* (pp. 557–574). New York: Macmillan.

Ödman, P. J. (1988). Heumeneutics. In J. P. Keeves (Ed.), Educational research, methodology and measurement: An international handbook (pp. 63–69). Oxford: Permagon.

Passantino, C. B. (1997). *Making connections: A cognitive analysis of children's problem-solving behavior involving fraction representations and strategies.* Unpublished doctoral dissertation, Rutgers University Graduate School of Education. (University Microfilms No. 97-17241)

Phinney, M. Y., & Ketterling, T. (1997). Dialogue journals, literature, and a sixth-grade urban Indian class. *Teacher Research, 4*(2), 22–41.

Pirie, S. E. B. (1988). Understanding—instrumental, relational, formal, intuitive..., how can we know? *For The Learning of Mathematics, 8,* 2–6.

Pirie, S. E. B. (1991a). Peer discussion in the context of mathematical problem solving. In K. Durkin & B. Shire (Eds.), *Language in mathematical education: Research and practice* (pp. 143–161). Milton Keynes: Open University Press.

Pirie, S. E. B. (1991b). Mathematical discussion: Incoherent exchanges or shared understandings. *Language and Education, 11*(3), 243–257.

Pirie, S. E. B. (1996a). Is there anybody listening? In P. E. Elliot (Ed.), *Communication in mathematics K–12: 1996 Yearbook* (pp. 105–115). Reston VA: National Council of Teachers of Mathematics.

Pirie, S. E. B. (1996b). *Classroom video recording: When, why and how does it offer a valuable data source for qualitative research?* Paper presented the 18th Annual Meeting of the North American Chapter of the International Group for the Psychology of Mathematics Education. Panama City, FL. (ERIC Document Reproduction Service No. ED 401 128).

Pirie, S. E. B. (forthcoming). Crossing the gulf between thought and symbol—language as slippery stepping stones. In M. B. Bussi, A. Sierpinska, & H. Steinbring (Eds.), *Language and communication in the mathematics classroom.* Reston VA: National Council of Teachers of Mathematics.

Pirie, S. E. B., & Schwarzenberger, R. L. E. (1988a). Mathematical discussion and mathematical understanding. *Educational Studies in Mathematics, 19,* 459–470.

Pirie, S. E. B., & Schwarzenberger, R. L. E. (1988b). Mathematical discussion—it's what you say *and* what you do. *Mathematics Teaching, 123,* 58–60.

Polanyi, M. (1958). *Personal knowledge.* London: Routledge & Kegan Paul.

Popper, K. (1959). *The logic of scientific discovery.* London: Hutchinson.

Pramling, I. (1991). Learning about "the shop": An approach to learning in preschool. *Early Childhood Research Quarterly, 6,* 151–166.

Pramling, I. (1994). Fenomenografi och pedagogisk praktik. (Phenomenography and pedagogical practice). *Nordisk Pedagogik, 4,* 227–239.

Putnam, H. (1975). *Mathematics, matter and method* (Philosophical Papers Vol. 1). Cambridge: Cambridge University Press.

Qualitative Solutions and Research. *Non-Numerical Unstructured Data • Indexing Searching and Theorizing* (NUD•IST) [Software package]. (1994). Melbourne: Qualitative Solutions and Research.

Radford, L. (1997). On psychology, historical epistemology, and the teaching of mathematics: Toward a socio-cultural history of mathematics. *For the Learning of Mathematics, 17*(1), 26–33.

Renz, P. (1997). An excess of jargon and a poor aim? *Focus, 17*(3), 1–3.

Research Advisory Committee. (1994). Reflecting on practice: New directions for NCTM research sessions. *Journal for Research in Mathematics Education, 25*(4), 371–374.

Research Advisory Committee. (1997). Clarifying the contributions of research within NCTM. *Journal for Research in Mathematics Education, 28*(4), 396–397.

Research report. (no date). Uma análise da construção do conceito de fração [An analysis of the construction of the concept of fractions]. Unpublished manuscript.

Resnick, L. B. (1983). A developmental theory of number understanding. In H. Ginsburg (Ed.), *The development of mathematical thinking* (pp. 109–151). New York: Academic Press.

Restivo, S. (1992). *Mathematics in society and history: Sociological inquiries.* Dordrecht: Kluwer.

Richards, J. (1991). Mathematical discussions. In E. von Glasersfeld (Ed.), *Radical constructivism in mathematics education* (pp. 13–51). Dordrecht: Kluwer.

Richards, J. (1996). Negotiating the negotiation of meaning: Comments on Voigt (1992) and Saxe and Bernudex (1992). In L. P. Steffe, P. Nesher, P. Cobb, G. Goldin, & B. Greer (Eds.), *Theories of mathematical learning* (pp. 69–75). Mahwah, NJ: Lawrence Erlbaum Associates.

Richards, T. J., & Richards, L. (1990). *Manual for Mainframe NUD•IST: A software system for qualitative data analysis on time-sharing computers.* Melbourne: Replee.

Richardson, V. (1994). Conducting research on practice. *Educational Researcher, 23*(5), 5–10.

Rorty, R. (1979). *Philosophy and the mirror of nature.* Princeton, NJ: Princeton University Press.

Roschelle, J. (1992). C-Video. [Software package]. San Francisco: Knowledge Revolution.

Rotman, B. (1993). *Ad infinitum the ghost in Turing's machine: Taking God out of mathematics and putting the body back in.* Stanford, CA: Stanford University Press.

Rowland, S. (1984). *The enquiring classroom: An approach to understanding children's learning.* New York: Falmer Press.

Russell, R., & Ginsburg, H. P. (1984). Cognitive analysis of children's mathematical difficulties. *Cognition and Instruction, 1,* 271–244.

Ryle, G. (1949). *The concept of mind.* London: Hutchinson.

Säljö, R. (1979). Learning in the learner's perspective: Some common-sense conceptions. *Reports from the Department of Education, Göteborg University, No. 76.*

Säljö, R. (1982). *Learning and understanding: A study of differences in constructing meaning from a text.* Göteborg: Acta Universitatis Gothoburgensis.

Sandberg, J. (1996). Are phenomenographic results reliable? In G. Dal'Alba & B. Hasselgren (Eds.), *Reflections on phenomenography: Toward a methodology?* (pp. 129–140). Göteborg: Acta Universitatis Gothoburgensis.

Saxe, G. B. (1991). *Culture and cognitive development: Studies in mathematical understanding.* Hillsdale, NJ: Lawrence Erlbaum Associates.

Saxe, G. B., & Bermudez, T. (1996). Emergent mathematical environments in children's games. In L. P. Steffe, P. Nesher, P. Cobb, G. Goldin, & B. Greer (Eds.), *Theories of mathematical learning* (pp. 51–68). Mahwah, NJ: Lawrence Erlbaum Associates.

Schoenfeld, A. (1994). A discourse of methods. *Journal for Research in Mathematics Education, 25*(6), 697–710.

Schubert, W. H. (1986). *Curriculum: Perspective, paradigm, and possibility.* New York: Macmillan.

Schütz, A. (1964). *Collected papers II: Studies in social theory,* A. Broderson (Ed.). The Hague: Nijoff.

Schütz, A. (1970). Concept and theory formation in the social sciences. In D. Emmet & A. MacIntyre (Eds.), *Sociological theory and philosophical analysis* (pp. 1–19). London: Macmillan.

Schütz, A. (1972). *The phenomenology of the social world.* London: Heinemann.

Sega, D. (1997). Reading and writing about our lives: Creating a collaborative curriculum in a class of high school misfits. *Teacher Research, 4*(2), 101–111.

Sfard, A. (1991). On the dual nature of mathematical conceptions: Reflections on processes and objects as different sides of the same coin. *Educational Studies in Mathematics, 26*(1), 1–36.

Short, K., & Burke, C. (1996). Examining our beliefs and practices through inquiry. *Language Arts, 73,* 97–103.

Short, K., Harste, J., & Burke, C. (1996). *Creating classrooms for authors and inquirers* (2nd ed.). Portsmouth, NH: Heinemann.

Shotter, J. (1993). *Conversational realities: Constructing life through language.* London: Sage.

Shulman, L. S. (1981). Disciplines of inquiry in education: An overview. *Educational Researcher, 10*(6), 5–12, 23.

Siegel, M., & Borasi, R. (1994). Demystifying mathematics education through inquiry. In P. Ernest (Ed.), *Constructing mathematical knowledge: Epistemology and mathematical education* (pp. 201–214). New York: Falmer Press.

Silver, E. A., & Kilpatrick, J. (1994). E Pluribus Unum: Challenges of diversity in the future of mathematics education research. *Journal for Research in Mathematics Education, 25*(6), 734–754.

Simons, H. (Ed.). (1989). *Rhetoric in the human sciences.* London: Sage.

Sinclair, J. McH., & Coulthard, M. (1975). *Towards an analysis of discourse.* London: Oxford University Press.

Skemp, R. R. (1976). Relational understanding and instrumental understanding. *Mathematics Teaching, 77,* 20–26.

Skolverket. (1995). *Diagnostiskt material i matematik, skolär 2.* (The Swedish School Council. Diagnostic material in mathematics, year 2). Stockholm: Skolverket.

Skovsmose, O. (1985). Mathematical education versus critical education. *Educational Studies in Mathematics, 16,* 337–354.

Skovsmose, O. (1994). *Towards a philosophy of critical mathematics education.* Dordrecht: Kluwer.

Sowden, S., & Keeves, J. P. (1988). Analysis of evidence in humanistic studies. In J. P. Keeves (Ed.), *Educational research, methodology and measurement: An international handbook* (pp. 513–526). Oxford: Pergamon Press.

Steen, L. A. (1990). *On the shoulders of giants: New approaches to numeracy.* Washington, DC: National Academy Press.

Steffe, L. P. (1991a). The constructivist teaching experiment: Illustrations and implications. In E. von Glasersfeld (Ed.), *Radical constructivism in mathematics education* (pp. 177–194). Dordrecht: Kluwer.

Steffe, L. P. (Ed.). (1991b). *Epistemological foundations of mathematical experience.* New York: Springer-Verlag.

Steffe, L. P. (1996). Preface. In L. P. Steffe, P. Nesher, P. Cobb, G. Goldin, & B. Greer (Eds.), *Theories of mathematical learning* (pp. ix–xi). Mahwah, NJ: Lawrence Erlbaum Associates.

Steffe, L. P., & Gale, J. (Eds.). (1995). *Constructivism in education.* Hillsdale, NJ: Lawrence Erlbaum Associates.

Steffe, L. P., & Tzur, R. (1994). Interaction and children's mathematics. In P. Ernest (Ed.), *Constructing mathematical knowledge: Epistemology and mathematics education* (pp. 8–32). London: Falmer Press.

Steffe, L. P., von Glasersfeld, E., Richards, J., & Cobb, P. (1983). *Children's counting types.* New York: Praeger Publishers.

Steffe, L. P., & Wiegel, H. (1996). On the nature of a model of mathematical learning. In L. P. Steffe, P. Nesher, P. Cobb, G. Goldin, & B. Greer (Eds.), *Theories of mathematical learning* (pp. 477–498). Mahwah, NJ: Lawrence Erlbaum Associates.

Stenhouse, L. (1975). *An introduction to curriculum research and development.* London: Heinemann.

Strauss, A. (1987). *Qualitative analysis for social scientists.* Cambridge: Cambridge University Press.

Strieb, L. (1993). Visiting and revisiting the trees. In M. Cochran-Smith & S. L. Lytle (Eds.), *Inside/outside: Teacher research and knowledge* (pp. 121–130). New York: Teachers College Press.

Stubbs, M. (1981). Scratching the surface: Linguistic data in educational research. In C. Adelman (Ed.), *Uttering, muttering, collecting, using and reporting talk for social and educational research* (pp. 114–133). London: Grant McIntyre.

Svensson, L. (1989). Fenomenografi och kontextuell analys. Phenomenography and contextual analysis). In R. Sälö (Ed.), *Som vi uppfattar det. Elva bidrag om inlärning och omvärldsuppfattning* (As we see it. Eleven papers on learning and understanding the world around us) (pp. 33–52). Lund: Studentlitteratur

Svensson, O., Hedenborg , M. L., & Lingman, L. (1976). On children's heuristics for solving simple additions. *Scandinavian Journal of Educational Research, 20,* 161–173.

Tall, D. (1991). The psychology of advanced mathematical thinking. In D. Tall (Ed.), *Advanced mathematical thinking* (pp. 3–21). Dordrecht: Kluwer.

Teppo, A. R., & Esty, W. W. (1994). Problem solving using arithmetic and algebraic thinking. In D. Kirshner (Ed.), *Proceedings of the Sixteenth Annual Meeting of the North American Chapter of the International Group for the Psychology of Mathematics Education* (pp. 24–30). Baton Rouge, LA: Louisiana State University.

Teppo, A. R., & Esty, W. W. (1995). Mathematical contexts and the perception of meaning in algebraic symbols. In D. T. Owens, M. K. Reed, & & G. M. Millsaps (Eds.), *Proceedings of the Seventeenth Annual Meeting of the North American Chapter of the International Group for the Psychology of Mathematics Education* (pp. 147–151). Columbus, OH: ERIC Clearninghouse for Science, Mathematics, and Environmental Education.

Tiles, M. (1991). *Mathematics and the image of reason.* London: Routledge.

Todarov, T. (1984). *Mikhail Bakhtin: The dialogical principle.* (W. Godzich, Trans.) Minneapolis: University of Minnesota Press.

Toulmin, S. (1972). *Human understanding, I.* Oxford: Clarendon Press.

Treffers, A. (1991). Didactical background of a mathematics program for primary education. In L. Streefland (Ed.), *Mathematics education in primary school: On the occasion of the opening of the Freudenthal Institute.* Utrecht: Center for Science and Mathematics Education.

Tymoczko, T. (Ed.). (1986). *New directions in the philosophy of mathematics.* Boston: Birkhauser.

van Oers, B. (1996). Learning mathematics as a meaningful activity. In L. P. Steffe, P. Nesher, P. Cobb, G. Goldin, & B. Greer (Eds.), *Theories of mathematical learning* (pp. 91–113). Mahwah, NJ: Lawrence Erlbaum Associates.

Vico, G. B. (1858). *De antiquissima Italorum sapientia.* (Pomodoro, Trans.). Naples: Stamperia de'Classici Latini. (Original work published 1719.)

Vico, G. B. (1961). *The new science.* (T. G. Bergin & M. H. Fisc, Trans.). Garden City, NY: Anchor Books. (Original work published 1744.)

von Glasersfeld, E. (1987). Learning as a constructive activity. In C. Janvier (Ed), *Problems of representation in the teaching and learning of mathematics* (pp. 3–18). Hillsdale, NJ: Lawrence Erlbaum Associates.

von Glasersfeld, E. (1989). Constructivism in education. In T. Husen (Ed.), *International encyclopedia of education* (Supplementary vol., pp. 162–163). Oxford: Pergamon.

von Glaserfeld, E. (1991). *Radical constructivism in mathematics education.* Dordrecht, Kluwer.

von Glasersfeld, E. (1995). *Radical constructivism: A way of knowing and learning.* London: Falmer Press.

Vygotsky, L. S. (1978). *Mind in society. The development of the higher psychological processes.* Cambridge: Harvard University Press.

Walkerdine, V. (1988). *The mastery of reason.* London: Routledge.

Walkerdine, V., & The Girls and Mathematics Unit. (1989). *Counting girls out.* London: Virago Press.

Wang, H. (1974). *From mathematics to philosophy.* London: Routledge.

Wells, G. (1994). *Changing schools from within: Creating communities of inquiry.* Toronto: Ontario Institute for the Study of Education (OISE).

Werner, H. (1973). *Comparative psychology of mental development.* New York: International Universities Press. (Original work published 1940.)

Wilder, R. L. (1981). *Mathematics as a cultural system.* Oxford: Pergamon Press.

Wittgenstein, L. (1953). *Philosophical investigations* (G. E. M. Anscombe, Trans.). Oxford: Basil Blackwell.

Wittgenstein, L. (1978). *Remarks on the foundations of mathematics* (rev. ed.). Cambridge, MA: MIT Press.

Wolcott, H. (1975). Criteria for an ethnographic approach to research in schools. *Human Organisation, 34*(2), 111–127.

Wolcott, H. (1982). Mirrors, models and monitors: Educator adaptations of the ethnographic innovation. In G. Spindler (Ed.), *Doing the ethnography of schooling: Educational anthropology in action* (pp. 68–95). New York: Holt Reinhart & Winston.

Woolgar, S. (1988). *Science: The very idea.* London: Ellis Horwood/ Tavistock.

Zang, R. (1994). *Inferring internal strategic problem representation and its development: A two-year case study with four elementary school children.* Unpublished doctoral dissertation, Rutgers University Graduate School of Education, (University Microfilms No. 95-14127).

Zang, R. (1995). Inferring internal strategic problem representation and its development: A two-year case study with Marcia. In D. T. Owens, M. K. Reed, & G. M. Millsaps (Eds.), *Proceedings of the Seventeenth Annual Meeting of the North American Chapter of the International Group for the Psychology of Mathematics Education* (Vol. 1, pp. 199–203). Columbus, OH: ERIC Clearinghouse for Science, Mathematics, and Environmental Education.

Zaslavsky, C. (1973). *Africa counts.* Boston: Prindle, Weber & Schmidt.